BLACK AND BLUE

BLACK AND BLUE

INSIDE THE DIVIDE BETWEEN
THE POLICE AND BLACK AMERICA

JEFF PEGUES

Prometheus Books

59 John Glenn Drive
Amherst, New York 14228

Published 2017 by Prometheus Books

Cover design by Jacqueline Nasso Cooke
Cover images © M. Stan Reaves / Alamy (*top*);
© Rena Schild / Shutterstock (*bottom*)
Cover design © Prometheus Books

Inquiries should be addressed to
Prometheus Books
59 John Glenn Drive
Amherst, New York 14228
VOICE: 716–691–0133
FAX: 716–691–0137
WWW.PROMETHEUSBOOKS.COM

21 20 19 18 17   5 4 3 2 1

Library of Congress Cataloging-in-Publication Data

Names: Pegues, Jeff, 1970- author.
Title: Black and blue : inside the divide between the police and Black America /
    Jeff Pegues.
Description: Amherst : Prometheus Books, 2017. | Includes index.
Identifiers: LCCN 2016055261 (print) | LCCN 2016059873 (ebook) |
    ISBN 9781633882577 (hardback) | ISBN 9781633882584 (ebook)
Subjects: LCSH: Police—United States. | Law enforcement—Moral and
    ethical aspects—United States. | Police brutality—United States. | Police
    misconduct—United States. | African Americans—Civil rights. | Police-
    community relations—United States. | BISAC: POLITICAL SCIENCE /
    Political Freedom & Security / Law Enforcement. | SOCIAL SCIENCE /
    Criminology.
Classification: LCC HV8141 .P34 2017 (print) | LCC HV8141 (ebook) |
    DDC 363.2089/96073—dc23
LC record available at https://lccn.loc.gov/2016055261

Printed in the United States of America

My parents, Joe and Bettye, inspire me to persevere and overcome.
My wife, Tareaz, motivates me to keep striving.
My daughters, Jordyn and Peyton, give me strength and hope.
My family sustains me. My mission keeps me reaching for the stars.

CONTENTS

FOREWORD

BY CHARLES RAMSEY,
CO-CHAIR, PRESIDENT'S TASK FORCE
ON 21ST CENTURY POLICING

I have been a member of the law enforcement community for forty-seven years. I began my career in my hometown of Chicago, Illinois. I have also served as chief of the Metropolitan Police Department in Washington, DC, and police commissioner in Philadelphia. I have witnessed a change in policing over the years, but nothing compares to the challenges we face today.

I first met Jeff Pegues while I served as police commissioner in Philadelphia. He had occasion to visit me in my office to interview me for the *CBS Evening News* about officer-involved shootings in the wake of the killing of Michael Brown in Ferguson, Missouri, and other highly charged incidents, some of which were captured on video. *Black and Blue* highlights many of the cases that have sparked controversy, tension, and protests in cities across America, as well as a growing rift between police and communities of color.

High-profile incidents, in particular, those involving questionable uses of force, have caused police leaders to find new ways to reach out to the community and repair the damage. Rising crime rates in some cities lead some to believe in the so-called Ferguson effect, meaning police officers are apprehensive when working in what they perceive as an anti-police environment and are therefore reluctant to be proactive when dealing with crime in the neighborhoods they patrol. And, as Pegues's book points out, some members of the community fear the police who are there to protect them.

Trust between police and the communities they serve is essential in a democracy. To establish trust, we must all first face hard truths, as FBI director James Comey indicated. Police officers and their supporters cannot pretend as if excessive force and unequal enforcement of laws do not exist in some cases. To say that is not an indictment of the entire policing profession, however. The majority of the men and women who serve in law enforcement do so with great honor and dignity. They are compassionate and caring people who do their best to bring a sense of safety and justice to the communities they serve. But we cannot ignore the fact that biased policing and even racism exists among a few in our ranks. Those individuals must be rooted out.

The history of policing in America shows us that law enforcement has not always performed its duties in a fair and impartial manner. Officers who abuse their authority or treat the public disrespectfully must be held accountable. Terry Cunningham, a past president of the International Association of Chiefs of Police, took the bold move at a recent gathering of hundreds of police chiefs, to apologize to communities of color for past injustices at the hands of police. At the same time, the community must recognize that not every officer-involved shooting or use of force is improper or the result of biased policing. The violence that plagues many of our communities will end only if police and the community work together to establish mutual trust and respect.

Jeff Pegues provides thoughtful insight into the challenges facing police as they attempt to build relationships and legitimacy in communities of color. He accurately captures the complexity of addressing the issue of race and policing in America by forcing us to look at ourselves and find ways to overcome the fear and distrust that exists on both sides. This book is a must-read for police and community members alike.

PREFACE

We don't always listen. Everyone is so busy trying to be heard that people aren't listening to each other. As a consequence, people often don't know what's really going on in the country, in their neighborhoods, or even in their homes.

I was sitting in a Philadelphia restaurant one night after my live shot for the *CBS Evening News*. It had been a long day and I was hoping to just unwind. I was led to a seat at a table in the bar area, and on the televisions in front of me I could see cable news. At the time, the nation was exactly two weeks away from electing Donald Trump as president of the United States. Trump and Hillary Clinton had slogged through one of the most divisive presidential campaigns in US history. So many wounds had been opened. So much pain had been exposed for so many people. Regardless of whether they disliked Clinton or Trump, there was a lot of bad blood spread across so many people. Thankfully, the volume on the televisions in the bar was down. Frankly, I didn't want to hear the talking heads anymore— prognosticating about what was coming next or who was up or down. Like the rest of America, I had heard enough! I was content to zone out at the table with the televisions in front of me, while at the same time trying to think of a way to finish writing this book.

It's not that I was feeling the pressure of getting everything done by the deadline, rather, I wanted to make sure that I covered all of the important topics. The deadline for the manuscript was now just days away, and the months of juggling my day job and the weekend work of writing was taking its toll. This was also a busy time on the Justice and Homeland Security beat. US intelligence sources had confirmed that they believed the Russians were trying to influence the election, and the prospect of a US cyberattack response was on the horizon. But looming right over my shoulder was writer's block.

I was kicking myself for committing to write the book in the first place! Writing a book is a major undertaking on its own, but then delving into the relationship between the police and the black community, well, that's a bear of a task all to itself. I had been advised that I had nothing to gain and a lot to lose. Several publishing companies and editors passed on the book a year earlier because they didn't feel that it was a big enough issue. But after several years of interviews and reporting, I knew that the problem was only getting worse and warranted further discussion and attention.

No matter where you live in the United States, whether we like to admit this or not, the relationship between our police and our communities of color affects all of us. You don't have to live in the inner city to feel the impact of this debate. Perhaps you're a police officer working in a wealthy suburb, and even you feel the sting of how confrontations caught on camera are affecting your routine traffic stops.

No matter who you are, there are lessons for all of us, regardless of race or income, in this book and in this story. I believe that this is a story about good people trying to work through a tough situation. Not only am I referring to police commanders and federal officials who are pushing for change but also to community activists whose peaceful demonstrations are motivated by a desire to change the system in a positive way.

But how do we get beyond the unrest we are seeing now? I believe it begins with understanding and listening. I've spent years listening to law enforcement. I see the challenges they are facing and how their jobs are harder than ever. As a black American man, I grew up listening to my parents and grandparents. While most kids played games or watched television, I eavesdropped on conversations. I heard the stories of how my mother marched for equal rights and how my father was arrested in Atlanta during a sit-in at the age of fifteen. How a white judge scolded him for protesting and demanded that he leave the state by sundown or face jail time. I also recall the stories about how my grandfather bravely integrated a middle-class white neighborhood in Birmingham, Alabama. How he owned guns to protect his family, because blacks did not trust that the police would come when they called 911 for help. Birmingham was at the center of the civil-rights struggle, where confrontations with police in the 1950s and '60s usually didn't end well. Blacks will never forget the images of Eugene "Bull" Conner's officers, with their dogs, fire-hoses, and clubs.

This brings me back to that restaurant in Philadelphia in late 2016. While I was sitting and staring at the television sets in front of me, the waiter led a woman to sit at a table next to me. She was a middle-aged white woman, and she squeezed between the tables and took a seat on the padded bench next to me. As I said, all I wanted was peace and quiet. I wasn't in the mood to be social, and she certainly didn't appear to be paying any attention to me. But, for whatever reason, we started talking. It may have been the waiter who sparked the conversation, or it may have been something we both saw on television. In any case, we started talking about the election, and that ultimately led us to another hot topic—race relations and the police.

Her name was Rhonda, and she was a married mother of four from Florida. She did not understand why nor did she like how blacks were, in her words, "rioting" after police shootings. She believed that the only way for there to be change and progress was for black Americans to demonstrate peacefully. In response, I did what I often find myself trying to do, and that is to explain that the majority of the demonstrators are peaceful. And that there is a reason why people are frustrated and angry about the police shootings. I told her that between 2014 and through 2017 a series of police-involved shootings of unarmed African American men trained the light on and exacerbated the divisions between black and blue. I also tried to explain how reform is unfolding in some police departments and why some officers are resistant to making the changes and feel unfairly targeted.

In a nutshell, Rhonda from Florida reminded me of why a book like this is important. Over the last twenty-five years of covering news and specifically law enforcement, I have interviewed thousands of people. In the last three years, on this topic, I have had conversations and interviewed a few hundred people. Those experiences are reflected in this book. What you will read are the unfiltered views of many of those people. Americans from all walks of life, police officers, commanders, federal officials and academics. The interviews, captured through my two cell phone recorders and reflected on these pages are an edited biography of reality.

CHAPTER ONE

REFORM IS IN THE AIR

I spent about ten years in New York City, working for a local television station. The station's success was built on a belief in covering the city by blanketing it with reporters in news vans ready to spring into action for breaking stories.

For nearly a decade, mostly during the late afternoon and into the night, that was my job. I would cover breaking news—shootings, multi-car pileup accidents, fires, and just about any other tragedy. But among the most memorable images I have of what I would witness in some of the city's toughest neighborhoods. It was often at night. The streetlights were out or dim, and my crew and I would race down a street in a news van heading to the next story. I would sit in the back of the van in the "captain's chair," sometimes reading e-mails but most of the time staring out of the back window. The brownstones would blend together as we rushed by, and the people walking down the street would become a mix of different indistinguishable colors. But then there would be a burst of dark blue. That's when I would see a young police officer, sometimes alone and standing with his or her back against a wall. I remember that the rookie officers were pressed to the brick of the building, head essentially on a swivel. Slowly, looking left and then right. They were brave but, boy, did they look terrified.

In certain neighborhoods where crime was a problem, their posture was important for survival because it limited their blind spots. The biggest blind spot, of course, was not being able to see what might have been coming up from behind. With their backs pressed against the wall, at least they could prepare and see what was coming at them.

Nowadays, police officers across the country see an even more challenging future. Reform is in the air in the wake of police shoot-ings in Ferguson, Baltimore, Baton Rouge, Minnesota, and Mil-waukee. It was the 2014 shooting of Michael Brown in Ferguson that really focused the public's attention on the issue. In subsequent years, there would be more incidents. Americans everywhere were becoming more attuned to the disparities in the way justice was being administered. By the time five police officers were killed in Dallas in 2016, the rhetoric had reached a fever pitch and voices on both sides of the divide knew that the time had come to lower the volume. Police departments have begun changing tactics just as some cities see disturbing spikes in crime.

In 2015 the number of homicides in major US cities increased 17 percent, which marks the greatest increase in a quarter century.[1] There are different theories behind the increase, but based on the data I've seen, the lack of trust between police and inner-city commu-nities of color may be a contributing factor. Police are also frustrated, tired, and angry.

FBI director James Comey had been trying to get the world to notice that the crime stats were heading in the wrong direction.[2] While some dismissed the sharp spikes in violence as a "blip," Comey knew that it was more than that and that there were underlying issues that had to be dealt with openly. Among the first few times he really made a point of sounding the alarm about rising crime was in a meeting with a small group of national reporters.

Comey walked into the room; the assembled reporters sat up in their chairs, pushed their notepads into place, and made sure their cell phone recorders were ready to capture the words of the most powerful voice in law enforcement. The director pulled a chair from under the table to take a seat. It was a boardroom-sized table, and assembled around it were about a dozen or so print and television reporters from the major publications and broadcasting outlets. Only they were granted access to the director like this every few months.

In the halls of the famed Hoover Building on Pennsylvania Avenue, these meetings were called "Pen and Pads" by the FBI.[3] But that was old-school. There were no cameras, only audio devices to record the director's words, to guard against misquoting him. There was an agree-ment in place that allowed reporters to record Comey's statements, but we couldn't use the audio for broadcast. They are the rules of the game or the price of admission, depending on how you look at it.

Comey sank into his chair at the head of the table. The man who is essentially the CEO of American law enforcement had a lot on his mind. He often spoke in very colorful language, and he was about to unleash another vivid portrait of the current threats to national security.

"How does it feel to have seven recorders in front of you?" a radio reporter asked Comey.

He replied, "It always freaks me out a bit." The reporters laughed, and so did Comey. It was perhaps his way of breaking the ice in these sessions, which can often turn tense.

For the record, very little seems to rattle Comey. At about 6′8″, he is one of the rare Washington "power players" who has worked for both Democratic and Republican administrations and seems to have no qualms speaking truth to power. That had also worked against him at times. Some former colleagues had called him "honest to a fault."

On October 1, 2015, with the nation embroiled in a national-security crisis in the Middle East, the most pressing threat to the American people may have been domestic. The rift between law enforcement and "communities of color" was growing. A blunt assessment may have been exactly what was needed. Crime was spiking across the country. At the same time, an Obama administration effort at criminal-justice reform had garnered bipartisan support, and it would ultimately result in the "rapid-fire" release of more than forty thousand federal prisoners from custody.[4] Separately, states across the country were in the middle of their own criminal-justice reforms to reduce prison populations.[5] It was a tsunami of potential problems that rank-and-file police officers on the nation's streets would be forced to confront first.

The men and women who make up police agencies were already coming under fire in more ways than one. They were on the defensive as a result of misconduct by some officers, and their actions were being scrutinized more than ever. Once-routine arrests were now escalating into fatal encounters. Cell phone videos of police in action were going viral, and it was having a negative impact on everyone associated with law enforcement.

The stain had pushed morale to a new low, and departments couldn't fill the ranks that were being depleted by retirement. How can you protect life and property if you don't have the number of police officers you need? Or if the officers you have lack the trust of the neighborhoods they patrol? You don't have to be a genius to figure out that there was a major problem in law enforcement.

As the news conference began, Comey had answers for most of the questions we asked of him. What he could not explain was *why* crime was spiking in the nation's major cities. When he was questioned about that, he told the assembled reporters that the spike in crime was, "very concerning."[6] He didn't stop there, "I think all of us need to figure out what is going on here [because]," Comey said, "the chiefs tell me that they're seeing huge spikes in violent crime, especially in homicide." As he reported, some of the chiefs were in panic mode, and so were some FBI agents who were aware of the trend. I had gotten a tip about it several weeks before and had begun to look into it. Eventually, I confirmed that the Department of Justice was kicking around the idea of expanding the number of cities in which it had increased its presence. In a select number of cities with increasing crime problems the DOJ had partnered the FBI, ATF, and DEA with local police. The feds were on the ground there, seeing firsthand how the tide had violently and unexpectedly turned.

During 2015, there were reported spikes in crime of 20 percent, 50 percent, and even 70 percent, and yet there was no clear indication why it was happening.[7] Even the FBI director was at a loss in attempting to explain the data. Then, for the first time publicly, the assembled reporters heard him use the term "Ferguson effect." Comey said, "Some people have suggested to me—look, a wind is blowing through law enforcement, sort of a 'Ferguson effect' that has changed the way people police—and some have said that police officers aren't getting out of their cars and talking to gang bangers on street corners anymore, and the answer is . . . I don't know."

"What I *do* know," Comey said, "is that a whole lot of people are dying. According to the chiefs, they are overwhelmingly young men of color dying, and we [have] got to care about that."

But that wasn't the only factor having an impact on crime. Heroin use was at epidemic levels.[8] Criminal-justice reform was having an impact by clearing out jails and prisons. And then there was a change in police tactics. It wasn't just the "Ferguson effect"; it was the end of stop and frisk as well. The latter had been discredited and branded a harsh police tactic that had alienated communities of color. A judge in 2013 found that it was being used in a manner that violated the US Constitution.[9] All of those factors combined had, in a way, tied the hands of law enforcement across the country.

Police departments were being forced to change their tactics, and that was a sign of law enforcement being at a crossroads. Stop and frisk, for example, had been used for years in New York City to stop, question, and frisk people suspected of crimes. But the tactic mostly targeted people of color. The New York branch of the American Civil Liberties Union (ACLU) found that, historically, blacks and Latinos were disproportionately targeted by police using this tactic. In 2011, blacks and Latinos in New York City made up 87 percent of the people stopped by police; of those people, 88 percent were totally innocent.[10] It was getting easier to draw a line from certain police procedures to the outcomes that were now being recorded by cell phone cameras across the country as evidence of unconstitutional policing. The targeting (or harassment) of certain populations, without probable cause, was taking a toll on people who were fed up with being singled out.

But Comey cautioned against rapid changes in how police and political leaders enacted reforms, "As we do it, we need to be very, very thoughtful." Imagine if you tried to reengineer a car while it was driving down the street. Attempting to revamp police tactics in the middle of an uptick in crime was a dangerous practice. It's one thing to do it if crime is up across the board and has been that way for some time. But at this point in history, if you look at the numbers, there are still historic lows in some categories of crimes. The FBI's Preliminary Semiannual Uniform Crime Report (UCR) showed declines in the number of property crimes reported for the first six months of 2015 when compared with the same point the year before.[11] Also, according to the numbers, cities with populations from 50,000 to 99,999 inhabitants saw a 0.3 decrease in violent crime; and cities with 500,000 to 999,999 in population experienced a smaller 0.1 decrease in violent crime.[12]

Meanwhile, the Brennan Center for Justice, which is a nonpartisan law and policy institute, published statistics that showed that over the last ten years, twenty-seven states had seen a 23 percent drop in crime since 2006.[13] While the numbers offered by the UCR continued to show a decline, law enforcement professionals knew better than to trust that data. Those statistics were old, and the 2015 numbers wouldn't be available to police and the FBI until 2016. The streets showed the real trends, and Comey was reading between the lines. He knew that trouble wasn't on the horizon—it was already here.

The FBI director had been working to change how such data are collected. It's been a mission of his to get local departments to gather and report the latest stats. He believes that having the data readily available means having facts. And having the facts, he said, "help[s] us find truth and understanding."[14] Comey believed that the nation could not address issues about use of force and officer-involved shootings or why violent crime was up in some cities if law enforcement didn't really know what was going on. He insisted, "we need to improve the way we report, analyze, and use information and crime statistics. And we need that information to be accurate, to be timely, and to be accessible to everybody—or it doesn't do much good."

The lack of current data was an obvious blind spot that was having an impact on how to respond to the changing dynamics of law enforcement. Comey pointed out that, nowadays, cell phones can give you up-to-date data on just about anything you need to make accurate decisions in your daily lives, and yet police could not call up the data they needed in order to make life-or-death decisions. According to Comey, "It just didn't make sense!"

Public-opinion polls did provide almost immediate results, and Americans' opinions on race relations were distressing. Negative views of race relations in the country had risen to a level not seen since the 1992 Los Angeles riots that followed the Rodney King verdict.[15] Just 26 percent of Americans now believed race relations in the United States "are mostly good"—an eleven-point drop from a year earlier—while 69 percent say they "are mostly bad."[16] A divisive presidential campaign season was having an impact, and the string of police shootings and takedowns caught on tape were dredging up hard feelings among blacks and whites. Every incident with a hint of race at its core seemed to rub salt in the wound. He's not a politician, but Comey sometimes makes speeches that sound as if he is running for office. He'll tackle a potentially divisive issue—like race and law enforcement—even though some believe he stands to gain very little and lose a lot. In February 2015, in an auditorium at Georgetown University, he weighed in on the current state of law enforcement just months after Michael Brown was shot in Ferguson, Eric Garner was killed by a police officer's illegal stranglehold in New York's Staten Island, and in 2014 two police officers were murdered in New York City by a man who claimed before taking his own life that he was angered by the deaths of Garner and Brown.[17] When I asked some of my law enforcement sources why he chose to deliver the speech, I was told that Comey had been thinking about it for a while and felt like he needed to say something.

It is surprising that Comey publicly broached the issue, considering that talking about race essentially sank the career of Attorney General Eric Holder. In 2009, the nation's first African American attorney general referred to America as "a nation of cowards" when it comes to discussing race.[18] Even President Obama has had a difficult time navigating the race-based complexities of police-involved shootings of unarmed black men. Every speech he has given about the subject has drawn the ire of his critics, who accuse him of being divisive. But Comey pushed ahead with his speech. "We are at a crossroads," Comey told a packed auditorium at Georgetown.[19] "As a society, we can choose to live our everyday lives, raising our families and going to work, hoping that someone, somewhere, will do something to ease the tension—to smooth over the conflict. We can roll up our car windows, turn up the radio, and drive around these problems, or we can choose to have an open and honest discussion about what our relationship is today—what it should be, what it could be, and what it needs to be—if we took more time to better understand one another. In places like Ferguson and New York City, and in some communities across this nation, there is a disconnect between police agencies and many citizens—predominantly in communities of color." The director's speech was well received. Comey had placed himself in the middle of one of the most divisive issues of the day, and it wouldn't be the last time he would do it.

CHAPTER TWO
BROKEN WINDOWS

We had heard the results of Department of Justice Civil Rights investigations before. Ferguson comes to mind. In March 2015, a DOJ report found systemic discrimination in the way the Missouri police department was serving its community.[1] The black residents had suffered the most in "nearly every aspect of Ferguson's law enforcement system." The report also found that the city's focus on revenue rather than public safety "contributed to a pattern of unconstitutional policing." The data DOJ Civil Rights units collected showed that despite making up 67 percent of the population, African Americans accounted for 85 percent of the police department's traffic stops, 90 percent of its citations and 93 percent of its arrests from 2012 to 2014. Those numbers said it all, and just over six months after a white Ferguson police officer had shot an unarmed black teen named Michael Brown, it was hard for anyone to legitimately deny that there was a problem when the streets erupted in protests and unrest.

That case shocked and saddened a lot of people, but what I knew then was that the DOJ's conclusions were just the tip of the iceberg and far from the whole story. Another DOJ Civil Rights investigation was also wakeup call. "Unconstitutional policing" was the term the DOJ used to describe what had gone wrong.[2] Baltimore Police had been in the eye of the storm before. Just over a year earlier, twenty-five-year-old Freddie Gray died after somehow suffering a severed spine on his way to jail in police custody. After his funeral, the city erupted in violence. High-school students may have sparked the rioting, but there were many blacks, young and old, who shared their anger.

For years, frustration had been bubbling beneath the surface in black neighborhoods as the number of problems within the Baltimore Police Department (BPD) grew. Now it appears that the department's commanders knew the day of "reckoning" was coming. In an exclusive interview with me for the *CBS Evening News*, several months after he was fired, former Baltimore Police commissioner Anthony Batts revealed that the writing was on the wall when he got the job in 2012. Looking back, he told me, "What I shared with my boss, who was the mayor, early on is that I thought that the police organization, the day that I walked in, was pretty much open to a consent decree."[3]

A consent decree is an agreement between two parties on a path forward. The DOJ enters into consent decrees to begin the process of reforming troubled police departments. Baltimore's had been on that path for some time. Still, the DOJ report revealed so many shocking statistics to the world when it was published. The bottom line: Discrimination had been engrained into the fabric of the police department. Top to bottom, officers were violating residents' rights—not on occasion but routinely. In this city of six hundred thousand, African Americans were being treated differently.[4] They made up a little over 62 percent of the population, and they were getting the brunt of the harassment.

Here's what the DOJ investigators found:[5]

- BPD makes stops, searches, and arrests without the required justification.
- BPD uses enforcement strategies that unlawfully subject African Americans to disproportionate rates of stops, searches, and arrests; uses excessive force; and retaliates against individuals for their constitutionally protected expression.

DOJ lawyers sought to prove their case, with data to back up this pattern of civil rights violations:

- BPD officers recorded over 300,000 pedestrian stops from January 2010-May 2015. These stops, the report noted, were concentrated in predominantly African American neighborhoods and often lack reasonable suspicion.

- BPD's pedestrian stops were concentrated on a small portion of Baltimore residents. BPD made roughly 44 percent of its stops in two small, predominantly African American districts that contain only 11 percent of the city's population. Consequently, hundreds of individuals—nearly all of them African American—were stopped on at least ten separate occasions from 2010-2015. Indeed, seven African American men were stopped more than 30 times during this period.

- BPD's stops often lack reasonable suspicion. DOJ's review of incident reports and interviews with officers and community members found that officers regularly approach individuals standing or walking on City sidewalks to detain and question them and check for outstanding warrants, despite lacking reasonable suspicion to do so. Only 3.7 percent of pedestrian stops resulted in officers issuing a citation or making an arrest. And, as noted below, many of those arrested based on pedestrian stops had their charges dismissed upon initial review by either supervisors at BPD's Central Booking or local prosecutors.

- BPD is far more likely to subject individual African Americans to multiple stops in short periods of time. In the five and a half years of data we examined, African Americans accounted for 95 percent of the 410 individuals BPD stopped at least 10 times. One African American man in his mid-fifties was stopped 30 times in less than 4 years. Despite these repeated intrusions, none of the 30 stops resulted in a citation or criminal charge.

- BPD also stops African American drivers at disproportionate rates. African Americans accounted for 82 percent of all BPD vehicle stops, compared to only 60 percent of the driving age population in the City and 27 percent of the driving age population in the greater metropolitan area.

- BPD disproportionately searches African Americans during stops. BPD searched African Americans more frequently during pedestrian and vehicle stops, even though searches of African Americans were *less likely* to discover contraband. Indeed, BPD officers found contraband twice as often when searching white individuals compared to African Americans during vehicle stops and 50 percent more often during pedestrian stops.

- Racial disparities in BPD's arrests are most pronounced for highly discretionary offenses: African Americans accounted for 91 percent of the 1,800 people charged solely with "failure to obey" or "trespassing"; 89 percent of the 1,350 charges for making a false statement to an officer; and 84 percent of the 6,500 people arrested for "disorderly conduct." Moreover, booking officials and prosecutors decline charges brought against African Americans at significantly higher rates than charges against people of other races, indicating that officers' standards for making arrests differ by the race of the person arrested.

To cap it all off, DOJ investigators concluded that there was a "perception that there are two Baltimores: one wealthy and largely white, the second impoverished and predominantly black."[6]

This DOJ civil rights probe so implicitly summarized the discrimination some blacks say they have been feeling at the hands of law enforcement. The 164-page report alleged a systemic process by which police had essentially kneecapped an entire community. When people debate why there is a cycle of violence, poverty, and despair in Baltimore's inner-city communities, they may point to this document.

But what the document didn't address is what happened to all of those people who were stopped, frisked, arrested, and thrown in jail even though they hadn't been breaking any laws. Did they lose a job? Did the false arrest lead to some sort of psychological trauma that affected work and family? The data the DOJ report presented is devastating in part because of what isn't mentioned explicitly but is there if you read between the lines. This type of law enforcement can be crippling for generations of people. This explains a lot.

There are young black men who run from the police even though they are innocent of any crime. They run because the police officers they know are not viewed as helpful, as the findings in this report substantiate. The police officers in their neighborhoods may stop and harass Dad and Mom, are disrespectful to Grandma and Grandpa, and look at these men as a threat. "Protect and Serve," which is the phrase that bonds police officers to the neighborhoods they patrol, clearly does not mean the same thing to many black Americans as it does to white Americans.

What is unsettling to black Americans is that they believe this type of policing has been happening in cities across the country. Since 2009, the DOJ has opened investigations into more than twenty-three police departments.[7] Many of these departments have the same problems. It has been described as systematic bias, and at the heart of the issue is zero-tolerance policing, which leads to unconstitutional stops, searches, and arrests. It had been happening in Baltimore for about sixteen years. But the tactics and the idea behind zero-tolerance policing originated in New York City. It was a more aggressive strategy that ended up driving down crime. The accomplishments were worth bragging about, and politicians and police chiefs did just that. But what they appeared to miss was the growing resentment in communities of color. Inner-city neighborhoods were essentially beaten and battered by police tactics that not only enabled but also led to constant and consistent harassment on city streets across the country.

Many feel that the root of the problem was the "Broken Windows" policy. "Broken Windows" was a policing theory first floated by James Wilson and George Kelling. In a 1982 article titled "Broken Windows," the duo discussed a crime-fighting strategy rooted in enforcing minor infractions that could lead to major crimes.

> In the 1960s, when urban riots were a major problem, social scientists began to explore carefully the order maintenance function of the police, and to suggest ways of improving it—not to make streets safer (its original function) but to reduce the incidence of mass violence. Order maintenance became, to a degree, coterminous with "community relations." But, as the crime wave that began in the early 1960s continued without abatement throughout the decade and into the 1970s, attention shifted to the role of the police as crime-fighters. Studies of police behavior ceased, by and large, to be accounts of the order-maintenance function and became, instead, efforts to propose and test ways whereby the police could solve more crimes, make more arrests, and gather better evidence. If these things could be done, social scientists assumed, citizens would be less fearful.
>
> A great deal was accomplished during this transition, as both police chiefs and outside experts emphasized the crime-fighting function in their plans, in the allocation of resources, and in deployment of personnel. The police may well have become better

crime-fighters as a result. And doubtless they remained aware of their responsibility for order. But the link between order-maintenance and crime-prevention, so obvious to earlier generations, was forgotten.

That link is similar to the process whereby one broken window becomes many. The citizen who fears the ill-smelling drunk, the rowdy teenager, or the importuning beggar is not merely expressing his distaste for unseemly behavior; he is also giving voice to a bit of folk wisdom that happens to be a correct generalization—namely, that serious street crime flourishes in areas in which disorderly behavior goes unchecked. The unchecked panhandler is, in effect, the first broken window. Muggers and robbers, whether opportunistic or professional, believe they reduce their chances of being caught or even identified if they operate on streets where potential victims are already intimidated by prevailing conditions. If the neighborhood cannot keep a bothersome panhandler from annoying passersby, the thief may reason, it is even less likely to call the police to identify a potential mugger or to interfere if the mugging actually takes place.[8]

In the 1980s under New York City mayor Rudy Giuliani and then police commissioner William Bratton, the "Broken Windows" theory attracted big-name backers because it was working. Most law-abiding citizens loved it. Politicians embraced the get-tough policies as campaign rhetoric, and its use became more widespread. Among the tactics developed was an approach to policing in which officers were encouraged to stop and question pedestrians and then frisk them for weapons. "Stop and frisk," as it is now more commonly known, was practiced mostly in inner-city communities of color. You never really saw it employed by the NYPD on Manhattan's wealthy Upper East Side or Upper West Side. Stop and frisk ended up targeting blacks and Latinos, and because it appeared to be working to drive down crime, variations of the tactic were then used in other cities and towns.

The NYPD's brightest commanders were hired away to cities across America, spreading the crime-fighting gospel. Meanwhile, "Broken Windows" tactics were shattering black families. Blacks were being stopped, frisked, and sent to jail in large numbers.[9] The tough-on-crime gospel ravaged black neighborhoods as men were wrongly accused—swept up by "zero tolerance" law enforcement strategies. Prisons swelled to record populations,[10] and the pressure increased on cops to make arrests and to write tickets to cut corners.[11]

Politicians who didn't want to run on a platform of raising taxes to fill city coffers instead pushed for police officers to hand out more tickets.[12] Being aggressive was encouraged as law enforcement essentially turned into a cash cow. Proactive policing was perverted and police officers turned into revenue-generating arresting machines. Politicians touted the successes as crime—at least according to the numbers—dropped. Those same politicians painted a rosy picture of how it was happening. And although many of the people living in black communities knew the truth, no one was listening to them. What do you expect to happen in neighborhoods if families are torn apart, men are thrown in jail and prison, schools are faltering, and unemployment rates are skyrocketing? As I mentioned before, young blacks would (understandably) routinely run from officers, whom they saw as agents stopping and frisking family members, disrespecting elders, and viewing them as threats to safety.

Instead of building allies in the fight against crime—in some cases, police departments across America gained critics and enemies. Zero-tolerance has led to animosity and frustration toward the men and women in blue policing communities of color. And now the job of a police officer is tougher than ever. Officers are leaving home and heading out onto the streets in pockets of cities that are more dangerous than ever before. Broken windows policies and three-strikes laws that significantly increased prison sentences may have begun with good intentions, but they morphed into albatrosses around the necks of communities that didn't have the power or influence to speak out against them. Today, the Black Lives Matter movement has been giving voice to communities that believe they have lived with the pain of oppression for decades. However, it's not just the people who identify themselves as supporters of the BLM movement. It's bigger than that. The people pushing for change aren't always marching or protesting, and they aren't always the ones you see on television or speaking out on social media.

In late May 2016, a young black activist in Chicago ominously told me, "Black people are starting to wake up to the systemic racism. I think people have known about it, but nobody has really taken action, or people have just dealt with it and said 'there's nothing we can do.'" But he said that is changing. Then he offered a warning. "People are now ready to fight back across the country." Within weeks, a crazed gunman armed with an AR-15-style rifle shot and killed five police officers in Dallas.[13] Then, just over a week later, three more police officers were shot and killed in Baton Rouge, Louisiana.[14] There was bloodshed on both sides of the divide, and no one seemed to have the right message to ease the heartbreak. On this issue, even the president seemed to be at a loss for words.

CHAPTER THREE

THREE DAYS AND SEVEN DEAD

resident Barack Obama was in the last year of his presidency. For most of 2016, his public-approval ratings were high, but the pollsters may not have been talking to a lot of cops. Among rank-and-file officers, the president had his critics. Many of them believed he was constantly taking sides after police-involved shootings of black men.[1] Granted, the issue was highly charged and emotional. No matter what was being done, the divide only seemed to grow wider; the protests, louder. Over the years, President Obama had succeeded in articulating how he was going to revive the economy, rescue Detroit's auto industry, and draw down the number of troops in Afghanistan and Iraq. But the nation's first black president was having a tougher time explaining the complexities of the lingering lack of trust between the police and the black community.

Terrence Cunningham, the president of the International Association of Police Chiefs, was deeply involved in those discussions, and even he was increasingly growing frustrated with some of the president's statements.[2] This was in part because Cunningham was getting heat from chiefs across the country who complained that President Obama was not being supportive of them. Cunningham is the chief of police in Wellesley, Massachusetts, and as the leader of IACP in 2016, he was an influential voice in the debate. He was also among a select group of law enforcement leaders working with the president to find solutions. The solutions seemed out of reach, but the tragedy in Dallas put a renewed focus and energy behind the effort to solve the problem.

America reached a new low during a week that should have been a high. It was July 4, 2016, and the country was celebrating its 240th birthday. Three days later, five Dallas police officers were shot and killed by a crazed, racist gunman who told police he hated white people.[3] The shootout, which like everything else these days was caught on camera, had once again exposed a huge crater in race relations in the country exacerbated by the tension between blacks and police.

The shooting occurred just as a peaceful Black Lives Matter protest was winding to an end. Armed with an AR-15-style rifle, Micah Johnson opened fire on the cops. The popping sound of bullets echoed through Dallas's downtown buildings. Protestors ran for cover, and cops ducked behind cars. I was watching on television as the horror unfolded live. The officers drew their handguns but couldn't pinpoint where the bullets were coming from. I remember seeing several officers looking up and around. They seemed confused at the time, unsure if there was one attacker or multiple shooters. Either way, it was a cowardly ambush, and we would later learn that the killer was targeting as many white cops as he could. Through our reporting, CBS News would learn that he was using skills he developed in the military. The Army Reservist was using "move and shoot" techniques that he had practiced in his backyard.[4] It was enough to keep police guessing. The killer survived long enough to talk to police negotiators. But ultimately Dallas police chief David Brown took the unusual step of approving the use of a bomb-squad robot to take the suspect down. The robot, which had been armed with a pound of C-4, moved in closer to Johnson's position. C-4 is a fairly powerful explosive. I've seen it blow a hole through half a school bus in a demonstration. What had been placed on that robot was more than enough to take out Johnson, and that's exactly what it did.

Typically, it can take a few days, weeks or months to determine a motive in shootings of that magnitude, but early on police knew why he did it. After having established contact with the crazed killer, investigators say that the twenty-five-year-old told them he took action in response to the deadly police shootings of Alton Sterling in Baton Rouge, Louisiana, and Philando Castile in a suburb of St. Paul, Minnesota.[5] Both shootings had happened that same week. Sterling was shot by police as he resisted arrest, and Castile was killed by a police officer who asked him for his identification. Castile had informed the officer that he had a permit to carry a handgun, and as he reached into his pocket to retrieve identification, the officer fired. Castile's girlfriend, Lavish Reynolds, activated "Facebook live" on her cell phone as the school-cafeteria worker bled out.[6] The officer was still shaking his revolver in Castile's face, as he drifted away. Not only did his girlfriend's daughter witness the encounter, but the whole world saw it. Two police shootings within a forty-eight-hour period, and black America doubted once again that anyone would be held responsible.

In the video, Reynolds says, "he let the officer know he had a firearm, and he was reaching for his wallet." The officer—who sounds shaken or panicked—says, "I told him not to reach for it. I told him to get his, told him to get his hand out . . ." His voice trailed off. Reynolds responds: "You shot four bullets into him, sir. He was just getting his license and registration, sir."

Blacks from different cities, states, socioeconomic backgrounds, and political beliefs were devastated. Castile's shooting was different. The video this time showed an innocent man needlessly dying. His blood-soaked undershirt in the foreground and the police officer's handgun just inches away. Castile had allegedly been pulled over for a broken taillight violation. He wasn't resisting. He was complying, and he still lost his life. Then the Dallas attacks happened. In the aftermath, Dallas's police chief—who happens to be black—used the pulpit he now commanded to say, "All I know is that this must stop— this divisiveness between our police and our citizens."[7] He made the statement during what had to be the darkest hour in the history of his department. But it was the right time for a message this divided country needed to hear. As I listened to the news conference and as investigators recounted what the killer said his motive was, what haunted me was what that young activist in Chicago had said to me a few weeks earlier. At the time, it stood out. But I brushed it off as hyperbole. Now it was ringing in my mind as significant.

He had said, "What you see is hate for the white man in these communities." Whenever white America hears blacks speak out in that way, it raises alarms. And in the wake of the shootings of police officers in Dallas and Baton Rouge just days later, it should. Especially when it's coming from a twenty-one-year-old who does not fit the mold of someone who is radical or potentially dangerous.

Over the Memorial Day weekend, I had gone to Chicago to begin working on this book. I knew that it would be a busy weekend, because the Windy City had been experiencing a deadly spike in crime. One thing I've learned while covering the crime beat is that, for some reason, hot summer weekends often lead to bloodshed in America's cities. I wanted to see firsthand how city residents, police, and politicians were reacting to the crime wave. I also wanted to get to the heart of the problem. Sometimes a TV camera can get in the way of that, and that's why I was traveling light with two iPhones and a notepad to record my meetings. I had several interviews set up, but it is the interview I stumbled into that became one of the most important voices in my research.

Chicago is a city I know, but not intimately. It's pretty obvious where the hotspots are, and that's exactly where I wanted to go. It was almost as if I was wearing a blindfold and throwing a dart at a target. I was going to go where the interviews led me—where the first person I called said "yes." That just happened to be Englewood, on the city's Southwest Side. When I arrived, I didn't hear the sound of gunfire or police sirens; what I heard was a celebration. Music was blaring, and Sherwood Park was rocking. There were children running around, playing games, and standing in line to get balloons twisted into different figures. The teenagers were listening and dancing to the music of forty-three-year-old Antoine Butler, who is known around here as DJ DAP.

His wife, Asiaha Butler, shook the dirt off a chair and offered me a seat next to her. I had a few questions about Englewood that only a lifelong resident would know the answers to. I was looking for honesty from someone who truly loved the community. Around here, the forty-year-old is known as "Miss Englewood." She doesn't hide her admiration for the community. Butler tells me, "I'm married to this community. All the negative perceptions that they say is wrong, I see what is right and I work to let others see what is right."[8]

She's the president of a group called RAGE, which is an acronym for Resident Association of Greater Englewood. It's a community association for the betterment of Englewood. Our conversation went as follows:

Pegues: How do you feel about this community?

Butler: I love my community. They call me "Miss Englewood" because I love it so much. I'm married to this community. All the negative perceptions that they say is wrong, I see what is right and I work to let others see what is right."

Pegues: Is that why you hold celebrations like this?

Butler: I do. Our parks are assets for this community, and I want the kids to enjoy it. Not to feel like they have to go out of the community to have a good time.

Pegues: Did you come up with the idea of forming RAGE?

Butler: I did. Members pay dues, and we do things together based on people's passions.

Pegues: Why RAGE?

Butler: The perception of Englewood is that it is horrible, so I actually had a play on names. You would think that we are the angriest people in the city. It's an acronym for Resident Association of Greater Englewood, and we actually are very calm. But, at the same time, we should be enraged by some of the things that go wrong in our community.

Pegues: What has gone wrong in your community that people who don't live here don't see?

Butler: Systematically, the resources that are here that are available, our housing market [for instance], we were targeted for predatory lending. Violence is rampant in our schools, which have been failing. There's a lot of things that most black communities face, and Englewood is just an example of that like any other urban area.

Englewood is three square miles of some of the most dangerous real estate in "Chicagoland." Year in and year out, it is hands down one of the murder capitals of the nation. In 2016, Englewood's homicide numbers were helping to fuel the city's record murder rate. Between June 11th and July 11th, there were nine homicides and a total of thirty-nine for the year. If residents don't fall victim to the deadly violence, the despair and lack of hope bearing down on them because they don't have jobs may kill them. The national unemployment rate heading into the summer in 2016 had ticked down below 5 percent.[9] By comparison, in Englewood it is more than 21 percent, and 42 percent of the households in the area live below the poverty level. Which, by the way, is more than two times higher than the rest of Chicago.[10]

>**Pegues:** I see all of the kids out here; they are having so much fun. But I also think about their future. What do you think about the future of the kids in this community? Is it bright, or is it grim?
>
>**Butler:** I think it's bright if they feel like it is and they work toward that. Like my daughter, who has been in Englewood her whole life. She's going to Spellman College on a full scholarship. So many people like her have that same opportunity. Our environment is not what makes us. It's what we do in this environment and how we thrive through it. We have to have this Englewood state of mind [that] regardless of what you're around, you have to be resilient and be very successful.
>
>**Pegues:** Do you feel the same way about black men here?
>
>**Butler:** The young men who are in danger . . . I wouldn't say it that way. I think it's just a small minority of young people trying to terrorize the community. The majority of our young people just want a safe and fun time and want to live. So I don't think they are all in danger. I think the people having that kind of lifestyle are in danger more so than the average Joe.
>
>**Pegues:** But do cops look at the bad apples and the good kids and see them all as one?
>
>**Butler:** They see [them] all the same 'cause they're young black males.
>
>**Pegues:** They see them all the same?
>
>**Butler:** They do.
>
>**Pegues:** So how do you feel about the cops here?
>
>**Butler:** I have some good relationships with some of the police officers here. I also have members of RAGE who are also police officers. But just living here as a citizen and sitting on my block watching them come through my block, they are very mean to a lot of the residents in the community.

Pegues: Mean?

Butler: Very disrespectful.

Pegues: How so? Do you have any specific examples for me?

Butler: Oh, tons of examples! Just sitting on our porch. We have a building across the street from us, and my husband was just going across to check on our building, and they grabbed him, locked him up.

Pegues: Your husband?

Butler: My husband. Grabbed him. Locked him up and put him in the car. And he's telling them, "I won these two properties." And they said, "You fit the description." The way they talk to you, it was just extremely disrespectful.

She says her husband works for the Cook County Criminal Court in a job he's had for over twenty years. But he still gets stopped by police all of the time. The police, she says, often say he's got a taillight out. It's difficult to stay positive about the police when you keep getting stopped or pulled over as you mind your own business and attempt to go about your daily life.

The divide between police and the black community in Chicago was a mile wide. The Windy City's police force, which as of August 2016 was being investigated by the Department of Justice's Civil Rights Division, had become the poster child for the problems in the relationship between police and the black community. The breaking point was Laquan McDonald's death. McDonald was shot and killed by police in 2014. The officer who shot him fired sixteen shots, all of which was captured by dashboard cameras. It took more than a year for the tape to be released, and many in the black community blamed the city's mayor for what they believed was a cover-up.[11]

Five years into his term, Mayor Rahm Emanuel had alienated the African American community, the very people who are among any Democrat's most important constituency. Blacks in Chicago felt betrayed by the mayor. No matter what he said, he was branded the architect of the cover-up that allowed what they viewed as the videotaped execution of the seventeen-year-old, to remain city hall's dirty little secret for far too long. Not only did it take Chicago officials more than a year to release the footage but a judge had to order them to do it.

Community activist Ja'Mal Green sees a little bit of himself in Laquan McDonald. He's just four years older. Green has a vision for the future and is intent on making changes in his community. He can back up the words he speaks with knowledge. He was the one who told me, "People are now ready to fight back across the country."[12] Green was home-schooled on Chicago's South Side, where he's better known for performing than for being an activist. He says he's been singing and dancing for as long as he can remember. He tells me he's done Broadway and movies, and he has always been passionate about giving back to the community. Green sees himself as a hybrid Martin Luther King Jr. and Malcolm X. He is now among those who are preaching about the simmering tension beneath the surface in inner-city communities. Asiaha Butler introduced me to Green in Sherwood Park that Saturday over Memorial Day weekend.

Green walks up in jeans, a bright neon-blue shirt and shoes. He greets everyone around him with a smile before he takes the stage. They love him here. Butler says she's surprised he even showed up, because he's been so busy leading some of the protests around the city.

As Green is about to sing, I'm told that there was a time when people admired him solely for his talent on stage. Now his intellect is also giving him a voice. "Would you describe yourself as militant?" I ask him. "No," he replies.

"I believe that we shouldn't just hate. I believe that we just shouldn't. That's what God wouldn't want us to do. But at the same time, we have to figure out a way to change the system to change these things and allow them to benefit us without just saying f— the police, f— the system, everybody's against them. I'm more in the middle, trying to figure out the middle ground and force that oppressive force to say, 'you got to come this way, to the middle, or else.'"

He believes the middle is a compromise that saves lives. Green says he was summoned to the mayor's office in 2015 in the hours before the release of the videotape showing Laquan McDonald's death. The police, city hall, and others had somehow managed to keep the video under wraps for over a year. Until, Green says, he and a handful of other Chicago inner-city leaders were summoned to the mayor's office.

> **Green:** November comes, and the mayor brought us in and told us he was going to release the Laquan McDonald videotape, and he joked, saying if it gets violent, don't look at me for resources. And so, yeah, that meeting happened.
>
> **Pegues:** 'Don't look at me for resources' . . . what did that mean?
>
> **Green:** Basically it was a joke, but it was probably the truth. So, [he's] basically saying if the city gets torn up, don't look at me to help you.
>
> **Pegues:** You had been working with the mayor's office in different capacities up until that point. Did you like him?
>
> **Green:** No, I never liked Rahm Emanuel.
>
> **Pegues:** Why?
>
> **Green:** He was a horrible mayor, number one, and he is a man who likes it his way or the highway. It's the stuff he says. It's his demeanor. He's been mayor five years, and it has still been a tale of two cities. He's honestly a ridiculous person. He doesn't get along with anybody. It's because of who he is. One thing politicians are good at is they're good at lying. They're good at showing or acting like they care. You can look, and you'll probably believe a politician. Rahm Emanuel, he's the total opposite. *I'm going to do what I want to do and I don't care about what you want to do. It's my way or the highway.* That's why nobody gets along with him—because he has no heart.
>
> **Pegues:** Do you think he has a heart for black people?
>
> **Green:** Hell to the no! Excuse my language, but not at all. No. All the way, no! if you can look at the last five years, you can tell that Rahm Emanuel does not care about the black community. I can call about fifty people [who] have pushed proposals. I myself have asked for a budget for the Put the Guns Down campaign. Okay, we want to actually reduce violence. Well, we got to put money behind it and bring awareness . . . do certain things and invest in certain programs. [We hear] "No money . . . city's broke . . . city's broke." But you can invest in DePaul's 100-million-dollar basketball arena . . . now they

want to build a museum . . . you can give 15 or 16 million to someone who is already rich to build a Marriott. You can expand the bike lane of Lakeshore Drive. You can give uptown 16 million dollars to build upscale apartments that are going to be 3,200 dollars a month. You can shut down fifty schools, but get a grant for the new South Loop school that's going to cost $8.2 million? They try to make it seem like it's not about [shortchanging black people], but if you really honestly look at the numbers and look at everything that's been going on, you'll say that there is definitely racism going on at city hall. You look at the police culture. You look at the fact that when Emanuel first came in he may have inherited a lot of these problems, but at the same time he still did the same thing that Daly did.

Pegues: Which was . . . ?

Green: He didn't care about changing the police culture. He kept it the same way. All these different policies stayed the same. The stop and frisk policies and the racism going on in the police culture kept going. They spent 664 million dollars in police misconduct since 2004. So it's really about how they are prioritizing the money down at city hall. They are spending the money on what they want to spend it on. And then you walk in these neighborhoods, and they are third world countries. You go in neighborhoods, and there is no economic development, no opportunities. They got the Red X program where they are just knocking down all the buildings, leaving the vacant land the same. No plans to redevelop anything in our neighborhoods. They shut down all the schools, with no plans to do anything about the buildings. Leaving them boarded up in our communities. So when you look at all this money that's going everywhere, you look in the neighborhoods and say not a dollar is coming into our neighborhoods? Then you got these same aldermen doing the bidding for Rahm Emanuel and standing next to him so they can be good and straight, but [they're] not feeding the communities. So does Rahm Emanuel really like black people? Probably not. But then people argue, well maybe he's not racist. Maybe it's a class issue? Maybe he only caters to the one percent? Maybe he only caters to the rich. Okay, maybe you can say that; but at the end of the day, those [who] are at the bottom, the majority of them, are the urban community. The majority of them are black. So it looks like a race issue.

Before the Laquan McDonald videotape was released, Emanuel called for calm: "I believe this is a moment that can build bridges of understanding rather than become a barrier of misunderstanding," he said.[13] It is "fine to be passionate, but it is essential that it remain peaceful." The dashcam footage of the seventeen-year-old's death is difficult to erase from memory. The video starts with a warning about its graphic content and "that viewer discretion is advised." On October 20, 2014, seventeen-year-old Laquan McDonald was shot sixteen times by police. His body absorbed some of the bullets as he lay dying on a Chicago street. He was shot so many times that you actually see smoke rising from his body. He died in the street alone. The cops who shot him didn't try to help him after he was down. After a while, one of them kicked a knife away from his hands and · walked away. The video fades to black.[14]

In some ways, the city went dark too after that shooting. Police officials, union officials, and city officials kept it under wraps. A man was shot by a police officer sixteen times in a matter of seconds, it was caught on camera, and there were questions about the shooting . . . and yet they sat on it for more than a year. Mayor Emanuel was orchestrating Chicago police reform, but he had a long way to go to win back the trust of the black community. Over the years, he had developed a reputation for going it alone. He was a member of Congress representing Illinois's Fifth Congressional District for three terms; he was President Obama's first chief of staff for about a year and a half;[15] and when he left Washington in 2010, he had friends in high places—but also a growing list of enemies.

But this didn't deter him from pursuing his dream job as the mayor of Chicago. It was a nightmare now as he tried to explain to a skeptical public all that had gone wrong in the police department and, by extension, his administration.

On December 9, 2015, Emanuel humbled himself and appeared before the city council to deliver a speech on police accountability. But there was a lot more than that on the line. Emanuel wasn't just trying to restore trust in the CPD; *he* needed the public's trust, too. His public approval was scraping the bottom of the barrel at 18 percent.[16]

JUSTICE, CULTURE, AND COMMUNITY

(Mayor Rahm Emanuel, Wednesday, December 9, 2015)

Members of the City Council, police officials and community leaders and religious leaders:

We are here today because Chicago is facing a defining moment on the issues of crime and policing—and the even larger issues of truth, justice, and race. We can either be defined by what we have failed to do—or what we choose to do.

To meet this moment, we need to come to a common understanding of how we got here and why. We need a painful but honest reckoning of what went wrong—not just in this one instance—but over decades.

We need to talk about what to do differently to ensure that incidents like this do not happen again, about the police culture that allows it and enables it, and the even larger cultural issues that devalue life in our communities.

Like every other challenge we have ever faced, this one is not bigger than us or beyond us. The only thing that stands between us and a better place is whether we have the collective will to admit to ourselves where we have fallen short and have the courage to do the hard but necessary things that it will take us forward.

Chicago needs your heart, your strength, and your spirit—because that is what it will take from all of us in this room and outside of this room.

What happened on October 20th, 2014, should never have happened. Supervision and leadership in the police department and the oversight agencies that were in place failed. And that has to change.

I am the mayor. As I said the other day, I own it. I take responsibility for what happened, because it happened on my watch. And

if we're going to fix it, I want you to understand, it's my responsibility with you. But we're also going to begin the healing process.
The first step in that journey is my step, and I'm sorry. Nothing
less than complete and total reform of the system and the culture
that it breeds will meet the standard we have set for our city. I have
reflected deeply on what happened that night: A young man with
a knife, agitated, and surrounded by police officers. But until the
point where Police Officer Jason Van Dyke got onto the scene and
got out of his car, this was a routine situation. It could have and
should have been contained and managed. Situations like this are
defused and resolved all the time without the loss of life, which
is why we never hear about them. The majority of our officers do
their job professionally every day. But thirty seconds after Jason Van
Dyke arrived, it was anything but routine or by the book. Sixteen
shots were fired. A young man from Chicago died in the streets of
Chicago.

Nothing . . . nothing can excuse what happened to Laquan
McDonald.

Our city has been down this road before. We have seen fatal
police shootings and other forms of abuse and corruption. We took
corrective measures, but those measures never measured up to the
challenge. So today I want to describe the challenges that we must
address. Every police officer is sworn to protect life; and, under the
most extreme circumstances, to take life. It is a staggering responsibility that requires officers to make split-second decisions.

In the millions of encounters each year between the police
and the public, it may be too much to expect that every officer
will always get it right. But it is not too much to expect that we can
put the right safeguards in place to hold officers accountable when
they get it wrong.

What makes an officer's job all the more difficult, dangerous,
and demanding is that it rests on upholding that sacred trust with
the citizens that he or she serves.

Nevertheless, I ask every police officer in Chicago to reflect
on your work, your training, your experience and—to be honest—
about the fears and frustrations you bring to the job. They are real.
They matter. And we as a city cannot be afraid to talk openly and
honestly about them.

We can define the rules of police-citizen engagement, but

everyday decisions will always be made by men and women in uniform, on the street, in the community, under extreme pressure in a dangerous world where guns easily fall into the wrong hands.

We are right to ask the best and the most of every officer. But the rest of us who do not put our lives on the line every day must be honest about our own responsibilities as well.

As a nation, we have done far too little to reverse the gun epidemic that makes every encounter between the public and the police potentially lethal. Shoot first and ask questions later too easily becomes the default practice and posture in a fearful world where mass killings are now a regular event and there is an increasing likelihood of a gun in every home, car, or backpack. The Chicago Police Department takes more illegal guns off the street than either New York or LA.

While we must hold accountable the fraction of officers who betray our solemn and sacred trust, we must also acknowledge the real dangers police face and the honorable work that the vast majority of them do every day.

My uncle was a police sergeant here in Chicago. And I respect the work that he did and other officers do today. But let me be clear. We cannot ignore nor can we excuse wrongful behavior, especially when it costs the life of another citizen. Police are not protecting the city of Chicago when they see something and then say nothing.

Our reforms will rely on the work of police, elected officials, and community leaders across our city who bring their experience, relationships, and close knowledge of the communities they serve.

We need your leadership and your involvement, because a big part of this effort is to empower your constituents to help police make our communities safer. We have to provide opportunities for the community to air their grievances with the police, and we need community leaders to foster those conversations and to keep those conversations productive, honest, and respectful.

I want to also speak directly to every resident of Chicago. I work for you. My first responsibility and your government's first responsibility is to keep you and your family safe and to make sure that you feel safe in your neighborhoods.

And we have clearly fallen short on this issue, and that needs to change. It starts by hearing your fears and frustrations—as well as your hopes and your expectations.

We also need to see what we can do in our communities to restore trust where it has been lost. I know some of you are afraid to work with police. You do not trust them.

And I want to be honest, when African American mothers, fathers, and grandparents feel it is necessary to train their sons and daughters to behave with extreme caution when they are pulled over by police to have both hands visible on the wheel, what does that say? We have a trust problem. It is not something I would ever tell my children. That's unacceptable.

When parents tell their children not to congregate on corners, especially in groups, out of fear for them encountering the police, what does that say? We have a trust problem.

So we—elected leaders, police officers, and community and religious leaders—have a responsibility to earn back the trust and to change that narrative.

This is not just about what the police need to do.

When a nine-year-old son is executed in retaliation against his father by someone who knew his mother, what does that say? We have normalized gun violence.

When an adult victim of gun violence himself gives his four-teen-year-old niece a gun to settle a score from social media, which then leads to the homicide of another child, what does that say? We have normalized gun violence.

All of us must set a higher standard of behavior for our children and help them understand that people can work out their problems responsibly and fairly with mutual respect. We need to reset our norms. We need to reset our expectations. We need to reset our values.

This is not just on the police or the community. I know that I—personally—have a lot of work to do to win back the public's trust, and that words are not enough. I will not rest until we take the concrete steps that are necessary to confront these issues—comprehensively and effectively. There will be many who doubt our efforts. I get that. I begin this effort with a request of every person in this city to bring out the best in themselves. To look for the best in others as we focus on the hard work ahead.

It falls into three overarching areas: justice, culture, and community.

The pursuit of justice on the issue of police misconduct is our most immediate and pressing goal. And several efforts are already underway.

First, Officer Van Dyke has been charged with murder, and the state's attorney is proceeding with the case. The public trust is the most important resource we have. But I recognize that a prolonged investigation served to undermine public trust and every day that we held on to the video contributed to the public's mistrust. And that needs to change.

Second, there is a federal civil rights investigation into this shooting and the conduct of the officers who responded to the scene. That investigation began a little over a year ago. And again, that is being handled by the US attorney.

Third, the Justice Department is now looking more broadly at the issue of police misconduct, police oversight, and civil rights here in Chicago. We welcome it. We will be a better city for it. It is in our self-interest, because we need their help and assistance to make the fundamental and necessary changes.

Fourth, on August 6th, the ACLU and the Chicago Police Department came to an agreement to have an independent evaluation of the CPD's investigatory stop practices and procedures, additional data collection on stops, better training for officers, and better transparency for the public. As part of this historic agreement, the Chicago Police Department will create enhanced training to reinforce the law and policy and to ensure respect for civil rights. Because civil rights and public safety go hand in hand.

Fifth, we announced a task force last week of respected and knowledgeable leaders in criminal justice and police oversight who will conduct a very public and thorough review of our existing system of training, oversight, discipline, accountability, and transparency. In a letter made public this week, the task force outlined a timeline and plans to hold public hearings with the community and with experts from across the country.

The task force is led by Lori Lightfoot, a distinguished former prosecutor with a deep history of investigating police misconduct. She currently chairs the Chicago Police Board, which rules on police disciplinary cases. It also includes Inspector General Joe Ferguson, retired Chicago police deputy superintendent Hiram Grau, former federal prosecutor Sergio Acosta, and University of Chicago law professor and former public defender Randolph Stone. In addition, Chicago native Deval Patrick, the former chief of the civil rights division of the US Department of Justice and former governor of Massachusetts, is serving as a senior advisor to the task force.

Collectively, the members of the task force bring decades of experience, knowledge, and different perspectives to these complex issues. They have committed to delivering a report to the public by the end of March that clearly identifies the problems and offers real solutions to each and every one of them.

They will look at the Bureau of Internal Affairs at the Police Department, which investigates corruption, and they will look at the Independent Police Review Authority, which investigates police shootings and citizen complaints. They will look at IPRA's record since it was created in 2007 and ask a simple question. Why—out of the hundreds of police shootings in the last eight years—only a handful of them have led to any charges. They will ask why some police officers with repeated and multiple citizen complaints of excessive force have yet to face any meaningful disciplinary action.

These facts defy credibility, which is why on Monday I appointed Sharon Fairley to head IPRA. She brings a wealth of experience from the public and private sectors to help reinvigorate IPRA and reestablish the integrity and independence it was originally designed to have.

The first recommendation by the task force is that we appoint a senior officer for civil rights at the Chicago Police Department who will have clear authority to implement the recommendations of the task force and ultimately the recommendations of the Department of Justice. They will also look at the report from former prosecutor Ronald Safer offering recommendations to strengthen police disciplinary procedures—although we have to cast a wider net than that effort. They have to examine decades of past practices that have allowed abusive police officers with records of complaints to escape accountability; they should revisit every policy and every protocol, including the timing and release of videos that are part of an ongoing investigation.

As you know, two new videos were released this week—raising even more questions about police actions. Although the state's attorney is declining to prosecute in one of them, IPRA will be doing another review of both cases. The task force will also look at what other cities are doing and the steps they took. Cities all across America are dealing with similar challenges. There are lessons to be studied, lessons to be learned, and lessons to be implemented.

We have all seen the videos from Cleveland, New York, North Charleston, and as recently as Miami. We have read the studies and articles on racial profiling, the lack of diversity in our police ranks across the country, and the disproportionate levels of enforcement towards people of color.

It is my deepest hope that we continue to address these issues in a peaceful, passionate, and productive way, but I fully understand that the public's patience is limited. You want answers. You want corrective action. You deserve both; and you will get both.

To be clear, this task force will not be guided or directed by my office. Their job is to get out all of the facts about the police department and the reforms and the changes that must be adopted. As we move forward, I am looking for a new leader of the Chicago Police Department to address the problems at the very heart of the policing profession.

The problem is sometimes referred to as the "thin blue line." Other times it is referred to as the "code of silence." It is the tendency to ignore. It is the tendency to deny. It is the tendency [to] in some cases cover up the bad actions of a colleague or colleagues. No officer should be allowed to behave as if they are above the law just because they are responsible for upholding the law. Permitting and protecting even the smallest acts of abuse by a tiny fraction of our officers leads to a culture where extreme acts of abuse are more likely, just like what happened to Laquan McDonald.

We all have grieved over young lives lost again and again to senseless violence in our city. Now more than ever we need good and effective policing. We cannot have effective policing if we turn a blind eye to the extreme misconduct we saw at its worst in the tragic case of Laquan McDonald.

We cannot ask citizens in crime-ravaged neighborhoods to break the code of silence if we continue to allow a code of silence to exist within our own police department. We cannot ask young men to respect officers if officers do not respect them in kind. Respect must be earned. Respect is a two-way street.

The search has begun for a new superintendent to lead the work in changing this culture and to lead the department. In the meantime, the acting superintendent John Escalante has already taken some initial steps. Last weekend, he announced that there will be zero tolerance for patrol officers who fail to properly engage dashcams. He has also taken the step to expand the use of body cameras to a third of our districts. He will also retrain police for de-escalating tense situations and minimizing the use of force.

And we will recommit to reinvigorating our community policing strategies. Chicago is where the whole idea of community policing began. It remains the best and most comprehensive approach we have in changing the everyday conditions that breed crime and violence and then breed mistrust. We have more work to do, and we need better training to live up to the values and the principals of community policing.

It is one thing to train officers on crime-fighting. It is a whole other thing to train them to build friendships and relationships, which are integral to fighting crime. This takes time, effort, and patience on the part of police officers. They have to sit with parents. They have to sit with their kids, and community leaders. They have to listen, collaborate, and in many cases be a mentor.

Over the last few years, we have trained ten thousand officers on the concepts of community policing, but, frankly, training is not enough. Our leadership needs to reinforce that training and set the example necessary for the principles to also be translated into action.

We also train police to understand the circumstances when they can use excessive force. But as one sergeant in the Fifteenth District said to me recently, there is a difference between *whether* someone can use a gun and *when* they should use a gun.

Just because extreme force is justified does not always mean it is required. This is where the right training is essential. But for this effort to succeed, we must rebuild the partnership with our communities—and that gets to the third principal: community.

In our city today, we have people of every background, race, and culture; and ethnicity and that is one of Chicago's great strengths. We have a vast well of talent, ideas, and energy. We have the skills and knowledge to lead the world in every field—and in many areas we do.

We have the love and strength of our mothers and fathers, and the hopes and dreams of our children. We need to direct our collective energy towards a common vision of a better tomorrow for this city. And every one of us needs to reflect on what we can do in our own lives to make our communities safer. That includes me.

How do we raise our kids? What values do we teach them? How do we help them negotiate those challenging years between childhood and adulthood so youthful mistakes do not lead to negative consequences? How do we give more young people more opportunities instead of a path to nowhere? For many of these young people, gang life is the only life they know.

When I was sworn into office in May, I said that when young men and women join gangs in search of self-worth, we as a city must and can do better.

I said when young men and women turn to lives of crime for hope, we as a city must and can do better.

I said when prison is a place we send young boys to become men, we as a city must and can do better.

When I talk to these young men who have had negative experiences with police, they tell me they just want one simple, human thing—respect. I was with a group of young men this weekend, having lunch. All who had had a history with the criminal justice system. All had a made a choice to do something different. And they are trying to get on the right path. Do the right thing. Acknowledge that what they did in the past was wrong. So I asked them, tell me the one thing I need to know. Rather than tell me something, one young man asked me a simple question that gets to the core of what we're talking about. He said, "Do you think the police will ever treat you the way they treat me?" And the answer is no. And that is wrong and that has to change in this city. That has to come to an end, and end now. No citizen is a second-class citizen in the city of Chicago. If my children are treated one way, every child is treated the same way. There is one standard for our young men. And we can do everything that we are talking about. But it comes down to one simple thing. It's what we are taught when we're children and what we hope to teach our children as parents, and that is the value of respect. We can have the training, we can have the leadership, we can have the manual. But it is what is in here that we need to call out onto the streets of Chicago. Because respect is earned. Respect is a two-way street. And that is what we will begin to demand from this day forward.

Now, while we have communities overrun by gangs and guns, I

want to be clear with everybody, we also have grandmothers who sit on porches watching kids go to school, people who mentor young men, and kids who are graduating and going on to college. We as a city cannot just show up when there is a basketball shot or a gunshot. We must be there every day, helping to nurture that sense of community.

Beyond the issues of policing and fighting crime, we must also address the underlying challenges of family, of poverty, of jobless-ness, of hopelessness, which demand greater action. Not just in this city but across the country. We cannot wait another day to address the current crisis that we face.

We have to have better oversight of our police officers to ensure that they are living up to the high standards we expect of them. And we also have to create a place for the community to vent their understandable feelings and fears about the police—without it devolving into acrimony and finger-pointing.

We have to have these difficult conversations if we are going to build trust. Not just have the conversations but also have the ability to hear each other. We have to enable people to speak freely, and we have to listen intently. We have to listen to the parents whose children were killed, and see their extraordinary grace, their strength, and their courage that is required of them to endure the infinite pain of burying a child. We have to listen to the men who have been in and out of the criminal justice system—and listen to the limited choices they faced, and understand them rather than simply condemn them.

And, finally, the community has to listen to our police offi-cers talk about their work and the challenges of working in com-munities overrun by gangs, drugs, guns and the loss of hope and opportunity.

At the same time, police have to listen to the community to understand the challenges they face and hear their hopes and expectations for their own future and their own children's future.

Both sides have to look beyond the surface to see the common humanity they share, instead of the differences that divide them. A young man can look at the uniform or see a father. The officer can see dreadlocks and tattoos or a student and an artist. Our efforts are to have them see past their roles to their souls. That is our work.

We have to be honest with ourselves about this issue. Each time when we confronted it in the past as a city, Chicago only went far enough to clear our consciences so we could move on.

This time must be different. It will be a bumpy road—make no mistake about it. It is a painful process. It is a long journey because of the issues we need to confront. But we as a city will not hesitate in pursuit of what is right. We cannot shrink from the challenge any more than we can ignore that wrenching video of a troubled young man, a ward of the state of Illinois, failed by the system, surrounded by the police, gunned down on the streets of Chicago.

This is not the Chicago we love and this is not the Chicago we know. This is not the police department we believe in and trust to protect our families and our neighborhoods. This is not who we are. And this will not stand.

Laquan McDonald's death was totally avoidable. Our only choice as a city is to do everything in our power to right that wrong.

It starts today. It starts now. It starts with us.

Thank you.[17]

The speech received a standing ovation. It played well in City Council Chambers, but in the neighborhoods? As emotional as it was, with the mayor appearing to get choked up at times, Emanuel's olive branch wasn't enough. Blacks were furious, hurt, and fed up. In the eyes of many African Americans, the ninety-second video spoke volumes about the state of black relations with law enforcement. The officer who fired his weapon sixteen times—Jason Van Dyke—was charged with first degree murder. Ja'Mal Green says that Van Dyke had become one of the poster boys for "protect and serve" gone bad.[18] He says that residents in Chicago's black neighborhoods have become consumed with anger and even hate:

What you see is you start seeing hate for the white man in these communities. Just because they'll start looking at the white man and picture Rahm Emanuel and picture what's going on and say, "Are you out to get me?" I just think it's coming to that point, and I don't want it to be a race war—it shouldn't have to be—but in our neighborhoods, the white man coming into our neighborhoods looks like the white man that's coming against us. Whether that's police or anybody else. It just looks like an oppressive force because of what's been done to us for so long.

CHAPTER FOUR
THIN BLUE LINE

Dean Angelo is the voice of what Ja'Mal Green calls the "oppressive force." Few people are more vocal about the challenges facing cops in Chicago than he is. Before we were to meet in person, he told me over the phone that he believes the political environment for police officers has never been more toxic. He doesn't think cops are getting the support they deserve, and he thinks that politicians are more worried about negative headlines, damaging video, or staying in office than in actually serving both the police and the community. He says, "Right now it is not politically correct to support police. We've got a system in Chicago that is very political and always has been."[1]

The sixty-two-year-old is as colorful a character as you will ever meet. He is Chicago through and through. The kind of guy you envision rooting for "DA-Bears" on Sundays. He believes in the men and women who make up the ranks of the Chicago PD, and he doesn't shy away from controversy. For example, he gave a job to the cop who shot Laquan McDonald. Officer Jason Van Dyke and his family were having a difficult time making ends meet, and so Van Dyke was offered a job as a janitor in the Fraternal Order of Police Union Hall. Public relations be damned.

Angelo, who is the president of the Fraternal Order of Police, defended the hiring with this statement to the local media:

Weeks ago, the FOP reached a decision to assist the Van Dyke family. Due to the notoriety of the incident, the ongoing threats of harm and intimidation and other issues caused him to become completely unemployable. Furthermore, after several threats against the safety of his spouse and her clients, his wife was forced to shut down her family-run business, resulting in zero household income.[2]

The Union Hall is in Chicago's West Loop. When I arrived, it was casual Friday and Angelo was dressed in an orange collared shirt with tan slacks. I was a couple minutes late, and he was in the middle of speaking with a colleague when he pointed down the hall to his office. As I walked through the office door alone, the first thing I saw behind his desk was a large police crest on the wall. There were framed photographs on the bookshelves, and both the Italian flag and an American flag were displayed. When he walked in, I made some sort of remark about his office and motioned over to the flags. Angelo told me that his dad was "half and half"—half Irish and half Italian. His mother? "All Italian." He is proud of his family heritage and about what it means to be a cop. This is something he no doubt inherited from his father, who was on the force for thirty-seven years. That makes three generations of Angelos in the Chicago Police Department, with the FOP president's son now in uniform.

Dean Angelo rose through the ranks, and his son is currently a cop following in Angelo's footsteps. It's pretty clear that this is a man who bleeds blue and sees red when he's asked about the current state of the Chicago Police Department. "Why would anyone want to be a cop anymore?" I ask.

"Good question," he replies. "It's a terrible job right now. You can't do anything right, you know, in the public's eye, in the media's eye, in the politician's eye."

Angelo believes police officers have become the "whipping boy" for politicians and the public in general. He says that city leaders are finding that it helps them if they run campaigns on anti-police plat-forms. "Although we have a lot of friends in the media [and] we have a lot of friends in politics, it's very difficult for our supporters now with the anti-police environment to stand up for us. I'm the only one that says it now. I'm trying to be the voice of support."

Angelo attests that cops feel more isolated than ever before, with fewer people willing to stand up for them. He believes that even other police union leaders—whose job it is to defend rank-and-file officers—aren't speaking up.

Angelo: You don't hear them. You don't see them. And, it's just me. Which is okay, it's a big chair, it's a big-boy chair, you know, I don't mind.

Pegues: But, you know, in a way, it's sad. I wonder sometimes if police officers feel ashamed to wear the uniform and walk the streets in some places. I mean, I'm sure you're scrutinized like never before?

Angelo: Well, I don't think they are ashamed at all, you know, I think they're very proud of what they do. And I think they love this job.

Pegues: What part of it?

Angelo: All of it!

Pegues: "Protect and serve"? Does that mean anything anymore, or . . . ?

Angelo: Oh, yeah, it has to. Otherwise, you get your s—and you go home.

Pegues: There are some who are going home, and just giving up?

Angelo: Well, they don't leave, you know. We can moan and groan and complain all we want, but nobody leaves. If you don't like it, go find another job. But, although we may be crabby and feel disenfranchised and be very frustrated with what's going on, we show up every day. And when someone calls, there's a woman screaming for help—you fly.

Pegues: No matter where it is?

Angelo: No matter where it is.

Pegues: Englewood?

Angelo: Englewood, my god, more times in Englewood than anywhere else.

Pegues: Because there's—

Angelo: More times on the West Side. There are so many people that live in Englewood that want us on every one of these corners, and they don't want us to leave, but they can't say it because they're afraid, and they live there, and they can't get out. We're their only source of protection, and they love us, but they can't go to a community meeting and say "I like the police," because guess who else is in the community meeting?

"I can't say that in an open forum because I'm targeted and because there are instances where, if I did that, my front steps and my back steps are burned at three o'clock in the morning when I'm sleeping, or when my grandkids are sleeping with me, my family's there. God forbid I open my mouth, I got to shut up and survive." That's who we're there for.

But despite what he says Chicago police officers are doing every day, he believes they are getting the blame for society's problems.

Angelo: Now everybody is writing about police. We got people that write about real estate, well, because of policemen the real estate has gone down, because of the lack of stops—real-estate prices, are going down—it's our fault. Education reporters are writing about the police not going into the schools as prevalently as they used to, and now, the disruptions in the classroom are out of control, and the police, my god, we should be everywhere, you know. We can't fix your kid. We can't raise them. We can't fix your marriage. We can't get you a job. We can't fix your addiction, you know. You know we certainly can't cure your psychosis, but everybody wants us to do everything now, because everything is related to crime and statistics; and the people that are on the streets wind up at the wrong end of a police-involved shooting. Well, you know what, he was off his meds—we should know that? He has a history of being homeless and being psychotic—and we should fix that? We should treat that? We can only judge what's in front of us at the time; and if it's a threat, we need to eliminate the threat because my li'l' ass is going home. So, how do you say that? And how do you continue to perform that way when everybody thinks you're conspiring? Everybody thinks the mayor says "code of silence" or "the thin blue line." The thin blue line is what keeps that beast from his front porch.

Pegues: What do you mean?

Angelo: We are there to be the line of separation between the good and the bad. That's what the thin blue line is. The thin blue line is the line of support for the families that cannot support themselves. The line of protection for the people that can't protect themselves. The line of defense for the people who can't defend themselves.

Pegues: In the inner cities?

Angelo: Everywhere.

Pegues: Everywhere. So, when the media writes about the thin blue line, you don't see it the same way that they do?

Angelo: They're way off base. They don't know the definition. They don't even know the meaning behind it, but it's adopted this new connotation, this new negative stigma that's way off base.

Chicago is now one of America's most violent cities. Through 2016, the city was experiencing a wave of murders the likes of which it had never seen.

When I was there that year during the month of May, according to the Chicago Police Department, there were 66 murders, 318 shootings, and 397 shooting victims.[3] That was a 40 percent increase over the previous year. The total for the year to date was another record at 243, which alone was a 48 percent increase over the year before. With good reason, Angelo calls some of Chicago's neighborhoods "the kill zone." It's harder than ever for citizens to stay alive, especially when cops are admittedly doing less. You don't often hear cops acknowledge that they are not doing their jobs as "proactively" as they used to. But Angelo confirms that some officers have thrown in the towel.

Angelo: I've got guys with twenty years [of experience] that can't wait to get out. They can't wait.

Pegues: Just in the last two years, because of what's been happening?

Angelo: Yes. More so now than before, but yeah. I got kids, and I tell them, "You're on your first pair of boots, you're done? You're on your first pair of boots, man, you got a long career." They say, "Hey, man, I'm done. I'm not going out there, and doing what I used to do."

It's the Ferguson effect. FBI director James Comey made the term famous while trying to explain why crime was shooting through the roof in some communities. Critics pounced on him for saying that. Even President Obama denied that it was happening.[4] But it is. Cell phone cameras have changed the way police officers are doing their jobs. People are watching them, and they do not like it. In Baltimore, there was cell phone video of Freddie Gray being lifted into a police wagon. He was dead a week later. Alton Sterling was shot and killed in Baton Rouge, and the encounter with two police officers was caught on cell phone cameras. Philando Castile was shot and killed on cell phone camera after a traffic stop, and in Chicago Laquan McDonald was shot sixteen times. It took more than a year, but eventually that (dashcam) video was made public, too. Angelo suggests that some of the officers he represents do not see videotape as a welcome addition to policing because it may reveal too much.

> **Angelo:** Just take into consideration the disrespect, the YouTube video, and sooner or later I'm going to hit one of them, because I'm a human, too. I can be an idiot if I get pushed to be an idiot. I'm not supposed to be, but I'm a human, too, and I have behavioral functions that are going to come out when I get put in a corner as well, whether it's verbally or physically. But if we don't take [suspects] down, if we don't search them, if we don't document them, if we don't roust them and try to get them to move off the corner or lock them up when they got a gun or when they got dope, and if we don't approach them, we don't know when the guns come or go, or when the dope arrives or doesn't.

On a sheet of paper, Angelo draws a diagram showing several city blocks. He says if cops pull back on one of the corners on those blocks by not cracking down, crime will go up. In his experience, if you don't stay on top of the people who loiter on the corners, by constantly engaging, the crime problem escalates.

> **Angelo:** I want all these corners. So I'm going to come by and confront them. I'm going to get them off that corner and

put my guys on that corner. If we don't take that corner back, [then] these are all different blocks in our neighborhood. We lose the corner, we lose the block. We lose the block, we lose the community, and it's half done. Now what do you do? Or how do you take that block back? And everybody that lives here, there are houses up and down these blocks . . . for lack of a better word, they're f—ed.

Over the holiday weekend, his theory appeared to be playing out on the streets, with the bloodshed being the ultimate proof that the system was failing some of Chicago's neighborhoods. By the time the sun set on Memorial Day, the nation's third largest city had capped its deadliest month of May in more than twenty years.[5]

CHAPTER FIVE

"SOMETHING IS HAPPENING IN AMERICA"

In May 2016, FBI director James Comey was still pressing the issue. Spikes in homicides continued to ravage inner-city communities. There would be some discussion about next steps and policing, but then something would happen to cause political leaders and their constituents to turn away to other matters. Comey clearly believed a lot more needed to be done when he decided to tackle another speech on race. Police relations with African Americans were still touching new depths. Comey and his aides settled on going to one of the most famous churches in America. It was to be used as a backdrop for what would turn out to be one of the most important speeches to date during Comey's term as FBI director.

The Sixteenth Street Baptist Church will always stand as a monument to the Civil Rights Movement. In 1963, a bombing there killed four black girls. It was another seminal moment on the march to equality. But the church is also known for hosting prominent visitors. Dr. Martin Luther King Jr., most memorably. Half a century later, Comey stood out like a sore thumb. He is among the tallest men in government, and there are few people more adept at grabbing headlines the way he is. He has a way of drawing attention to his actions. There is no reining in his words with a script, as he routinely speaks his mind. Over the years, colleagues had described Comey as "honest to a fault." But during the summer of 2016, his reputation for being independent and above politics was beginning to unravel. His decision to announce the result of the FBI investigation into Secretary Hillary Clinton's private e-mail server brought a torrent of negative headlines for the FBI director.[1] And the pressure on him increased when he essentially reopened the investigation eleven days before the election, after having cleared Clinton nearly four months earlier. Democrats ultimately blamed Comey, in part, for Hillary Clinton losing the 2016 presidential election.[2]

In July 2016, Comey was viewed as a voice of reason in law enforcement. During the first half of the year leading up to his speech at the Sixteenth Street Baptist Church, he had been able to reach law enforcement in a way others in the Obama administration could not. The president's relationship with police had frayed. So, it was Comey who had become the administration's "public face" for reform. His speech was a call to action. "Something is happening in America," he told the mostly black crowd filling the church's pews.[3] "A whole lot more people are dying. In some places more this year than last year and more last year than the year before, and I do not know why. And those homicides are happening nearly entirely in communities of color. You've seen it right here in Birmingham."

Alabama's largest city had seen its deadliest year in almost two decades.[4] According to Comey, some were attributing the violence to the drug trade or the high poverty rate. But, like in other cities, an exact cause seemed to elude the experts.

That was the story in city after city. According to the violent crime survey for the first quarter of 2016, homicides, rape, robbery, aggravated assault, and nonfatal shootings were all up.[5]

Comey referred to the teachings of Dr. King and implored the audience and America at large to pay attention and do more:

> Those spikes in violence seem to be happening in what you could call "cities within cities." Over here is a city with safe neighborhoods, clean streets, and good schools. People can wash their cars in the evenings, sit on their porch, and walk their dogs. Over here is a city where parents are afraid to let their kids play outside, where a good education is an uphill battle, and the street corners are becoming war zones. Most of us in America can drive around this city, right? Because we live apart from that violence. We don't live in that city within the city. We can escape it. We think: "Hey, it's not my neighborhood. It's not my problem." But these neighborhoods belong

to every single one of us. It is our problem. Not just the police, not just teachers or city council members or community leaders, but everyday citizens. The same citizens who so often show the peculiar indifference to something that is not immediately part of their reality. We are all guilty of that.[6]

But there was evidence that rising crime was everyone's problem. Sometimes people forget that a crime spike in a major city might eventually spill out into the suburbs. The latest data from the 2015 Uniform Crime Report showed that violent crime in suburban cities was up 3.4 percent compared to 2014.[7] Crime in the suburbs was trending in the wrong direction—which was another reason why police reform, as Comey at one time noted, needed to happen carefully and thoughtfully everywhere. Finally, Comey channeled Dr. King:

It will take all of us, every single member of every community, to fight for and deliver change. To fight for equality and fairness, to stop driving around problems. To be agitators and insiders in the best way. In the way that Dr. King taught us.

On television, 2016 was turning into the year of Trump. The Republican nominee was dominating news coverage. The FBI director's speech in Birmingham was largely overshadowed. He wanted law enforcement and communities of color to "continue to talk to each other," because he knew what was at stake, and the divide seemed to be growing.

That was certainly the case in Chicago, where recommendations for reform were being implemented . . . just not as fast as many in the black community wanted. In the midst of it all, cops were "stepping back" with their tactics under fire and under review. Consequently, about six months after the Laquan McDonald video was made public, crime in the city seemed to be out of control. Residents in several Chicago neighborhoods compared living there to inhabiting a war zone. Cook County commissioner Richard Boykin has his own theories about why the situation devolved the way it has. The Austin neighborhood is one of Chicago's most notorious "kill zones."

Like Englewood, it ranks near the top in homicides. But there is also a 21 percent unemployment rate (two times higher than the Chicago average), and 27 percent of the nearly one hundred thousand households live below the poverty level.[8]

Commissioner Boykin says that he has constituents who tell him that when they call police, the cops don't show up. For instance, he was contacted by a homeowner who said that she hears gunshots and every night sees people on the street corners dealing drugs; Boykin reports that she told him, "I call the police, and they don't come."[9]

When Boykin isn't representing his constituents, he works as a lobbyist. He is a lawyer who spent ten years as the chief of staff of longtime congressman Danny Davis. But he came back to Chicago to run for commissioner. He grew up in Englewood, where his father worked for the Ford Motor Company for more than thirty years. He said, "Love my mom dearly, but my dad taught us the values that kept us out of jail, that kept us out of gangs, [and] that kept us from having guns. He demanded that we get an education. That we do the right thing." Boykin says residents in the community have to do better: "We all have a responsibility and an obligation. Never before in the history of this country have blacks killed each other in Chicago at the alarming rates we're doing that now. We get very emotional when a police officer shoots somebody [who is] black. When a black person kills another black person, we don't see the same level of emotion. It's just another casualty of war. Unacceptable. You know, I wish the Black Lives Matter movement would be zeroed in and focused in on this black-on-black crime and figure out how we reduce the violence."

But Boykin's list of people to blame extends well beyond Black Lives Matter. He also points to police. "Right now, we got a crisis." He says, "We got a state of emergency in Chicago with respect to this gun violence and with respect to police sitting on the sidelines and allowing this to go on." Later, he tells me, "We've got to protect our neighborhoods, and right now the neighborhoods are not being protected. If this was happening in the white community, there would have been a state of emergency declared. There would have been a massive response."

For all intents and purposes, the city is in a state of emergency as its mayor and Police Department attempt to win back trust. After the

Laquan McDonald shooting, the Police Accountability Task Force was formed. The stated goal of the panel was to "actively seek out, listen, and respond to voices from all over the city" who had stories to tell about the Chicago Police Department.[10]

Investigations into the McDonald shooting alleged that Chicago police officers involved in the shooting lied about how it happened. As the task force pointed out in its findings, initial reports of the shooting were "false," and the "false narrative about the shooting originated with comments from the scene by formal Fraternal Order of Police Spokesperson, Pat Camden."

According to the task force, Camden told reporters: "Officers got out of their car and began approaching McDonald, again telling him to drop the knife"; "The boy lunged at police, and one of the officers opened fire"; "Officers were forced to defend themselves"; and "[McDonald] is a very serious threat to the officers, and he leaves them no choice at that point but to defend themselves."[11]

The video—when it was finally released thirteen months later—told a different story. Van Dyke fired the first sixteen shots, and Laquan McDonald was leaning away from the officer. The CPD's so-called code of silence had been exposed along with other systemic problems going back decades.

According to the task force, the problems manifested themselves in various ways:

- Death and Injury at the Hands of the Police
- Random but Pervasive Physical and Verbal Abuse by the Police
- Deprivation of Basic Human and Constitutional Rights
- Lack of Individual and Systemic Accountability[12]

But there was also an acknowledgement that racism plays a role:

The Task Force heard over and over again from a range of voices, particularly from African Americans, that some CPD officers are racist, have no respect for the lives and experiences of people of color, and approach every encounter with people of color as if the person, regardless of age, gender, or circumstance, is a criminal. Some people do not feel safe in any encounter with the police.

Some do not feel like they have the ability to walk in their neighborhoods or drive in their cars without being aggressively confronted by the police. The consistent theme of these deeply held beliefs came from a significant cross-section of people: men and women; young, middle-aged, and older; doctors, lawyers, teachers, and other professionals; students; and everyday workers. Regardless of the demographic, people of color loudly expressed their outrage about how they are treated by the police.

These encounters leave an indelible mark. Long after the officer moves on to chase the next call or make the next stop, the citizen involved remains affected; and if the encounter involved physical or verbal aggression, even if there was no arrest, there is a lasting, negative effect.

The linkage between racism and CPD did not just bubble up in the aftermath of the release of the McDonald video. Racism and maltreatment at the hands of the police have been consistent complaints from communities of color for decades. And there have been many significant flashpoints over the years—the killing of Fred Hampton (1960s), the Metcalfe hearings (1970s), federal court findings of a pattern and practice of discriminatory hiring (1970s), Jon Burge and his midnight crew (1970s to 1990s), widespread disorderly conduct arrests (1980s), the unconstitutional gang loitering ordinance (1990s), widespread use of investigatory stops and frisks (2000s) and other points. False arrests, coerced confessions and wrongful convictions are also a part of this history. Lives lost and countless more damaged. These events and others mark a long, sad history of death, false imprisonment, physical and verbal abuse and general discontent about police actions in neighborhoods of color.[13]

The CPD's own data gives validity to the widely held belief that the police have no regard for the sanctity of life when it comes to people of color. Police officers shoot African Americans at alarming rates.[14]

The report found that of 404 shootings between 2008 and 2015, 74 percent of the people hit or killed by police officers were African Americans. Blacks made up just 33 percent of Chicago's population. The report also found that police officers disproportionately used Tasers against African Americans as well. Seventy-six percent of the people getting tasered were African American.

Also, black and Hispanic drivers were searched four times as often as white drivers, even though contraband was twice as likely to be found on whites.

In conclusion, Chicago's task force decided to do the following:

- Create a Community Safety Oversight Board, allowing the community to have a powerful platform and role in the police oversight system.
- Implement a citywide Reconciliation Process beginning with the Superintendent publicly acknowledging CPD's history of racial disparity and discrimination, and making a public commitment to cultural change.
- Replace CAPS [Chicago Alternative Policing Strategy] with localized Community Empowerment and Engagement Districts (CEED) for each of the city's 22 police districts, and support them accordingly. Under CEED, district Commanders and other leadership would work with local stakeholders to develop tailored community policing strategies and partnerships.
- Renew commitment to beat-based policing and expand community patrols so that officers learn about and get to know the communities they serve, and community members take an active role in partnering with the police.
- Reinvigorate community policing as a core philosophy and approach that informs actions throughout the department.
- Evaluate and improve the training officers receive with respect to youth so that they are prepared to engage in ways that are age-appropriate, trauma-informed and based in a restorative justice model.
- Require CPD and the police oversight system to be more transparent and release to the public incident-level information on arrests, traffic and investigatory stops, officer weapon use and disciplinary cases.
- Host citywide summits jointly sponsored by the Mayor and the President of the Cook County Board to develop and implement comprehensive criminal justice reform.
- Encourage the Mayor and President of the Cook County Board to work together to develop and implement programs that address socioeconomic justice and equality, housing

segregation, systemic racism, poverty, education, health and
safety.[15]

According to Boykin, economic development may be among the
most important aspects of any reform. But is the political will there
to make those changes? Boykin says, "it hasn't been to date."[16] It is
his belief that had Mayor Emanuel, the governor, and others gotten
together in a room and discussed ways to deploy resources, the situation might have gotten better. "How can we target communities that
have unemployment rates upwards of 25 percent—unemployment
rates at the rate of the Great Depression?" he asks. "During the Great
Depression, the highest unemployment rates were between 16 and
25 percent. The community you are sitting in today, Austin, has an
unemployment rate of 22 percent. West Garfield, which is not too far
from here, has an unemployment rate of 25.8 percent. East Garfield,
upwards of 20 percent. These are West Side communities. So you
have these communities with high unemployment rates, and then
if you dig down deeper and look at the black male unemployment
rate . . . it's horrific!"

CHAPTER SIX
LIVESTOCK

I'd been in Englewood's Sherwood Park for a couple of hours when the new Chicago police superintendent arrived. He was in a black SUV when it pulled up to the curb. Eddie Johnson's visit came as a surprise to most of the people in the park. But not Ja'Mal Green, who says he invited Johnson to come.

It was a noble effort by the new police boss to reach out to the community in one of the toughest neighborhoods, where his officers by and large are not viewed favorably. As Johnson mingled with the crowd, I interviewed Jermont Montgomery, a community organizer and the program manager of a youth league who also works nights at General Motors. On this day, he's dressed in a white T-shirt and jeans, and his hair is in dreads.

He wasn't among those in the park who rushed over to introduce themselves to the superintendent. I asked him what his thoughts on the police were. He responded, "The relationship between the community and police . . . where do I begin? . . . As a youth myself, growing up [here, you] can be confused. You met great police, and you met aggressive, very judgmental police."[1]

Pegues: What do you see the majority of?

Montgomery: I see a department rooted in a radicalized system of justice to perpetuate a system where some lives are considered livestock.

Pegues: "Livestock"?

Montgomery: Livestock.

Pegues: You think that some cops look at black people as livestock?

Montgomery: Yes, as a commodity. Arrest quotas, drug laws that

make the war on black men and the black community—when
there are just as much drugs being rotated around the white
community. We could talk about the war on guns, which
is now the war on the black community as well. There's a
number of different systems, I think, put in place that suggest
that the law is to discriminate.

Montgomery, who will be forty this year, admits to having been
arrested "plenty of times." He acknowledges that he was once "a par-
ticipant in something illegal as a teenager." He wouldn't get into spe-
cifics or tell me exactly why he was arrested, but he says he has turned
his life around with a college degree and has since been working in
the community. There, he believes, he has a pulse on what many
think about the cops.

He continued, "For too long, the police department became
a place for people to take frustrations out on disenfranchised
communities."

That's why he believes some of the tension exists. But does the
community share some of the blame?

I tell him that I've spoken with law enforcement officials who
believe the kids in the black community, especially, are disrespectful
to the police. "If the kids don't respect the badge," he says, "it's
because cops never demonstrated respect for them. The one way to
reach these kids is simple, come down to Earth. Step out of your
uniform for a second."

It looks like that's what Superintendent Johnson is trying to do. He
didn't have to show up at this Englewood celebration, but he did; and,
like a politician, he's "pressing the flesh," so to speak, at least trying
to bridge the gap. He is a veteran of twenty-seven years on the police
force, and he was handpicked by the mayor to take the reins at a difficult time. But the African American superintendent's introduction
to the people in the city was not exactly flawless. He probably regrets it
now, but he said publicly, "I've actually never encountered police misconduct."[2] That kind of statement does not inspire confidence when
the community is looking for someone to lead the reform of a troubled police force. One critic of the superintendent wrote:

When he says he never witnessed misconduct, not even once, a lot of people, including me, asked how that could be true. Did Johnson come down with a case of temporary misconduct blindness? Did he suffer from some rare "see-no-evil disease" that manifested as a crick-in-the-neck that forced him to look the other way when misconduct was nearby? Twenty-seven years on the job is a long time to go without seeing a fellow officer break any department rules.[3]

In the *Crain's Chicago Business,* writer Tracy Siska called Johnson, "wholly unqualified to reform CPD."

In the most quintessential Chicago move ever, Mayor Rahm Emanuel and the Chicago City Council picked an insider to lead the Chicago Police Department. This comes at a time when everything signals the need to break from past practices, from the mayor's own task force to the ongoing investigation by the Civil Rights Division of the Department of Justice.

The mayor's pick, Eddie Johnson, is wholly unqualified to bring about the revolution in policing policies and practices that Chicago so desperately needs. If ever there was a time to not hire a rank-and-file cop's cop from the patrol division—one who says he's never witnessed a single incident of misconduct in his 27 years on the force—this is it.

The supreme irony of Johnson's appointment, though, is that it comes just as Emanuel's task force on accountability is calling for massive, dramatic, game-changing reform in the wake of the release of the Laquan McDonald video. Johnson's appointment is the exact opposite of that.[4]

Ja'Mal Green has his concerns as well, but he says he's known Johnson for a long time.[5]

Pegues: Do you like him?

Green: So, Eddy . . . he's humble . . . he listens . . . and I think that he's a good cop. He's a good man. He's very popular around Chicago. Of course, Rahm appointing him kind of tainted him and [set] everyone against him. I mean, it made him look like Rahm's boy when Rahm didn't really know him at all. But Rahm was just trying to get some cool points because everybody else knew [Eddy]. I think what Eddy has to do, and this is what I tell him, he has to start being a little more radical; and what people want to see are people who are going to stand up for them, and so the bad thing is that he's really a pawn—because at the same time he has no power to do anything. He can't fire an officer if he wants to; he has no authority to discipline officers.

Pegues: Why?

Green: Because they have police union contracts in place that prevent him from doing anything. If he does anything, they can sue him and get rich. The only thing he can do is put an officer on desk duty. So what people want to see is a superintendent that is really a boss. You do something, and your boss can fire you. They want to see some justice, and because of the process in place, it is preventing him from doing any justice. He's just really being a pawn, being a black superintendent that can hopefully gain some trust within the department . . . but he's a pawn. so I think he needs to start advocating for a new contract [with] FOP. He's got to start going against them—but then he's fighting the inside forces in the police department, and when he's doing that he's also fighting city hall. Even though he's not elected by the people, he still has to do right by the people so that they can support him; because at the same time, if a new mayor comes in, he'll be gone. So he's in a bad position. But he can take advantage of it by speaking out. Say, "The FOP contract is ridiculous and we need to change it. I want to have more authority to do my job and discipline officers, but the contract in place is preventing me from doing it." If you get the people behind you, you are unstoppable."

Pegues: Do you trust him?

Green: I don't trust anyone. I'm giving him a chance. The moment it goes south is the moment I will be his harshest critic.

Johnson spent about an hour in the park that day. It wasn't something that made headlines, nor was it mentioned in the news; but it may have been an important step in the right direction about a month after he got the job. However, many more important steps were needed to rebuild trust.

Three months later, Johnson made a bold statement. It wasn't so much what he said, though, as it was his actions. Not only did he announce a shake-up in leadership in the department but, perhaps most importantly for the image of the CPD, he recommended that seven officers be fired for making false statements. The officers were part of the alleged cover-up in the Laquan McDonald shooting in 2014.[6]

CHAPTER SEVEN
GHOST SKINS

The vast majority of police officers across the nation are doing the right thing. But there is a small percentage who are tarnishing the badge. Over the last several years, in addition to the police shootings that have sparked calls for reform, there have been scandals in departments from coast to coast. Some of those scandals have highlighted explicit racism within the ranks. Once again, technology plays a role in how that racism is exposed, as text messages often unearth bigotry in the rank and file. In 2015, an internal investigation in Miami Beach, Florida, revealed that sixteen officers had sent hundreds of racially offensive, sexist, and pornographic e-mails.[1] Two of the officers were high-ranking and were believed to be the main instigators.[2]

According to CBS reporting, Miami Beach police chief Daniel Oates informed reporters that the internal investigation uncovered 230 e-mails that were demeaning to African Americans and women or pornographic in nature. Many were reported to be depictions of crude racial jokes involving President Obama or black celebrities such as golfer Tiger Woods. One showed a woman with a black eye and the caption, "Domestic violence. Because sometimes, you have to tell her more than once."[3] One of the racially offensive e-mails depicted a board game called "Black Monopoly" in which every square says "go to jail."

The county's top prosecutor, Miami-Dade state attorney Katherine Fernandez Rundle said at the time that the officers' behavior had jeopardized about 540 cases in which the officers were witnesses. Rundle called the officers' actions "a breach of trust" and "disgusting."[4]

On the opposite side of the country, in San Francisco, California, the stain of racism was arguably much greater on that city's police department. It was a story that probably didn't get as much attention as it should have, and it's hard to figure out why. Perhaps it was because it was on the West Coast? Or because it was simply overshadowed by other similar stories happening in other cities across the country. But, regardless, looking back now—what was happening within the SFPD was probably among the most shocking cases to roil law enforcement in some time. This was so shocking in part because the city is seen as such a beacon of tolerance.

A corruption probe exposed the underbelly of the police department when San Francisco police sergeant Ian Furminger was stripped of his badge and then sentenced to 41 months in federal prison. The forty-eight-year-old was convicted of stealing money and property from drug dealers. He was clearly a bad cop who was also terribly reckless. According to court papers, his behavior as a police officer included throwing small explosives out of moving cars for fun and stealing antique call boxes.[5] Such papers also pointed out that he was a "virulent racist and homophobe who, even while a police officer, felt free to share his views with other individuals, including other San Francisco police officers." As investigators dug for evidence in the corruption case, they obtained the cop's cell phone and text messages between October 2011 and June 2012. He was still a police officer during that time, and he was sending text messages to friends and to other officers. The messages were racist:[6]

> "Don't worry about my height, worry that I'm white!"
> "White Power!"
> "We got two blacks at my boys [sic] school and they are brother and sister! There cause dad works for the school district and I am watching them like hawks."
> [In response to a text asking, "Do you celebrate quanza [sic] at your school?" Furminger wrote] "Yeah we burn the cross on the field! Then we celebrate Whitemas."
> "Its [sic] worth every penny to live here [Walnut Creek] away from the savages."
> "Those guys are pretty stupid! Ask some dumb ass questions

you would expect from a black rookie! Sorry if they are your
buddies!"

"The buffalo soldier was why the Indians Wouldnt [*sic*] shoot the
n—s that found for the confederate They [*sic*] thought they
were sacred buffalo and not human."

"Gunther Furminger was a famous slave auctioneer."

"My wife has 2 friends over that don't know each other the cool
one says to me get me a drink n— not knowing the other is
married to one just happened right now LMFAO."

"White power."

[In response to a text saying, "N—s should be spayed"] "I saw one
an hour ago with 4 kids."

"I am leaving it like it is, painting KKK on the sides and calling
it a day!"

"Cross burning lowers blood pressure! I did the test myself!"

[In response to a text saying, "All n—s must f—ing hang," Furminger wrote] "Ask my 6 year old what he thinks about
Obama."

[In response to a text saying, "Just boarded train at Mission/16th,"
Furminger wrote] "Ok, just watch out for BM's" [black males].

"I hate to tell you this but my wife friend [*sic*] is over with their
kids and her husband is black! If [*sic*] is an Attorney but
should I be worried?" [Furminger's friend, an SFPD officer,
responded: "Get ur pocket gun. Keep it available in case the
monkey returns to his roots. Its (*sic*) not against the law to
put an animal down." Furminger responded] "Well said!"

[In response to a text from another SFPD officer regarding the
promotion of a black officer to sergeant, Furminger wrote]
"F—in n—."

During Furminger's appeal for bail, a prosecutor wrote in court
documents:

If the medals and awards Furminger received as a police officer
are somehow relevant to the analysis of his character, his views
regarding black citizens, who were part of the population he was
sworn to protect, also are relevant. He not only possessed but felt

free to articulate these views to others while he was a San Francisco Police Officer. Although these sort of overtly racist views sadly are still expressed in some communities, it is shocking and appalling to find a police officer in San Francisco who would give voice to them. Furminger's willingness to do so—which exemplifies his erratic and anti-social behavior—should be taken into account.[7]

Furminger called his conviction "disgusting."[8] He added, "I'm well-educated, 20 years a cop, never had a complaint, civil or suits."

It wasn't just Furminger, though. More SFPD cops would fall in the scandal. In April 2015, San Francisco's police chief said he had moved to dismiss seven officers who sent or received text messages that spoke of lynching African Americans and burning crosses.[9]

According to the *New York Times*, Police Chief Greg Suhr said the texts, "are of such despicable thinking that those responsible clearly fall below the minimum standards required to be a police officer."[10] The texts were sent or received by as many as fourteen police officers in the department. Prosecutors and public defenders announced that they would be conducting a review to see if the cases the officers worked on had been tainted in anyway by their "animus toward racial minorities or gays."[11] The *New York Times* wrote that the lawyers for the officers have said the texts did not represent their clients' opinions and were little more than naïve banter meant to blow off steam in their high-stress jobs.[12]

It almost doesn't make sense that racist text messages would be shared over and over again between more than a dozen officers in a department with a good record for hiring diverse candidates. The DOJ investigation, which was concluded in the fall of 2016, found that between 2013 and 2015, minority candidates accounted for 50.2 percent of all candidates entering the SFPD Academy. But "gender, racial, and ethnic minority recruits were terminated at a higher rate from recruit training than white male recruits."[13]

San Francisco's population of 824,834 residents is comprised of 49.3 percent whites and 5.8 percent African American.[14] The police department was more than 9 percent African American. While that number was higher than the percentage of blacks making up the city's population and at least appeared to demonstrate a commitment to increasing diversity, the lack of it in any major numbers seemed to give some officers in SFPD a "green light" to share racist text messages. What did that say about the culture within the department? Look at what precipitated the Department of Justice investigation. There was a slew of incidents in addition to the Furminger investigation.

According to the Department of Justice:

> In a 2010 criminal investigation, a series of racist, sexist, and homophobic text messages was found to have been shared among a group of SFPD officers. The public was not informed about this issue until February 2014.
>
> In a similar incident made public in early 2016, prosecutors investigating an alleged sexual assault involving an SFPD officer discovered a series of racist and homophobic texts shared among the accused officer, his supervisor, and several additional SFPD officers in 2015.[15]

When the DOJ report on San Francisco was announced, it sounded similar to the investigations into the police departments in Ferguson, Missouri, and Baltimore, Maryland. Just as they did in those cities, DOJ investigators found clear patterns of behavior by police officers that negatively impacted people of color.

- African American residents were disproportionately stopped compared to their representation in the driving population.[16]
- African American and Hispanic drivers were more likely to be stopped and searched compared to white drivers.
- The majority of incidents involving the use of deadly force also involves residents of color; furthermore, the SFPD does not adequately investigate police use of force.

Once again, the DOJ found "numerous indicators of implicit and institutionalized bias against minority groups."[17]

A number of indicators highlighted the disparities in the way San Francisco police were doing their jobs.

A summary of data analysis is as follows:[18]

Analyses of the SFPD's traffic stop data reveal racial or ethnic disparities in stops, warnings, citations, arrests, searches, and contraband discovery. Citywide, African-American drivers were 24 percent more likely to be stopped by the police than their estimated representation in the driving population, and they were 9 percent more likely to be stopped than their estimated representation among potential traffic violators. Hispanic and Asian drivers, on the other hand, were considerably less likely to be stopped than their representation in the estimated driving and traffic violating populations in the city. African-American drivers were more likely to be warned, arrested, and searched (for both consent and high discretionary reasons) but less likely to be cited or found to be in possession of contraband than White drivers. Hispanic drivers were more likely to be arrested and searched (for both consent and high discretionary reasons) but less likely to be cited or found to be in possession of contraband than White drivers. Finally, Asian drivers were more likely to be cited or found with contraband but less likely to be warned, arrested, or searched based on consent than White drivers.

While these results indicate patterns of disparity, no definitive conclusions can be drawn regarding the underlying motivation for these outcomes including the possibility of racial or ethnic bias. Nonetheless, the patterns of disparity in post-stop outcomes are consistent with those found for the initial stop decision and warrant further monitoring, investigation, and analysis—possibly by drilling down to the officer or unit level using officer-to-officer comparison ("internal benchmarking") techniques as part of an early warning approach by the SFPD.

Bias in the actions of police officers erodes community trust and support. The SFPD as a whole exhibits a level of organizational understanding and awareness of bias and its implications for policing. Yet there are few demonstrable and measurable outcomes that assist in ensuring that biased policing is removed from the department's culture.

The SFPD must address the issue of bias directly and make the cultural changes needed not only to create a procedurally just and fair organization but also to account for those officers who engage in biased behaviors. Training and accountability must function in tandem with institutional cultural change to make a sustainable difference. When the police act outside the law or contravene their own policies on a regular basis, their legitimacy and the public's trust is negatively impacted. The SFPD must develop an ongoing institutional vision that addresses bias as part of an overall strategic plan, one that is transparent and gives voice to the community.[19]

But it's more than just traffic stops and "stop and frisk." In Chicago, it was literal torture; and in April 2015, the city agreed to a $5.5 million settlement for victims of a former cop.[20] CPD commander Jon Burge was alleged to have tortured 120 African American men between 1972 and 1991. He never went to prison for torturing the men, because the statute of limitations ran out. So the only case that would stick was perjury, because he lied under oath when he denied his role in the horror. According to the *Washington Post*, when Burge wanted to get people to confess to a crime, he would pull out a box. The box had two wires and a crank. His alleged victims told prosecutors that Burge would attach one wire to the suspect's handcuffed ankles and the other to his (handcuffed) hands. Then Burge would place a plastic bag over the suspect's head. He would crank the little black box, and electricity would pump through the suspect's body. One witness told prosecutors, "when he hit me with the voltage, that's when I started gritting, crying, hollering. It [felt] like a thousand needles going through my body."[21]

As the *Washington Post* describes, Burge would ask suspects, "You going to talk, n—?" And the suspects confessed. They were confessing to crimes they never committed. But that wouldn't come out until some of them had served thirty years behind bars. Mounting evidence of torture led to Burge's firing in 1993. He went to prison on that perjury charge but spent about four and half years locked up until he was released with a monthly $4,000 CPD pension. When the *Washington Post* reported on the story, some of Burge's alleged victims were still behind bars.[22] Burge's story should have been a cautionary tale for all of America, but most people aren't even aware that it happened, or they choose to forget.

San Francisco and Chicago are just a couple of examples of police departments that have had shocking bias incidents beyond police shootings of black men, which some argue points to other issues in the rank and file that may be harder to root out. A police chief I spoke with says the key to rooting out the bad cops starts when they fill out an application. His department tries to thoroughly screen candidates, and he says you'd be surprised about what comes up when people apply for the job.[23]

> **Pegues:** What kind of things come up?
> **Unidentified Police Chief:** Substance abuse. Gang relations. White supremacy.
> **Pegues:** White supremacy?
> **Unidentified Police Chief:** If you want me to say that that doesn't exist anywhere, I don't think I can give you a 100 percent answer. But there's obviously problems, because things are happening. There's obviously problems. I think we have a long road ahead of us.
> **Pegues:** When you say "things are happening" [what do you mean]? Have you seen cases?
> **Unidentified Police Chief:** I certainly saw it when I first came on about twenty years ago. It was sort of an us-against-them kind of mentality. I would hear statements like, "I have three of THEM stopped." If someone says something like that today, they can be terminated.

While times have changed, should a 2006 FBI report titled "White Supremacist Infiltration of Law Enforcement," be ignored? The bureau often compiles reports on domestic and international threats as a way of informing the nation's local police departments. Some of these reports seem rather routine and go unnoticed by the media, but this one really stood out. Several sections of the report were redacted, but what was made public said a lot about the severity of what the FBI believed was the threat of white supremacists infiltrating the ranks of police.

In a section the document titled "key judgements," investigators wrote:

- White supremacist leaders and groups have historically shown an interest in infiltrating law enforcement communities or recruiting law enforcement personnel.

- The Primary threat from infiltration or recruitment arises from the areas of intelligence collection and exploitation, which can lead to investigative breaches and can jeopardize the safety of law enforcement sources and personnel.
- White supremacist presence among law enforcement personnel is a concern due to the access they may possess to restricted areas vulnerable to sabotage and to elected officials or protected persons, whom they could see as potential targets for violence.
- The intelligence acquired through the successful infiltration of law enforcement by one white supremacist group can benefit other groups due to the multiple allegiances white supremacists typically hold.

According to the FBI, white supremacists have a name for their sympathizers among law enforcement: "ghost skins." Ghost skins are white supremacists who avoid overt displays of their beliefs and blend into society while covertly advancing white-supremacist causes. The FBI report says, "at least one white supremacist group has reportedly encouraged ghost skins to seek positions in law enforcement. . . ."[24]

CHAPTER EIGHT

SIXTEEN SHOTS

T wenty-one-year-old Chicago activist Ja'Mal Green is wise beyond his years. The young man is very clear about what he believes the city should be doing to heal the wounds of a police department run amok. After we met for the first time in Sherwood Park in Englewood, we decided to reconnect for an interview in downtown Chicago. It was a Monday morning, and we were meeting for breakfast. We sat down at a table, I put my cell phones in front of him and began recording.

Green believes that part of the solution to healing the wounds caused by police shootings is investing in the community. A change in police culture alone is not enough. "At the end of the day," he said, "what should have happened immediately is there should have been millions of dollars of economic development to change these urban communities. Millions of dollars in programs."[1] Too often, he says, politicians in Chicago claim poverty when inner-city neighborhoods ask for money for development. But then they steer millions of dollars to the wealthier areas and Chicago's Magnificent Mile, which is perhaps the most recognizable section of the city, with its luxury stores and apartments. There are also police officers on every corner of the Magnificent Mile. The area is representative of what Green sees as the mayor's central focus. He calls Emanuel, "the mayor of one city but not the entire city of Chicago."

The activist adds, "he's still building a museum, still trying to expand the bike lane. They said there is a budget for that, but there is no budget for the black community. Rahm Emanuel does not care about the black community." Green says when the black community asks for the city to invest, the reply is usually, "No money . . . city's broke . . . city's broke." Green's assessment that there is a lack of opportunity in many of the inner-city communities is supported in a study by the University of Illinois in Chicago that shows that the suffering in Chicago's black community goes well beyond police tactics. The report found that in 2014, blacks aged sixteen to nineteen had a jobless rate of 88 percent; that number dwarfed the national figures, which were also disturbing.[2] In the United States during that same year, this demographic (blacks aged sixteen to nineteen) was facing jobless rates of 79 percent.

Green says it comes down to survival for a lot of people in the inner city, because the problems with the police and crime are systemic. He says, "You have these systemic conditions where people are trying to survive. . . . It's not, 'let's go be successful.' It's, 'I got to figure out how to survive to the next day. How am I going to feed my family? Whether it be selling drugs . . . ?' Selling drugs is a way people in the urban community survive."

Pegues: Do you see drug dealers as bad?

Green: The only way I see a drug dealer as bad is if they are selling drugs in a community that has everything. So let's say in Englewood? You see drug dealers and killers as bad because you think they can injure your kids—that's understood. Let's look at the root of the problem. Let's look at why they are that way. The politicians will say, "We don't care why they are that way, we're just going to put them in jail and kill them." We need neighborhoods that look like your neighborhoods [wealthier neighborhoods]. Everybody should get the same treatment.

Everybody should have the same education, but our education is bad in the urban community. You are getting taught based on class. You go to a school in Englewood, and you are probably going to pass eighth grade with a basic education. You go to school up north in a white school or private school, whatever the case may be, you'll learn how to open up a bank account—know about credit and how to play the stock market. They are not going to teach you that in a black school. You get a basic education, and nobody really wants to go to college because they can't pay for it and they can't see themselves being in school that long 'cause there is no way to have income. They are growing up in neighborhoods where there is nothing. You look at TV and how they depict Africa—primitive. It's really how these neighborhoods look. You may have a few houses on the block—everything is torn up. People live in trap houses; there are no jobs or businesses in the community.

There are no businesses in the community that's giving jobs to the community. You got all these other races that are building in our neighborhood and hiring their own and taking money back to their neighborhood and communities. Then the only way you're going to get a job is that you have to travel, maybe downtown, and get lucky and get a job. But you shouldn't have to do that, and not everyone is going to do that. But then if you do something illegal, you grow up in these conditions . . . you may be on the block . . . something may happen and you may get arrested for it. You go to jail . . . come back, and now it's even worse for you. *Nobody* is going to give you a job now. You're going to go back to that community and be a menace to society. Nobody is going to give you a second chance.

When you go to Ravenswood [which is an area where real-estate values have skyrocketed over the years], people interact with the police because police don't have that much to do. They are not going into situations where they have to take down a killer or they feel threatened. So when the crime lowers, police won't feel threatened in our neighborhoods; [then] we can build on those relationships. But at the same time, we got to get those racist cops out of the force, too. That's why one thing I was always pushing for are cops to either work in the district they live in, or more black cops in black neighborhoods. So if there were black cops who understood our neighborhoods and policing our community . . . basically we would be policing ourselves and you won't see a lot of police killings and you'll see better relationships because people can relate to those cops. And once you have the cops blending in the community and becoming people within the community, then you'll have people saying, "Hey, what's up, Officer Tom? . . . I saw this—don't tell anyone." And you can have an anonymous call. There's trust. There's a relationship.

Back at the Union Hall in the West Loop, Dean Angelo, the head of the Fraternal Order of Police, agrees that police are confronting more than just crime. There are social issues that police cannot handle alone, "We can't fix your addiction, you know. You know, we certainly can't cure your psychosis; but everybody wants us to do everything now, because everything is related to crime and statistics, and the people that are on the streets wind up at the wrong end of a police-involved shooting."[3]

Police, he says, can't stop and cure it all, "We can only judge what's in front of us at the time; and if it's a threat, we need to eliminate the threat." Angelo seems agitated as he tells me how he really feels about all of the criticism Chicago cops are getting. He's critical of politicians who derisively refer to the "thin blue line" as a policing culture that rewards loyalty and silence over protect and serve. Angelo believes the people who criticize it, like Mayor Rahm Emanuel, don't really know what it means. "The thin blue line is what keeps that beast [crime] from his front porch. We are there to be the line of separation between the good and the bad. That's what the thin blue line is."

Angelo, who is sixty-two years old, says he didn't retire from the CPD—he was thrown off, because he had nine surgeries on his knees. One of the injuries happened when he was executing a search warrant. He said, "I've had a lot of reconstructions, and I always came back to work."

During his career, he went through gang crimes unit, bomb and arson, and patrol. When he was pushed out due to injury, he says his first reaction was, "Get the f— out of here!" But "just like that," he says, he was out. At the time, his two sons were in college and his two girls were in a private school. He remembers it being an emotional day. He's had many of those days as president of the FOP.

But among those days, he recalls that defending Laquan McDonald's shooter was a headache unto itself.[4]

Pegues: Sixteen shots, and he was walking, he was walking away. I mean, how does that get out of control?

Angelo: I don't know about walking away, walking is . . . he's—his back is—

Pegues: But he didn't seem like a threat, you know? How does it get—?

Angelo: Every one of those situations is [about] compliance.

Pegues: He wasn't listening?

Angelo: Drop that knife, it's over with.

Pegues: But *sixteen* shots?

Angelo: But he had been ordered to drop that knife for fifteen minutes, and you know the situation is going to court, so I got to watch what I do and say. But there are so many different things that were not available that night that could have eliminated this from occurring.

Angelo says the video the city has released doesn't tell the whole story because there is no sound. "When you hear the audio, it's different," he says. "But we see a silent movie. And we see a kid spin, and we see dust coming up, and it's like *oh my god!*" The FOP president sees it differently than most of the world: "You don't hear anything. We don't realize there's no other options out there, tactically." Angelo argues that it appears to him that McDonald is heading toward officer Van Dyke; "people are saying, 'Oh, McDonald's walking away,' but he angles towards the sidewalk, and that last step, he's coming—"

Pegues: Toward the officer?

Angelo: And that one last step, the shoulders square off for a split-second. Am I supposed to wait for him to close even further? He hasn't complied. He hasn't dropped it. . . . It's easy for us to look at that and go, "What's going on?"

Pegues: Should [Van Dyke] be acquitted?

Angelo: I don't know. I don't know. I don't know what's going to happen.

Pegues: If you were on the jury, would you acquit him?

Angelo: If I was on the jury, I would have to look at everything and take it all into consideration, and then I see an opportunity, a big opportunity for acquittal.

Pegues: You do?

Angelo: Yes.

Pegues: Do you think [Van Dyke] should be a cop? Based on what you know now, based on what you saw in that tape, should he be a police officer?

Angelo: I don't know the impact that this event has had on Officer Van Dyke or any other officer that's involved in these circumstances . . . but the residual impact that happens to somebody involved in a shooting needs to be evaluated. The stresses and the accusations that occur on a regular basis for this individual officer in particular have got to be something that needs to be brought in consideration. When you and I open the paper to look at a box score—how'd the St. Louis Blues do? How'd the Yankees do? How'd the White Sox win when the Cubs lose? We're looking for a sports story or we're looking for the weather report or a puzzle. He opens the paper every day and looks for his name. What does that do? And how do you absorb that? . . . Let's say acquittal happens and it's over. How do you recover? What do you do with your life from this point forward? Can you stay here? Can you get your job back? Are you healthy enough, behaviorally, to get your job back? Do you even *want* your job back? We have other officers that are still dealing with PTSD from incidents that they were involved in. People think, "Oh it's a cop, it's TV. Boom, boom, you're good." You're not good. You don't want to do that. You don't want to be that person that is in this situation that winds up taking someone's life.

Pegues: Have you talked to him?

Angelo: Yes.

Pegues: Is he remorseful?

Angelo: Yeah. He is. He's already said so. He's sorry for the incident happening.

Pegues: Would he ever want to meet with McDonald's family?

Angelo: I don't know about his family. His family was completely removed from this poor kid. This kid had no contact with his family whatsoever. I don't think his mom had seen him for years. Again, it's a failure of a structure, a social structure that wound up ending with police. You know, educationally, emotionally, psychologically, this kid was a throwaway kid. . . . You have people that have been abused in our system, and exposed to levels of crime that are worse than third world countries and war zones. Nobody gives a s—, because it's in Englewood. It's in Gresham. It's in Rosewood. It's in Austin.

Angelo's candor was surprising. He and I talked for about two hours, and most of his responses were laced with profanity. Perhaps I caught him at just the right time, in that he had a lot to get off his chest and he didn't feel the need to sugarcoat how bad the situation in the Windy City had become. For months, Chicago police were taking a beating from all directions, and they felt like they had targets on their backs just as they were being asked to step up and do more. Crime was rising and they were needed now more than ever on the streets to prevent further bloodshed. Meanwhile, state lawmakers were considering legislation that would dramatically change the way the cops were doing their jobs. Many in the rank and file were not comfortable with that, because the last thing they felt they needed was to be "handcuffed" while confronting the reality in the "kill zone." Dean Angelo was speaking up for them.

CHAPTER NINE

EXECUTIVE ORDER 13684

About five months after Michael Brown's death at the hands of police in Ferguson, Missouri, President Barack Obama gathered together a group of law enforcement officials and experts. Their task was to come up with solutions to solve one of the most pressing concerns of the president's two terms in office. This would be among the topics that would shape his legacy decades from now. It was a bit ironic that the nation's first black president would be confronted with solving the divide between law enforcement and the black community.

On December 18, 2014, with Executive Order 13684, the President's Task Force on 21st Century Policing was empowered to deliver a report on how to improve policing in America. It was given an initial ninety days to gather information. It met seven times and had "listening sessions" in three cities. Six months later, its final recommendations were published. The executive summary of these recommendations included the following:

> Law enforcement culture should embrace a guardian—rather than a warrior—mindset to build trust and legitimacy both within agencies and with the public. Toward that end, law enforcement agencies should adopt procedural justice as the guiding principle for internal and external policies and practices to guide their interactions with rank and file officers and with the citizens they serve. Law enforcement agencies should also establish a culture of transparency and accountability to build public trust and legitimacy. This is critical to ensuring decision making is understood and in accord with stated policy.[1]

Those ninety-three words were, perhaps, at the core of solving the ills that plagued law enforcement and some communities. But getting to the point where police departments were reaching critical milestones like that would require persistence and focus from police leadership in thousands of departments across the country—at least those that were willing to make the recommended changes:

- Build Trust and Legitimacy: "The public confers legitimacy only on those whom they believe are acting in procedurally just ways. In addition, law enforcement cannot build community trust if it is seen as an occupying force coming in from outside to impose control on the community."[2]
- Policy and Oversight: "If police are to carry out their responsibilities according to established policies, those policies must reflect community values. Law enforcement agencies should collaborate with community members, especially in communities and neighborhoods disproportionately affected by crime, to develop policies and strategies for deploying resources that aim to reduce crime by improving relationships, increasing community engagement, and fostering cooperation."[3]
- Technology and Social Media: "The use of technology can improve policing practices and build community trust and legitimacy, but its implementation must be built on a defined policy framework with its purposes and goals clearly delineated. Implementing new technologies can give police departments an opportunity to fully engage and educate communities in a dialogue about their expectations for transparency, accountability, and privacy."[4]
- Community Policing and Crime Reduction :"Community policing emphasizes working with neighborhood residents to co-produce public safety. Law enforcement agencies should, therefore, work with community residents to identify problems and collaborate on implementing solutions that produce meaningful results for the community. Specifically, law enforcement agencies should develop and adopt policies and strategies that reinforce the importance of community engagement in managing public safety. Law enforcement agencies should

also engage in multidisciplinary, community team approaches for planning, implementing, and responding to crisis situations with complex causal factors."[5]

- Training and Education: "Today's line officer [*sic*] and leaders must be trained and capable to address a wide variety of challenges including international terrorism, evolving technologies, rising immigration, changing laws, new cultural mores, and a growing mental health crisis."[6]
- Officer Wellness and Safety: "The wellness and safety of law enforcement officers is critical not only for the officers, their colleagues, and their agencies but also to public safety. The US Department of Justice should enhance and further promote its multi-faceted officer safety and wellness initiative. Two specific strategies recommended for the US Department of Justice include (1) encouraging and assisting departments in the implementation of scientifically supported shift lengths by law enforcement and (2) expanding efforts to collect and analyze data not only on officer deaths but also on injuries and 'near misses.'"

There is a lot to digest and implement from the report, and the president had been holding meetings throughout the year. In one of those gatherings six days after five police officers were shot and killed in Dallas, the president said:

The bad news is, as we saw so painfully this week, that this is a really hard job. We're not there yet. We're not even close to being there yet, where we want to be. We're not at a point yet where communities of color feel confident that their police departments are serving them with dignity and respect and equality. And we're not at the point yet where police departments feel adequately supported at all levels.

. . .

I do not want to gloss over the fact that not only are there very real problems but there are still deep divisions about how to solve these problems. There's no doubt that police departments still feel embattled and unjustly accused. And there is no doubt that minority communities, communities of color still feel like it just takes too long to do what's right.[7]

The commander in chief had become the therapist in chief, cautioning against complacency on the path to righting a ship that had gone off course for years. Progress had been haltingly slow in bringing reform to police departments across the country. Every setback, such as the killing of police in Dallas, had the effect of slowing progress in other cities, such as Baltimore. The interconnected world made everything seem closer to home.

The President's Task Force on 21st Century Policing came up with a total of fifty-nine recommendations and ninety-two action items. It was another blueprint for local government, law enforcement and members of the community to follow. It was a tall order to fill—especially with a nation still grieving after a horrific week that commenced with the deaths of two innocent black men at the hands of police (Alton Sterling in Louisiana and Philando Castile in Minnesota) and culminated in the ambush attack of police officers in Dallas, Texas.

"The roots of the problems we saw this week date back not just decades, date back centuries," the president said.

> There are cultural issues, and there are issues of race in this country, and poverty, and a whole range of problems that will not be solved overnight. But what we can do is to set up the kinds of respectful conversations that we've had here—not just in Washington but around the country—so that we institutionalize a process of continually getting better, and holding ourselves accountable, and holding ourselves responsible for getting better.
>
> . . .
>
> The pace of change is going to feel too fast for some and too slow for others. And sadly, because this is a huge country that is very diverse and we have a lot of police departments, I think it is fair to say that we will see more tension in police—between police and communities this month, next month, next year, for quite some time.
>
> The one thing I think we all have to do, though, is not paper over those differences or paper over those problems, but we do

have to try to constructively solve them and not simply win talking point arguments.[8]

In that last comment, President Obama may have been making a reference to some of the Sunday news shows. The weekend before the president's statement, Dallas police chief David Brown and the city's mayor, Mike Rawlings, were both able to thread the needle when it came to choosing the right words to characterize the moment and the difficult path forward.

On *Face the Nation*, host John Dickerson had a few questions for Mayor Rawlings:

DICKERSON: Before the shooting, Dallas was actually a model for community and police relations.

So, as people struggle all over the country after this week, what was Dallas doing right? Excessive force complaints were at a two-decade low. What can they learn from Dallas before the shooting?

RAWLINGS: Well, first of all, I think training of our police officers is first and foremost.

I'm so proud of our police force. They were one of the first to train in de-escalation, how do you deal with individuals, protect yourself, protect them, get them dealt with in the right manner. Second, community policing is important. But, third, also, supporting police officers [is] important in this.

Recruiting is down across the nation for our police officers. And we have got to make this a noble profession. And we can't let a very, very small few impact this noble profession. And so doing all three of those, getting the right officers on board, and then training them correctly is what we're all about.

DICKERSON: Finally, Mr. Mayor, the *Dallas Morning News* has a front-page editorial that says, "Now we face a [new] test." What's the test for Dallas, as you see it?

RAWLINGS: Well, I think we are a laboratory for the United States.

Can we, in a moment of crisis, when officers are fallen, forgive? Can we disagree without demonizing? Can we see a better narrative, as opposed to just absurdity, that there's redemption as we build this great city?

I believe we can. And I believe we will.[9]

Minutes later on the same broadcast, former New York City mayor Rudy Giuliani seemed intent on ignoring the sentiment Mayor Rawlings was trying to convey to the country.

DICKERSON: Mr. Mayor, I want to ask you about something former speaker Newt Gingrich said, which is that he said, "white Americans can't understand the extra risk that comes with being black in America and that whites instinctively underestimate the danger of the black experience." What do you think about that?

GIULIANI: I agree with that completely. I agree largely with the sentiments of Congressman Elijah Cummings. The reality is, we have to look differently at race in America if we're going to change this. We've been looking at it the same way for 20 years and—and here's where we are. And we both have to try to understand each other.

First let me say, my deep sympathy for the people of Minnesota, the people of Louisiana, the people of Texas and of Dallas and I'd like them all to remember that though these incidents happened in different ways, they all share it together as Americans. And we—we share this violence together as Americans. So—so maybe whites have to look at it differently and blacks have to look at it differently. Whites have to realize that African American men have a fear and boys have a fear of being confronted by the police, because of some of these incidents. Some people may consider it rational. Some people may consider it irrational. But it's a reality. It—it exists.

And there's a second reality in the—in the black community. And the second reality in the black community is, there's too much violence in the black community. So a black will die

1 percent or less at the hands of the police and 99 percent of the hands of a civilian, most often another black. So if you want to protect black lives, then you've got to protect black lives, not just against police, which happens rarely, although with tremendous attention, and which happens every 14 hours in Chicago. Every 14 hours and we never hear from Black Lives Matter.

That day, I was on *Face the Nation* with the former mayor. I was part of a panel that included Sherrilyn Ifill of the NAACP Legal Defense Fund. Giuliani's comments angered her. Ifill accused him of having a twentieth-century vision of policing at a time when the country needed a twenty-first-century approach. Giuliani, she alleged, had "presided over one of the most discredited areas and periods of policing in the city of New York."[10] Ifill blamed the type of police tactics Giuliani advocated for "a lot of the tension that exists between police officers and people in African American communities." Finally, she said, "Parents of African American men and boys are scared to death of their children's encounter with police and encounters with criminality."

If there was to be reform, some cities were pushing for reconciliation. But words can often make that more difficult to achieve.

CHAPTER TEN

TRUTH AND RECONCILIATION

In 1996 the hearings began. For anyone going through it, the process was emotional and grueling. But it was necessary for the country to move forward. There was so much horror in its past that the country had to confront, or it was doomed to fail again. Ultimately, more than twenty-one thousand people testified before South Africa's Truth and Reconciliation Commission. One by one, the victims of apartheid looked their tormentors in the eye. There were accounts of rape, torture, murder, and kidnapping. The commission's chairman, Reverend Desmond Tutu, said at the time, "we needed to acknowledge that we had a horrendous past. We needed to look the beast in the eye, so that the past wouldn't hold us hostage anymore."[1]

I thought of the Truth and Reconciliation Commission when I read Chicago's Police Accountability Task Force's recommendations. Halfway down page 18 of the executive summary was a recommendation to "Implement a citywide Reconciliation Process beginning with the Superintendent publicly acknowledging CPD's history of racial disparity and discrimination, and making a public commitment to cultural change."[2]

No one is recommending a process that goes as far as South Africa's, but this divide in the United States between law enforcement and black Americans shows that our country is still grappling with a troubled past when it comes to race. It may require some sort of reconciliation process—not only in Chicago but nationwide—where these issues are discussed openly and honestly.

FBI director James Comey acknowledged in his Georgetown speech in February 2015 that the pain in the black community did not develop overnight. "First, all of us in law enforcement must be honest enough to acknowledge that much of our history is not pretty," he said.[3] "At many points in American history, law enforcement enforced the status quo, a status quo that was often brutally unfair to disfavored groups."

Some historians and researchers trace the origins of policing back to the "slave patrols" of the early 1700s. According to Eastern Kentucky University School of Justice Studies professor Victor Kappeler, in 1704, the colony of Carolina developed the nation's first slave patrol. The slave patrols, he wrote, "helped to maintain the economic order and to assist the wealthy landowners in recovering and punishing slaves who essentially were considered property."[4] The slave patrols spread to other states and regions, followed by the Fugitive Slave Acts of 1793 and 1850. Federal laws paved the way for the return of escaped slaves to their owners. Penalties were slapped on anyone who helped them escape. As authors K. B. Turner, David Giacopassi, and Margaret Vandiver noted, "the literature clearly establishes that a legally sanctioned law enforcement system existed in America before the Civil War for the express purpose of controlling the slave population and protecting the interests of slave owners. The similarities between the slave patrols and modern American policing are too salient to dismiss or ignore. Hence, the slave patrol should be considered a forerunner of modern American law enforcement."[5] Then came Jim Crow laws in the South, which set different rules for blacks and for whites. The laws were based on the theory of white supremacy, and they were a reaction to both Reconstruction and a fear among whites of losing their jobs to blacks. In Mobile, Alabama, there was a Jim Crow curfew that prevented blacks from leaving their homes after 10 p.m. Signs were put up over doors or water fountains saying, "white only" or "colored." In the South, it was the police who enforced Jim Crow laws, which perpetuated segregation and discrimination.

Also, throughout the South and in other parts of the country, blacks policed themselves and protected their own homes and families, as they knew that they would be harassed or thrown in jail without cause if they reached out to the majority white police departments. Or they were resigned to the realization that the police wouldn't show up to help them anyway. Also, during the civil rights era, police officers turned their water hoses on black men, women, and children; released their dogs on peaceful demonstrators; and lowered their billy clubs to the heads of grandmothers, grandfathers, and children.

Those are the images stamped into the minds of African Americans across this country. Accounts of discrimination and segregation are still discussed around the dinner table. The parents or grandparents who were there still tell the stories of how they were arrested or mistreated or disrespected or harassed by a police officer.

Is it any wonder, then, that the public-opinion polls show a disparity between how blacks and whites view the police? According to a Pew Research Center Poll, the divide "runs deep."[6]

Surveys once again show the disparity in how blacks and whites see the world around them: According to a 2013 survey conducted just before the fiftieth anniversary of Martin Luther King Jr.'s March on Washington, 48 percent of whites claimed that a lot of progress has been made since 1963, yet only 32 percent of blacks agreed with that assessment of police relations.[7]

A year later, after Michael Brown was shot and killed in Ferguson, the gap between black and white was wider: 80 percent of black respondents said the incident raised important issues about race; in contrast, only 37 percent of white respondents agreed.[8]

It was almost as if whites and blacks were living in a different universe. In some ways they were—especially when it came to law enforcement and the criminal justice system.

A McClatchy-Marist survey reported that 76 percent of blacks, compared with 33 percent of whites, believed that there was a problem with the justice system when it comes to law enforcement and race.[9] The survey in 2015 also found that half of whites had a great deal of confidence in the police to gain the trust of those they serve; compare those findings against the 22 percent of African Americans who felt similarly.

There is also a sense of pessimism about whether things will get better, according to a December 2015 Pew Research survey. About half of blacks, or 52 percent, expected relations between local police and minorities to worsen over the next year, while 31 percent said that they would remain about the same, and only 16 percent predicted improvement.[10] While fewer whites, or 34 percent, saw relations getting worse, only 21 percent expected improvement, and 43 percent said things would remain the same.

Recent shootings caught on video, like the shooting of Laquan McDonald in Chicago, and Department of Justice investigations showing discriminatory police tactics further engrain a belief among blacks that bias in law enforcement persists and that police do not treat African Americans fairly or with dignity.

Deep in the DOJ patterns and practice investigation into Baltimore's police department are details of incidents that to African Americans serve as a haunting reminder of the past. Federal investigators point to public strip searches being used to humiliate people who, ultimately, were never charged with a crime.[11] The DOJ report also found that sometimes, if complaints were filed against the officers involved, the penalty would be *another* strip search:

> Strip searches are "fairly understood" as "degrading" and, under the Fourth Amendment, are reasonable only in narrow circumstances. Safford Unified Sch. Dist. #1 v. Redding, 557 US 364, 375 (2009). Strip searches are never permissible as part of a pre-arrest weapons frisk. See Holmes, 376 F.3d at 275 (weapons frisks must be limited to the outer layers of a suspect's clothing). Following a lawful arrest, the reasonableness of a strip search turns on "the scope of the particular intrusion, the manner in which it is conducted, the justification for initiating it, and the place in which it is conducted." Bell v. Wolfish, 441 US 520, 559 (1979). Absent specific facts indicating that an arrestee is concealing a weapon or contraband, officers may not strip search a person incident to arrest for an offense that is not "commonly associated by its very nature with the possession of weapons or contraband." Logan v. Shealy, 660 F.2d 1007, 1013 (4th Cir. 1981). Moreover, courts have "repeatedly emphasized the necessity of conducting a strip search in private." Amaechi v. West, 237 F.3d 356, 364 (4th Cir. 2001) (finding strip search unreasonable where it was conducted in public view). BPD policy likewise recognizes that strip searches should be conducted only "under very limited and controlled circumstances" and that "strip searching suspects in public view or on a public thoroughfare is forbidden."

Nevertheless, our investigation found that BPD officers frequently ignore these requirements and strip-search individuals prior to arrest, in public view, or both. Numerous Baltimore residents interviewed by the Justice Department recounted stories of BPD officers "jumping out" of police vehicles and strip-searching individuals on public streets. BPD has long been on notice of such allegations: in the last five years BPD has faced multiple lawsuits and more than 60 complaints alleging unlawful strip searches. In one of these incidents—memorialized in a complaint that the Department sustained—officers in BPD's Eastern District publicly strip-searched a woman following a routine traffic stop for a missing headlight. Officers ordered the woman to exit her vehicle, remove her clothes, and stand on the sidewalk to be searched. The woman asked the male officer in charge "I really gotta take all my clothes off?" The male officer replied "yeah" and ordered a female officer to strip search the woman. The female officer then put on purple latex gloves, pulled up the woman's shirt and searched around her bra. Finding no weapons or contraband around the woman's chest, the officer then pulled down the woman's underwear and searched her anal cavity. This search again found no evidence of wrongdoing and the officers released the woman without charges. Indeed, the woman received only a repair order for her headlight. The search occurred in full view of the street, although the supervising male officer claimed he "turned away" and did not watch the woman disrobe. After the woman filed a complaint, BPD investigators corroborated the woman's story with testimony from several witnesses and by recovering the female officer's latex gloves from the search location. Officers conducted this highly invasive search despite lacking any indication that the woman had committed a criminal offense or possessed concealed contraband. The male officer who ordered the search received only a "simple reprimand" and an instruction that he could not serve as an officer in charge until he was "properly trained."

An African-American teenager recounted a similar story to Justice Department investigators that involved two public strip searches in the winter of 2016 by the same officer. According to the teenager, he was stopped in January 2016 while walking on a street near his home by two officers who were looking for the teenager's older brother, whom the officers suspected of dealing narcotics.

One of the officers pushed the teenager up against a wall and frisked him. This search did not yield contraband. The officer then stripped off the teenager's jacket and sweatshirt and frisked him again in front of his teenage girlfriend. When this search likewise found no contraband, the officer ordered the teenager to "give your girl your phone, I'm checking you right now." The officer then pulled down the teenager's pants and boxer shorts and strip-searched him in full view of the street and his girlfriend. The officers' report of the incident disputes this account, claiming that they did not conduct a strip search and instead recovered narcotics from the teenager during a consensual pat down. No narcotics were ever produced to the teenager's public defender, however, and the State's Attorney's Office dismissed the drug charges for lack of evidence. The teenager filed a lengthy complaint with BPD describing the incident and identifying multiple witnesses. The teenager recounted to us that, shortly after filing the complaint, the same officer approached him near a McDonald's restaurant in his neighborhood, pushed the teenager against a wall, pulled down his pants, and grabbed his genitals. The officer filed no charges against the teenager in the second incident, which the teenager believes was done in retaliation for filing a complaint about the first strip search.

Other complaints describe similar incidents in which BPD officers conduct public strip searches of individuals who have not been arrested. For example, in September 2014, a man filed a complaint stating that an officer in the Central District searched him several days in a row, including "undoing his pants" and searching his "hindquarters" on a public street. When the strip search did not find contraband, the officer told the man to leave the area and warned that the officer would search him again every time he returned. The man then filed a complaint with Internal Affairs and identified the officer who conducted the strip search by name. When Internal Affairs investigators pressed the man to provide a detailed description of the officer, the man recalled that the officer "had red patches with sergeant stripes" on his uniform. The investigator recognized this description as patches worn by the officer in charge of a shift and confirmed that the officer named by the man was working as an officer in charge in the Central District on the dates the man alleged he was strip-searched. Internal Affairs nonetheless deemed the complaint "not sustained" without further explanation.[12]

According to DOJ investigators, there was a pattern of police officers routinely "stripping away" the dignity of the people they were sworn to protect. Sadly, in the eyes of the DOJ, it wasn't isolated to Baltimore. The allegations contained in many of these reports mirror what was happening in cities across the country. Including in Ferguson, where police had been using similar tactics deemed discriminatory and biased:

FPD's Use of Canines on Low-level, Unarmed Offenders Is Unreasonable

FPD engages in a pattern of deploying canines to bite individuals when the articulated facts do not justify this significant use of force. The department's own records demonstrate that, as with other types of force, canine officers use dogs out of proportion to the threat posed by the people they encounter, leaving serious puncture wounds to nonviolent offenders, some of them children. Furthermore, in every canine bite incident for which racial information is available, the subject was African American.

FPD currently has four canines, each assigned to a particular canine officer. Under FPD policy, canines are to be used to locate and apprehend "dangerous offenders." FPD General Order 498.00. When offenders are hiding, the policy states, "handlers will not allow their K-9 to engage a suspect by biting if a lower level of force could reasonably be expected to control the suspect or allow for the apprehension." Id. at 498.06. The policy also permits the use of a canine, however, when any crime—not just a felony or violent crime—has been committed. Id. at 498.05. This permissiveness, combined with the absence of meaningful supervisory review and an apparent tendency to overstate the threat based on race, has resulted in avoidable dog bites to low-level offenders when other means of control were available.

In December 2011, officers deployed a canine to bite an unarmed 14-year-old African-American boy who was waiting in an abandoned house for his friends. Four officers, including a canine officer, responded to the house mid-morning after a caller reported that people had gone inside. Officers arrested one boy on the ground level. Describing the offense as a burglary in progress even though the facts showed that the only plausible offense was trespassing, the canine officer's report stated that the dog located a second boy hiding in a storage closet under the stairs in the base-ment. The officer peeked into the space and saw the boy, who was 5'5" and 140 pounds, curled up in a ball, hiding. According to the officer, the boy would not show his hands despite being warned that the officer would use the dog. The officer then deployed the dog, which bit the boy's arm, causing puncture wounds.

According to the boy, with whom we spoke, he never hid in a storage space and he never heard any police warnings. He told us that he was waiting for his friends in the basement of the house, a vacant building where they would go when they skipped school. The boy approached the stairs when he heard footsteps on the upper level, thinking his friends had arrived. When he saw the dog at the top of the steps, he turned to run, but the dog quickly bit him on the ankle and then the thigh, causing him to fall to the floor. The dog was about to bite his face or neck but instead got his left arm, which the boy had raised to protect himself. FPD officers struck him while he was on the ground, one of them putting a boot on the side of his head. He recalled the officers laughing about the incident afterward.

The lack of sufficient documentation or a supervisory force investigation prevents us from resolving which version of events is more accurate. However, even if the officer's version of the force used were accurate, the use of the dog to bite the boy was unrea-sonable. Though described as a felony, the facts as described by the officer, and the boy, indicate that this was a trespass—kids hanging out in a vacant building. The officers had no factual predicate to believe the boy was armed. The offense reports document no attempt to glean useful information about the second boy from the first, who was quickly arrested. By the canine officer's own account, he saw the boy in the closet and thus had the opportunity to assess the threat posed by this 5'5" 14-year-old. Moreover, there were no exigent circumstances requiring apprehension by dog bite. Four officers were present and had control of the scene.

For example, in July 2013 police encountered an African-Amer-ican man in a parking lot while on their way to arrest someone else at an apartment building. Police knew that the encountered man was not the person they had come to arrest. Nonetheless, without even reasonable suspicion, they handcuffed the man, placed him in the back of a patrol car, and ran his record. It turned out he was the intended arrestee's landlord. The landlord went on to help the police enter the person's unit to effect the arrest, but he later filed a complaint alleging racial discrimination and unlawful detention. Ignoring the central fact that they had handcuffed a man and put him in a police car despite having no reason to believe he had done anything wrong, a sergeant vigorously defended FPD's actions, characterizing the detention as "minimal" and pointing out that the car was air conditioned. Even temporary detention, however, constitutes a deprivation of liberty and must be justified under the Fourth Amendment. Whren v. United States, 517 US 806, 809-10 (1996).

Many of the unlawful stops we found appear to have been driven, in part, by an officer's desire to check whether the subject had a municipal arrest warrant pending. Several incidents suggest that officers are more concerned with issuing citations and generating charges than with addressing community needs. In October 2012, police officers pulled over an African-American man who had lived in Ferguson for 16 years, claiming that his passenger-side brake light was broken. The driver happened to have replaced the light recently and knew it to be functioning properly. Nonetheless, according to the man's written complaint, one officer stated, "let's see how many tickets you're going to get," while a second officer tapped his Electronic Control Weapon ("ECW") on the roof of the man's car. The officers wrote the man a citation for "tail light/reflector/license plate light out." They refused to let the man show them that his car's equipment was in order, warning him, "don't you get out of that car until you get to your house." The man, who believed he had been racially profiled, was so upset that he went to the police station that night to show a sergeant that his brakes and license plate light worked.

At times, the constitutional violations are even more blatant. An African-American man recounted to us an experience he had while sitting at a bus stop near Canfield Drive. According to the man, an FPD patrol car abruptly pulled up in front of him. The officer inside, a patrol lieutenant, rolled down his window and addressed the man:

Lieutenant: Get over here.
Bus Patron: Me?
Lieutenant: Get the f*** over here. Yeah, you.

Bus Patron: Why? What did I do?
Lieutenant: Give me your ID.
Bus Patron: Why?
Lieutenant: Stop being a smart ass and give me your ID.

The lieutenant ran the man's name for warrants. Finding none, he returned the ID and said, "get the hell out of my face." These allegations are consistent with other, independent allegations of misconduct that we heard about this particular lieutenant, and reflect the routinely disrespectful treatment many African Americans say they have come to expect from Ferguson police. That a lieutenant with supervisory responsibilities allegedly engaged in this conduct is further cause for concern.

This incident is also consistent with a pattern of suspicionless, legally unsupportable stops we found documented in FPD's records, described by FPD as "ped checks" or "pedestrian checks." Though at times officers use the term to refer to reasonable-suspicion-based pedestrian stops, or "Terry stops," they often use it when stopping a person with no objective, articulable suspicion. For example, one night in December 2013, officers went out and "ped. checked those wandering around" in Ferguson's apartment complexes. In another case, officers responded to a call about a man selling drugs by stopping a group of six African-American youths who, due to their numbers, did not match the facts of the call. The youths were "detained and ped checked." Officers invoke the term "ped check" as though it has some unique constitutional legitimacy. It does not. Officers may not detain a person, even briefly, without articulable reasonable suspicion. Terry, 392 US at 21. To the extent that the words "ped check" suggest otherwise, the terminology alone is dangerous because it threatens to confuse officers' understanding of the law. Moreover, because FPD does not track or analyze pedestrian Terry stops—whether termed "ped checks" or something else—in any reliable way, they are especially susceptible to discriminatory or otherwise unlawful use.[13]

There are many more examples of racially motivated abuse in these DOJ reports and elsewhere. These reports provide confirmation of what people of color say has been happening to them in disproportionate numbers in Baltimore, Ferguson, Chicago, and so many other cities across this country—for decades. The summaries of these federal findings offer a glimpse of what any type of national reconciliation process would likely reveal.

It may not be official, but such a process may already be underway—whether or not America is prepared for it. In Baltimore, community activist Ray Kelly referred to the DOJ report as another "tool that we can use to get these systemic issues addressed and get actual change put in place."[14] He sounds optimistic, but that optimism is fleeting. I ask him whether he is surprised it took people this long to listen. "I'm sad that it took this long and I'm still not convinced that people are going to listen," he replied. "Just to see the way young black men are frisked and stopped on our streets compared to any other affluent neighborhoods has been disheartening for years. And we've been going through that my whole life. I don't remember a time of being able to walk up and down the streets and not be worried about what my interaction is going to be with a police officer if he pulls me over."

CHAPTER ELEVEN
FEAR OF THE BADGE

Chicago alderman Chris Taliaferro was in his office when I went to see him. It was located in an old storefront building. I walked in and was greeted by his assistant, who led me to his back office. Taliaferro was sitting behind a desk and motioned for me to pull out one of the two chairs across from him.

Taliaferro straddles a lot of different worlds. He's a politician, a police officer, and an African American. I wanted to get his take on what was happening in Chicago.[1]

Taliaferro: I think we've got folks that fear the police because of what they've seen and what they've experienced on the negative side of policing.

Pegues: So what have they seen? A Laquan McDonald videotape?

Taliaferro: Yes. We [cops] are not, to include myself, we're not removed from that. We're not removed from misinterpretations, from believing by cell phone; you know, cops get nervous too. As a police officer, I can honestly tell you I've been nervous under certain circumstances. So cops get nervous as well. That's why we scream, "Show me your hands! Show me your hands!" Because as long as I've been in the business, fear never harmed you. Hands harm you, because hands carry guns. Hands carry knives. So that's why we scream, "Show me your hands." We want to go home as well. And, so it's not an easy job, and that's what we ask, you know, not just the politicians, but the community, to look at that as well. It's not an easy job at all. And I'm fortunate because I can see it from different perspectives.

As an officer with the Chicago Police Department, Taliaferro taught at the police academy, was an investigator with the Internal Affairs Division, and supervised a foot patrol. But after twenty-one years on the force he took a leave of absence when he was elected as alderman to represent constituents who live in the Austin neighborhood. Among the things that stick with him from his days walking the beat is the power individual police officers hold when they have a badge and a gun.

> **Taliaferro:** Although it is a position of authority, it is a position of power as well. . . . You can look at any person in any job in the United States of America—it's always just been my personal opinion—but the position of a police officer is probably the most powerful. Now, a lot of people would say President Obama or any US president is a powerful position—it is. But the president [does not have] the power of arrest. The power to take away one's freedom through arrest. And that's what a police officer has an authority to do—that's to take someone's freedom—albeit temporary in many cases—they have the power to take someone's freedom away. And that [freedom] is probably one of our greatest rights as US citizens. That's power. Now, if you are the average Joe, coming from a country environment like I did where my next door neighbor was down the road, or you were a quiet, timid guy in high school, you now have been placed in a position where you have more power than anyone in the United States. You could pull over an attorney and arrest him. You could pull over a US congressman and arrest him. Take away his freedom. You could pull over a US senator and arrest him. So, that's power. And that often leads to abuse. For a long time, I think we did very well in protecting our citizens from abuse. I think we've relaxed a little bit. I think we've relaxed a lot.
>
> **Pegues:** Are politicians here, in your opinion, anti-cop right now?
>
> **Taliaferro:** No.
>
> **Pegues:** You don't think so?
>
> **Taliaferro:** No. I don't think they're anti-cop. I think they are

more, "let's get it right." We know that there are problems. Let's get it right. Now, we have a police department, to include myself, that says it's already right, we [just] need to put some oil on the squeaky parts. But I don't certainly think that the politicians are anti-cop. I think we're far from it. I can't tell you an alderman that is not pro-police. In fact, I think there are five of us, six of us, that are currently on city council.

Pegues: Really?

Taliaferro: We may be projected as [anti-cop], you know, by the police union, or because of what's going on. When you have an incident that just occurred . . . like the Laquan McDonald shooting, of course you're going to see it from two different perspectives. In fact, I've heard everyone say they have great police officers in their individual ward, an overwhelming number of police officers are good and do their job fine, but you do have some out there that don't do their job the way it should be done. We need better policing. I'm a police officer. I support the police. But I recognize that we need changes in our police department. Not just in the disciplinary realm, but we need change in how we police.

Pegues: What's the most important takeaway from the Police Accountability Task Force report?

Taliaferro: Discipline. I personally believe that we lack in training. I believe that there needs to be continuous training. What they're not talking about, and what they're not addressing, is the quality of any training that each investigator receives. As an investigator for nine years with the police department, I had one week of training, my second month as an investigator. One week. And that's extraordinary, because they stopped that about a year after I became an investigator. So it becomes on-the-job training. I believe that we should have good transparency, accountability, but these are things we already have. What's not being addressed in my opinion is *quality*—quality of an investigation. If you had better quality, you'll have better outcomes.

Pegues: So corners are being cut because police aren't trained properly? Or they're missing things because they're not trained?

Taliaferro: Well, I think that's one of those things that's going to naturally occur if you're not trained. It's almost asking me to become a rocket scientist and I have no training.

Pegues: So some investigators are getting just one week of training?

Taliaferro: One week of training, and I'm not sure, I'm not sure what IPRA [Independent Police Review Authority] gets, but if an internal affairs division officer is not trained as an investigator, receives no training at all, and he's expected to do an investigation which might lead to the firing of an officer, you got to question the quality of that investigation. You have to question the quality of an investigation where an officer has had seventy-five, eighty allegations all of the same nature.

The task force report found that from 2011 to 2015, 40 percent of complaints against police officers were not investigated.[2] "CPD has missed opportunities to make accountability an organization priority," the report says. "Currently, neither the non-disciplinary interventions available nor the disciplinary system are functioning." As a consequence, "the public has lost faith in the oversight system." A broken disciplinary system meant that cops who were violating procedures were not being held accountable. After a while, that lack of discipline leads to cutting corners and even unnecessary use of force. The system begins to break down and, with it, trust between community and police erodes. It's that simple. Taliaferro says that, years ago, the implementation of the Chicago Alternative Policing Strategy—which is commonly referred to as the CAPS program—helped rebuild trust between police and the community. The CAPS program sought to build relationships between police and the community with quarterly meetings. The goal was to open up the lines of communication to discuss chronic problems and how to address them.[3]

Taliaferro: The implementation of CAPS was very strong. The city put a lot of effort and a lot of funding into building bridges between the community and the police department. Because of the funding, and because of the manpower that was allocated toward that program, I think police and community relations were at an all-time high.

Pegues: How did they build those bridges?

Taliaferro: Well, the community was very much involved in policing. The meetings, what they called the "CAPS meetings" were well attended, were well publicized; and we even had police officers that were welcoming the new concept of policing. In the 1990s, as you could imagine, there was a lot of federal funds that were put into these programs as well. And, I believe, they've been successful; because if we look at it statistically, you know, when I became a police officer in '94, the homicide rate was very high. Year after year after year, those rates continued to drop, to a point where Chicago went from approximately five hundred to six hundred murders a year, down to two hundred. Now, you can manipulate data, but you can't manipulate data that much. Now that we see that the resources have been cut, we see those rates going right back up. So I think that's probably the main factor. Meetings were packed. The rooms were packed. Now if you have five people in there, that's considered a good number.

Pegues: Now you have five people?

Taliaferro: Yeah. There's no funding. There's no more marketing. There's no more relying on it. When you get away from those things, when you get away from marketing, when you get away from openly saying that we want the community to play a role in policing, we want to be able to depend on the community, it doesn't happen.

Pegues: Do you remember the point where they got away from saying it? Was it a change in leadership?

Taliaferro: I don't think it was a change of leadership. I think it was the economic downturn [between 2007 and 2010].

Pegues: Without that direct connection, you're saying there is this breakdown in trust?

Taliaferro: There's a breakdown in trust. It's hard to trust someone that you don't have a working relationship with.

And, so, I think that coupled with some of the incidents that our city has experienced over the past year or so, or couple years, maybe even more, only tend to widen that gap.

Pegues: What I hear from cops is that there is no respect for the badge, you know, "Eff you" this, "Eff you" that.

Taliaferro believes there is a difference between respect for the badge as opposed to fear of the badge.

Taliaferro: One of my good friends was saying, "Man, it was so different many, many years ago. When you saw the cops coming and they told you to leave the street, you left the street. You didn't come back." And I said, "Was that respect or was that fear?"

Pegues: [You mean that] it was fear; and for black men it has always been fear?

Taliaferro: It's fear. The CAPS program taught respect. Now, we're back to fear. So we've gone from, in my short years on the police department, we've gone from fear, to respect, back to fear. Now if you look at that, that correlates to how homicides have [vacillated]—[first they] were high, [then] low, [now] going up again. High under fear, low under respect, now back to high under fear.

When you have respect, you have community policing where you have a good relationship between police and community. When you don't, you deal with fear. People fear the police, and that's never healthy. When you have that, you have increasing crime. You have an increase in crime in neighborhoods that fear the police, or don't respect the police. And in communities that respect the police, it's low in crime because there is no fear. They don't have a reason to fear. The young men and young women in the Austin community, they fear the police in many instances to a point where—or I should say, they lack the respect for police for one reason or another—and I'm not saying it's right or wrong. I'm just saying for one reason or another, there's a lack of respect, which leads to high crime.

Pegues: Can you name maybe three reasons why they lack that respect?

Taliaferro: Sure. Abuse. Two hours ago, I had a young gentleman sitting where you are who is an understanding citizen, owns a building, and is trying to get tenants evicted because he just purchased the building and they refuse to pay rent. So, he relied on the court system, which is the right thing to do rather than becoming an intimidator himself. This is a gentleman that served in the armed forces for many years, and as a result of his services, he's now disabled. But he was actually driving and wanting to relax, and he was driving past his property and decided to—when he saw the police at his property—be engaged and say, "Hey what's going on?" He immediately, immediately, became disrespected and abused by the police officer. He went into the station to make a complaint, and [then he] came to me because he wasn't sure that they took his complaint. And so I called as his alderman just to make sure that they took his complaint. . . .

Then there's the other aspect of how [police officers] engage with young men and young women on the street. I know a gentleman that has probably more credibility on the street than anyone in this area. But rather than use that credibility with young gang members to the bad, for years, he has been out there influencing them to [do] good, and has worked with one of the best organizations in the city. But yet, he was strolling two weeks ago, and because of his look, he was thrown against the car and treated with disrespect as if he was one of them [a gang member]. This is a man that's not afraid to say "Hey," to approach a young man or a gang member, drug dealer, and say, "Hey, let's talk about what you're doing. What can I do to change your life?" But the police didn't see that.

Pegues: What do you think police saw instead?

Taliaferro: They saw the possibility that he was either a gang member or a drug dealer.

Pegues: Based on . . . ?

Taliaferro: Looks. Based on looks.

Pegues: Were they white cops, black cops?

Taliaferro: I don't know. I didn't even ask him.

Pegues: Because that doesn't matter?

Taliaferro: It really doesn't.

Pegues: It comes from black cops too?

Taliaferro: Of course, yeah. And that's maybe a police officer trying to justify policing, or that style of policing. But, ultimately, what it does [is] it lends to the disrespect we just talked about. And it lends to fear. Now, this gentleman would probably never fear the police; but, you know, what we would rather see is not necessarily whether or not if you fear the police, but whether or not you respect the badge, and respect the authority. Because it is a powerful position, and, you know, as I said, I believe it is one of the most powerful—if not the most powerful—but if you don't respect the person[who] has that authority, it never ends good.

Pegues: That's one thing that you said that really stands out, because I think you're right, it is a powerful position.

Taliaferro: It is.

Pegues: One stop could ruin somebody.

Taliaferro: And that's been done. You know there's, in many cases, no recourse.

Pegues: How much responsibility does the black community share for what has gone wrong in terms of the breakdown in trust between the community and law enforcement?

Taliaferro: It's hard to say, . . . to answer that with a percentage or with a quantification of how much. I say that we all share in what's happened; and when I say *all*, we share in it as mothers and fathers, who have not probably in some instances raised children as we could have. We share it as business owners when we allow certain people to hang out on the street in front of our stores. We share that burden as police officers when we police improperly. We share it as politicians. So I think all of us share that burden of trying to change this thing—community organizations as well. . . . Here's something that I've said, and that I stand by, even with me as a politician, or should I say, a person that's elected to office. I consistently hear Mayor Emanuel over my year in office say how much he loves the city of Chicago; and, you know, somebody asked me, "What did you learn your first year in office?" And I've said, "I've learned a lot of things, but what stands out the most is we have a mayor that loves the city of Chicago. Loves it—to a fault. And, he loves money. But what I've not heard him say is, 'I love the *people* in the city of Chicago.'" And when you have that perspective of loving people, you get a different outcome every single time. I mean, I love the people of this ward. I think every alderman should love the people of their ward. If you proclaim that "I love the people and the city of Chicago," and when you do that . . . Man, you get a different, you get a whole different result.

Pegues: You're a critic of the mayor?

Taliaferro: No.

Pegues: You're not?

Taliaferro: I'm a supporter of the community.

Pegues: Would you want him to serve another term?

Taliaferro: No. I think our mayor has done the best he could. But I'm not a critic of him. I just think that, you know, there's someone out there that could do it better. Our city stops at downtown, unfortunately.

Pegues: In his eyes . . . ?

Taliaferro: Yes. The Austin community, where we led in homicides late last year. We've not had any significant investment from a capital standpoint since he's been around.

Pegues: But why would people want to invest money in a community that's killing itself?

Taliaferro: That's how you build a community. You build a community like that. You build a community by investing. Because, if not, you continue to get high crime. No community that's a high-crime community or an impoverished community where the recidivism rate is in the 30 percent range, unemployment rate is in the 30 percent range, the crime rate is as high as it is . . . No community can pull out of that, *unless* *you invest in it.* It's almost like being a mother and a father. Your children will not become what you want them to become unless you invest in them. And if you don't invest in them, they won't become close, not even close, to what you want them to become. They won't go to college, unless they're self-driven—but where did they learn that from? They look at the examples that are in the house with them—mothers and fathers. So it's an investment. That same investment is what separates us as a community and a place.

Pegues: So you think there's an economic component to rebuilding that trust?

Taliaferro: That is a major part of it.

That is the one common denominator linking many of the communities where police shootings have occurred. A lack of opportunity and hope permeate many of the neighborhoods where crime is rising and where there is a lack of trust between the police and the community.

CHAPTER TWELVE
POLICING SYSTEM IS BROKEN

When we met, Richard Boykin had been Cook County commissioner for District 1 for about a year and a half. He wanted to grab a bite at one of the Austin neighborhood's signature restaurants. MacArthur's on Madison Street is a neighborhood staple for soul food. Turns out it was closed on the day we scheduled our interview, but we met there anyway and sat outside at one of the tables.

As he invited me to take a seat, I took a look around the outside of the restaurant and noticed that the streets and stores nearby were not bustling with activity. There weren't people window shopping or kids playing. It was Memorial Day and in most neighborhoods across the country you would see families gathering—maybe around a picnic table or at a backyard barbecue. But here—sadly—given the high level of crime, there's a sense that an extended stay outdoors invites danger and violence.

Something else seemed to be missing—a visible police presence. Twenty-four hours before meeting Boykin, I had been in downtown Chicago—strolling along the fabulously opulent Magnificent Mile. All of the high-end stores were buttressed with private security and Chicago police officers standing in pairs on just about every corner. I didn't see that in Austin, even as most of the police reform task force reports I had read—even Chicago's—called for an increase in community policing.

Boykin says while community policing is important, what may matter the most is doing some house cleaning in the Chicago Police Department.

Boykin: Now you have so many police who have just sort of been bad actors, and, quite frankly, my dad used to always say that if you have a bushel of apples and you have one rotten apple in the bushel, before long the whole bushel will be rotten if you don't get that apple out.

Pegues: Why is that important?

Boykin: There can be no trust without accountability. You want citizens to be accountable, but if the police aren't being held accountable to that standard, then how can you expect the citizens to follow suit? I mean, you'll have anarchy. You'll have two sets of rules. One set for the police officers and one set for the citizens. It shouldn't be that way.

I always wanted to be a policeman when I was growing up. My dad told me not to do it. He said it's too dangerous that you'll mess around and get killed. But I grew up watching shows like *Starsky & Hutch*. Shows like *T.J. Hooker* and shows like that. . . . I'm showing my age. But I liked those shows. I liked the fact that the police went around policing and doing the right thing and catching the bad guys—not being on the take themselves. In a lot of instances, people feel like police plant drugs, they lie on police reports, they wind up giving the citizen the shaft . . .

Pegues: That's the way many of your constituents feel?

Boykin: Many of them. And obviously you can restore the trust, but again there has to be accountability and people have to see it front and center. Just like they saw that police officer shoot that kid sixteen times, Laquan McDonald. That officer stayed on the job, and the narrative they gave was that Laquan McDonald lunged at the officer; and that they hid the tape for over a year. They hid the tape for over a year! And Mayor Emanuel, of course, fought [to keep] the tape from being released. The state's attorney—and that's why she lost her job—she wouldn't release the tape. And so then, right before her election, she decided to release the tape—after, of course, a five-million-dollar settlement of hush money to the family. And this kid was in DCFS [Department of Children and Family Services], he wasn't even with his family. But they paid the family to keep quiet, and then, when everybody saw the tape released, they were like, "Wow. The guy didn't lunge at him; he was walking away. The officer executed him."

So what happens if that police officer is not found guilty? You know he's charged with murder. [For] murder, you have to prove premeditation; so how do you prove that on a police officer? It's a high bar to prove. So what happens if that officer walks away, because the prosecutor didn't charge the right way? The community is going to be up in arms.[1]

Case in point: Baltimore. Boykin sees Baltimore as an example of the failures in the system. In 2015, Baltimore City state's attorney Marilyn Mosby charged six police officers in connection with the death of Freddie Gray. The twenty-five-year-old was arrested and taken into custody in one of the city's toughest neighborhoods. He suffered a severed spine during the ride to jail and died about a week later.[2] The officers faced a range of charges from misconduct in office to second-degree, depraved-heart murder. With the latter charge, prosecutors do not have to establish that there was an intent to kill.

But even that proved elusive for prosecutors, who ultimately ended up having to drop all of the charges against the officers after failing to make their case in court through four trials. When she made the announcement that all charges had to be dropped, Mosby read a blistering statement that highlighted the obstacles she believes prosecutors face when taking police officers to court.

For those that believe I am anti-police, it's simply not the case. I'm anti–police brutality. I need not remind you that the only loss, and the greatest loss, in all of this was that of Freddie Gray's life. For over a year, my office has been forced to remain silent in all six of the cases pertaining to, and surrounding, the death of Freddie Gray. Despite being physically and professionally threatened, mocked, ridiculed, harassed, and even sued, we've respected and fulfilled our obligation in dutiful silence in accordance with Judge Barry William's gag order restricting any commentary from the state. In accordance with my oath to pursue justice over convictions, I refuse to allow the grandstanding of some and the hyperbole of others to diminish our resolve to seek justice on behalf of this young man. I was elected the prosecutor, I signed up for this and I can take it! Because no matter how problematic and troublesome it has been for my office, my prosecutors, my family, and me personally, it pales in comparison to what mothers and fathers all across this country, specifically Freddie Gray's mother, Gloria Darden, or Richard Shipley, Freddie Gray's step-father, goes through on a daily basis, knowing their son's mere decision to run from the police proved to be a lethal one. Please know that even though the media has made this about everything but the untimely death of your son [she looks over at Freddie Gray's stepfather] my office has never wavered in our commitment to seeking justice on his behalf.

As the world has witnessed over the past fourteen months, the prosecution of on-duty police officers in this country is unsurprisingly rare and blatantly fraught with systemic and inherent complications. Unlike other cases, where prosecutors work closely with the police to investigate what actually occurred, what we realized very early on in this case is that police investigating police—whether they are friends or merely their colleagues—it was problematic. There was a reluctance, an obvious bias, consistently exemplified not by the entire Baltimore PD but by individuals within the BPD at every stage of the investigation. Which became blatantly apparent in the subsequent trials. Lead detectives that were completely uncooperative and started a counter investigation to disprove the state's case by not executing search warrants pertaining to text messages among the PO involved in the case. Creating videos to disprove the state's case without our knowledge. Creating notes that were drafted after the case was launched to contradict the medical examiner's conclusion. Turning these notes over to defense attorneys months prior to turning them over to the state, and yet doing it in the middle of trial. As you can see, whether investigating, interrogating, testifying, cooperating, or even complying with the state, we've all bore witness to an inherent bias that is a direct result of when police police themselves.[3]

Throughout the trials, Mosby faced accusations that there was a rush to judgement in the case and that she failed to properly investigate the allegations. But as the data shows,[4] the reality is that prosecuting a police officer for any type of crime is difficult. In addition, when officers who have been charged with a crime are given a bench trial, as they were in the Freddie Gray case, their chances of acquittal rise dramatically.[5]

Philip Stinson, a criminologist at Bowling Green State University, says that attorneys representing accused cops know that the best course of action is to choose a bench trial. He says without a jury, the emotion is taken out of the deliberations. "I'm not saying the judges are doing anything wrong," he told me.[6] "They deal with crazy stuff every day. They can separate out the facts and apply the law. Prosecutors just can't prove these cases." Stinson, who was in law enforcement for seven years, says prosecutors often over charge or "charge with the wrong things." As a police officer in Dover, New Hampshire, and also as a dispatcher in Arlington County, Virginia, he claims that during those years he witnessed police misconduct firsthand, and he has his own theories about why it happens.

Pegues: What causes a good cop to go bad?

Stinson: I think a lot of it has to do with the police subculture where it becomes an us-versus-them mentality and that especially if they are working a permanent midnight shift that certain types of police crimes—on-the-job stuff—some of it just comes out of that sense of entitlement as a police officer.

Pegues: Did you ever feel that [sense of entitlement] when you were working in law enforcement?

Stinson: No, but I wasn't there long enough to. But I was tested. I was asked to lie about something. That's why I left New Hampshire, actually. I was asked to lie about something and chose not to. So I think I was supposed to lie.

Pegues: Something major?

Stinson: No. Not really. It had to do with the whereabouts of a supervisor at a particular time. It was a stupid thing to be told to lie about. I didn't see the reason to lie about it.

After his career in law enforcement came to a close, Stinson became an attorney and then got a master's degree. What really interested him, he says, was the misconduct for which cops were not getting arrested, and the crimes committed by police that never came to light. While he was on the job, he remembers wondering why police officers were breaking laws and getting away with things others weren't. He also noticed that no one was keeping track of that kind of data.

So, in 2004, Stinson began cataloguing the numbers simply by setting up forty-eight Google alerts that would notify him of new cases; and then, he says, he "let it rip." He created a database that is now widely recognized as one of the most comprehensive examinations of alleged crimes and acts of violence by police officers. The database has reviewed more than eleven thousand court cases.

Pegues: Does your research show that police officers are being convicted more or acquitted more when charges are brought?

Stinson: If we limited the discussion to police shootings where cops kill someone on duty . . . so not Freddie Gray. . . . As of mid-2016 we have seventy-four officers who have been charged with murder or manslaughter resulting from an on-duty shooting [in which] the officer shot and killed somebody. Since January 2005. A third [of those officers] ended up in conviction, and a third ended up in non-conviction as the result; and with the convictions, it was half—so far—half by guilty plea, half by jury trial . . . none by bench trial.

Pegues: None by bench trial?

Stinson: And the cases that are dismissed, sometimes they are dismissed by the prosecutor, sometimes by the judge, more often by the prosecutor. One of the limitations of my research [is that] we do not code for the race of the victim, because the materials that we have access to don't provide that information. We did start tracking about six years ago the race of the officer, and what I can tell you by looking at the race of the officers—exactly what I didn't want to show—I think black officers are treated more harshly than white officers. Black officers who get arrested for a crime are treated more harshly by the courts than white officers who get arrested for a crime. I haven't published anything on that yet; that's just preliminary [information,] but that's what the numbers are looking like. I wish I could come up with some other conclusion. And they lose their jobs quicker too! When they are in trouble. They are quick to be fired.

Pegues: But there has clearly been an uptick in prosecutions?

Stinson: Well, we don't know. Over the decade 2005 to the end of 2014, about 4.8 officers a year are charged. But eleven were charged in 2006. And [in] one year none were charged, 2007. I don't know if you remember in Atlanta, police barging into an elderly lady's house.[7] She thought it was a home invasion, she gets her gun, and they blew her away. They were in the wrong house. That one was the same year that several New York officers were charged in a case. That made up a good bit of the eleven officers. That was like four or five of them right there. Then we have eighteen last year; and we have, what, eight, so far this year that I'm aware of. We're dealing with outliers. We're dealing with small samples. I'm not pre-pared to say that there is a spike or a surge. Yes, there was an uptick last year, but I don't know. But I can tell you that eleven of those eighteen—at least eleven of those eighteen involve some sort of video evidence.

Pegues: Body cameras or cell phone cameras?

Stinson: Well, you got dashcam, body cam, smartphones, surveil-lance video, and security video. . . .

Pegues: So, in a sense, is that a game changer?

Stinson: It is a game changer because it catches cops in lying, creative report writing, inaccurate report writing, inaccurate statements, false memories, improper memories, whatever it's the result of.

[With] Freddie Gray, remember, you had surveillance video that showed the [police van] was in a different place than the officers claim they went. Or it stopped when they claimed it hadn't stopped somewhere. So people forget about that. That's not a shooting case, but that had an impact on the decision to bring charges. The most horrible case is the Michael Slager case in North Charleston, South Carolina.[8] Where that's just a f—ing execution. Slager's so f—ing casual in shooting [Walter Scott,] but then his very first thought was to plant evidence. His very first thought, which is quite telling. He moved the Taser, right? It's quite telling, because that's not behavior you learn in the police academy. So we're seeing officers—the behavior is learned behavior on the street, apparently; or they just do whatever the hell they want. Or the training is so bad that it doesn't kick in in stressful situations. Because you expect [that] if people are trained, they are going to act according to their training—they are just going to do it.

Pegues: How would you describe the state of law enforcement now and policing across the country?

Stinson: In my opinion, in many places the policing system is broken in this country. It is so messed up that it is truly broken [to the point that] I'm not so sure we even know what we want our police officers to do, and I'm not sure that we are hiring and training the right people. I don't think that's at all clear. I do think that Ferguson has really opened people's eyes to this idea of the police departments being a revenue source. I have friends who are black who have to have discussions with their teenage sons that I never had to have—you know, about how to behave around a police officer. I don't think a lot of middle-class white people thought a whole lot about this until we started to see some of the videos.

Pegues: But why should they care? Why should people who are white—maybe live in an affluent neighborhood—why should they care about how police are doing their jobs in the inner city?

Stinson: If so many people's lives are touched by heroin, for example, where they have somebody in their family who's become an addict or overdosed on pills—whatever. So sooner or later, somebody or everybody's family has a brush with the law, and you want your family member to be treated fairly. And I think it's as simple as that. It may take a few generations, but sooner or later the shoe's going to be on the other foot; and I think it matters for no other reason than that.

Pegues: Your assessment of policing is harsh.

Stinson: I have read the files of almost twelve thousand arrest cases involving over ten thousand police officers. So I've seen it all. We've followed these cases, and over time these are conclusions I've drawn based on my research. And I suppose our life experiences get us to where we are, but I have to remind myself on occasion . . . You know, my parents gave me a book about police heroes a few years ago for Christmas— reminding me—that most cops are good cops.

CHAPTER THIRTEEN
THE RECRUITS

Jim Pasco, the executive director of the national police officer's union, the Fraternal Order of Police, has been quoted as
saying that the number of police officers arrested is "not particularly
notable."[1] He has a point, if you put the numbers in perspective.
There are currently—according to Justice Department figures—
more than 750,000 state and local law enforcement officers nationwide.[2] The number of officers arrested and charged with murder or
manslaughter is a tiny fraction of officers on the job, and it is far
from an indication of a broken law enforcement system. As Pasco
noted in an interview with the *Washington Post*, "the level of media
scrutiny of police is way up."[3] This focus on police misconduct is
making it harder for departments across the country to recruit. If
you are going to "clean house" and reform police departments, then
you have to be able to bring in reinforcements.

When I went to Philadelphia over the summer in 2015, then
police commissioner Charles Ramsey told me that his department
was about two hundred officers short of its recruiting goal. "Right
now policing is not the most attractive occupation that they could
probably get into," Commissioner Ramsey said.[4] After a celebrated
career leading Washington, DC's police force and Philadelphia's
department, Ramsey was chosen as one of the co-chairs of the President's Task Force on 21st Century Policing. He has a pulse on what
is going on in law enforcement and acknowledges that the image
of the job has been battered and bruised; and he suggests that the
shine has been scratched off badges across the country because of
the actions of a relative few.

"I think police officers are proud of what they do, but I think that that doesn't mean they haven't been hurt by the images that have been shown repeatedly, and the portrayal of police as if it just paints us all with one brush," Ramsey told me in a report for the *CBS Evening News*. "It's got to hurt a little bit."[5]

It wasn't just Philadelphia having problems recruiting new officers, though—other major cities like New York and Los Angeles have also seen significant drops in the number of applicants. But the recruiting numbers didn't start to fall as a result of Ferguson or Baltimore. Interest in becoming a police officer has been trending down since the 1990s.

According to the *Police Chief*—a law enforcement magazine—there are many factors at play that have diluted the application pool. Among them, unemployment is down and students are looking to other fields. Tech jobs and the private sector are providing alternatives, and the wars in Iraq and Afghanistan have "siphoned off public-service-minded people to the military."[6] Not to mention, the negative publicity over high-profile incidents of police misconduct has also worked as a drag on police departments.

To make up for recruiting shortfalls, some departments are lowering standards. According to the Bureau of Justice Statistics, "in order to increase the pool of applicants for sworn positions, an estimated 84% of agencies had a policy in 2008 that allowed for some applicant screening criteria to be relaxed at times." This means that people who might have otherwise been passed over for hiring by a police department are given a break, which doesn't always end well.[7]

One case comes to mind in particular. Timothy Loehmann was hired by Cleveland's police department in 2014. But prior to being hired there, he was working for a small suburban department in Independence, Ohio. There were signs early on that suggested that he was not qualified to carry a gun. According to a local report in Cleveland.com, when Loehmann showed up for a state gun qualification session, he was "sleepy and upset," and he was "not following simple instructions."[8] A supervisor noted in an evaluation that "Loehmann lacked the maturity to understand the severity of his breakdown on the shooting range."[9]

A letter dated November 29, 2012, that was in Loehmann's personnel file from Independence said that during firearms qualification training he was "weepy."[10] In addition, the letter said that Loehmann's "handgun performance was dismal." That letter was written by the department's deputy chief and recommended parting ways with Loehmann. The deputy chief wrote, "I do not believe time, nor training, will be able to change or correct the deficiencies."

Loehmann left that department, and about two years later he was hired in Cleveland, where, according to his father, he wanted "more action."[11]

As a Cleveland police officer, Tim Loehmann shot and killed twelve-year-old Tamir Rice.[12] The rookie cop shot Rice less than two seconds after pulling up to investigate a complaint about a child carrying a gun. The gun was fake.

The shooting sparked protests and calls for reform. Ultimately, a grand jury did not indict Loehmann, but Cleveland police eventually acknowledged that they never reviewed Loehmann's file from Independence. Cleveland police officials subsequently changed their policies for potential hires. Going forward, they pledged to include checking publicly available records.[13]

Loehmann's case is far from isolated. Other incidents have not received as much attention, but they also highlight how hiring standards have been lowered in police departments as they struggle to fill the ranks.

The reality is that it's difficult to keep track of troubled cops who often slide between town after town and job after job, in part because demand is so high. Ron Hosko, who is president of the Law Enforcement Legal Defense Fund, says, "there are declining pools of candidates in massive numbers" and "far diminishing pools of the right candidates."[14] Hosko, who is also a former assistant director of the FBI says, "There are some people who don't belong in this profession. . . . Their willful conduct can destroy trust."[15]

But that's not the only thing that Hosko believes has been eating away at the foundation of law enforcement across the country. He likens the demise of some police agencies across the country to a crumbling building or road.[16] "Police are critical infrastructure," he says. "They are the backbone in trying to keep civility. If we don't invest in our infrastructure, what happens? It breaks down. There hasn't been enough investment. Investing in psychological testing to determine who we hire—they don't do that to sufficient standards, and not uniformly around the country. So if I'm not hiring and selecting the right people, training them throughout their career at every level, and hiring and paying the right leadership to build a culture and fabric; if I'm not training them on a firing range enough and in the law enough, then I'm not building the right police force."

Hosko believes that part of building the right police force is hiring the right people, and he admits that police departments are still struggling to do that. In Washington, DC, officers in charge of recruiting are pulling out all of the stops to get the best and brightest through their doors. The department is using social media to attract new recruits—basically anything and everything goes. They are stepping up their social media strategies to attract applicants and even considering an app that would appear on smartphones. Anything, it seems, to reach the millennials. A shortage of applicants is a trend nationwide that is forcing departments to adjust. According to the *Washington Post*, in the spring of 2016 Dallas canceled two police academy classes for lack of interest.[17] Chicago lowered its minimum age for rookie officers from twenty-five to eighteen. And Philadelphia dropped requirements for college credits.[18]

While attracting recruits remains an obstacle, departments across the country are reforming tactics. Many are following the ideas in the President's Task Force on 21st Century Policing, which found that training was another important pillar of reform. The task force recommended "more and better training" to meet a "wide variety of challenges including international terrorism, evolving technologies, rising immigration, changing laws, new cultural mores, and a growing mental health crisis."[19] It also called for "all states and territories and the District of Columbia" to "establish standards for hiring, training, and education."

Departments also lack the ongoing training of police officers. That was one thing that kept popping up while conducting interviews and research for this book. It is something the task force emphasizes, concluding that "in order for training to be effective it must continue throughout an officer's career" in a variety of areas:

- Community policing and problem-solving principles
- Interpersonal and communication skills
- Bias awareness
- Scenario-based, situational decision making
- Crisis intervention
- Procedural justice and impartial policing
- Trauma and victim services
- Mental health issues
- Analytical research and technology
- Languages and cultural responsiveness[20]

Bias-awareness training has already begun to filter down from the top. In late June 2016, Deputy Attorney General Sally Yates sent a department-wide memo to announce a new "implicit bias" training program. She felt a need to explain the program to the 23,000 agents in the four Department of Justice law enforcement agencies and the approximately 5,800 attorneys in the ninety-four US attorney's offices. Yates insisted that the training was "essential to the mission of our Department."[21]

Implicit bias is what's in the unconscious, she wrote in her memo; it is the subtle associations we make between groups of people and the stereotypes we associate with certain groups of people. According to research, whether we like it or not, implicit bias is in us. It is a part of human nature, "a byproduct of our diverse, multicultural society." This is distinct from "explicit bias," which is overt prejudice. For example, you would put someone who makes racist remarks in the "explicit bias" category. Conversely, "implicit bias" is harder to define because it something that happens, and we don't realize it.[22] In other words, it is happening in an unconscious manner. For example, when you avoid certain neighborhoods because they have a particular racial composition.

Yates wrote in the memo that implicit bias "presents unique challenges to effective law enforcement, because it can alter where investigators and prosecutors look for evidence and how they analyze it without their awareness or ability to compensate." But there is good news, she wrote, which "is that research suggests the vast majority of people can counter these effects if they are aware of which biases they possess—and are trained to recognize when they creep into their reasoning or situational awareness."

While some state and local law enforcement agencies across the country had already instituted this training, the DOJ was putting its money where its mouth is—leading by example in a very public way. But whether "implicit bias" training is a good start or enough to root out the "bad apples" and bias in law enforcement is up for debate.

Phil Stinson, the criminologist from Bowling Green State University, believes you can't repair the damage done that way. "You can't fix it by sending somebody to a workshop for a day and a half on implicit bias."[23]

Pegues: You don't think that works?

Stinson: No. I think it's symbolic. I suppose on some level it might have some impact, but I just don't think in the long term it's going to have any impact at all.

Pegues: How hard is it for these departments to retrain veteran officers?

Stinson: I think it is almost impossible to do. Let's take the example of the combat veteran who returns from his reserve or National Guard duty to be a police officer. We've seen cases where officers are put right back on the street as a police officer after having been deployed in the military, and they make the wrong decision. The rules of engagement on the streets of Seattle are different from the rules of engagement in Fallujah and northern Iraq. And we see the wrong decisions being made. The wrong judgement calls with force and guns. And I assume their military training is very good, but those experiences, combat experiences, coupled with their military training—that's a huge mistake to put these cops back on the street as cops in North America and the United States.

Pegues: You're saying that it's going to take a batch of new recruits and training them the right way for this?

Stinson: Yeah. I think we need to reevaluate or evaluate what it is we want cops to do and what type of people we should be hiring for those jobs. Do we want everyone to have a four-year degree, for example? I'm not sure you're going to find anybody anymore that will take the job. I really think the system is broken, and it's not just big-city police departments. The amount of misconduct we see in small agencies across the country—especially in the South—it'll just blow you away. . . . Policing is local, and the policing culture is local, and it's very different in different places. But the police subculture, the idea of that, is very, very strong. I don't think there's quick fixes here. I think systemically there's huge problems in this country; and I think that every summer we're going to have powder-keg environments, and more so with advances in technology as people see what's going on.

It's unclear whether any amount of training can prepare an officer for the level of scrutiny they are facing now. Hosko says that police are feeling threatened "by the presence of cameras": "They are threatened in a way that suggests everybody [should] come out and armchair quarterback me and reevaluate me; and I will quickly be fired for something that is a stumble. . . . It has the police more apprehensive around the country. The cameras are a piece of it. You also have the right people thinking, 'Wait a minute, I'm going to have my decisions dissected on the nightly news,' and they are going to decide, 'No . . . I don't want to be a cop.'"[24]

That is what many now call the "Ferguson effect"—the idea that arrests and police officers' actions are increasingly being recorded by people on the streets. Cell phones are recording video capturing officers making arrests that fit with protocol but may not appear that way. Then the video is edited and put out on social media for the world to see. Sometimes the cameras are catching the bad cops in action or, at the very least, officers who require more or better training. The concern is that all cops are being painted with the same brush. During my interview with Commissioner Ramsey, the veteran police chief told me, "It's the good cops who deserve more attention. They should hold their heads high; they should be proud of what they do, because what they do makes a difference, it makes a huge difference."[25]

CHAPTER FOURTEEN

THE RACE CARD

The police cruiser was heading to a meeting when the officers inside saw two people arguing in the middle of the street. In police jargon, what they were witnessing was a rolling disturbance. There was a woman in a car and a man standing in front of the moving vehicle, pounding on the hood. Traffic was slowing down, and everyone involved was getting angry. The officers pulled up, got out of the police cruiser, and walked up to the man and the woman—who were still arguing. They were black, and the officers were white. Before I tell you what occurred next, consider where it was happening.

It was unfolding near the border between Norwalk and Westport, Connecticut. The latter is one of the wealthiest communities in the country, where the average homeowner has a household income of about $170,000 and where more than 60 percent of the homes are valued at more than $1,000,000.00.[1] It is home to hedge funds, business tycoons, media superstars, and Hollywood royalty. Paul Newman, Joanne Woodward, Martha Stewart, Harvey Weinstein, Christopher Lloyd, Phil Donahue, Marlo Thomas, Michael Bolton, and many others have called Westport home.

But while few cities and towns can match its wealth—Westport is just like Chicago, Baltimore, Charlotte, Tulsa, and New York City in one important way: it too must confront the conflict between the police and the black community. Its officers and citizens are also dealing with such conflicts, even though blacks make up less than 2 percent of the town's population. Yes, even wealthy suburbs are dealing with the ramifications of police shootings.

I grew up in Westport, Connecticut. My mother and father purchased a home there in the late '70s and became one of a handful of black families living among a population of about twenty-five thousand. The town is located in Fairfield County along the Long Island Sound, about an hour's drive from Manhattan. From elementary school through high school, I always felt comfortable in Westport. That's not to say that there weren't instances in which I felt the sting of racism. That would happen on occasion. But those instances were rare. Westport welcomed me; and my friends there remain a big part of my life to this day.

Westport welcomed the town's current police chief as well. Foti Koskinas and his family immigrated to the United States from Greece almost forty years ago. Koskinas was just nine years old when he moved to town without knowing any English. He and I moved there at about the same time, and we would eventually become friends while playing varsity football for the town high school. I was about two years older, but I always remember him with a smile on his face— except when he was drive-blocking an opponent down the field.

After thirty years, we reconnected in the fall of 2016, and it was like old times. We bumped into each other at a football game where I was to be inducted into the Staples High School Football Hall of Fame. He was wearing his police uniform—having recently been appointed the new police chief. At the time, I was close to finishing the manuscript for this book, which is why we began talking about how challenging policing had become—even for smaller departments. His department, like so many others, had moved to provide officers with body cameras; and what they were seeing was eye-opening. The video was increasingly showing confrontations between officers and blacks. Traffic stops were often escalating into verbal confrontations. So much of the discussion had been focused on major US cities, while the conflict between black and blue was seeping into the fabric of policing in every city in America.

About a month later, I interviewed Koskinas as he was preparing for a meeting with a group planning to unfurl a Black Lives Matter banner. The chief wanted to make sure it went smoothly. Times have changed—something as simple as putting up a banner can quickly turn into a call to 911. Chief Koskinas is forty-four years old, with twenty-one years' experience in law enforcement and a lot of grey hair. His department has sixty-five officers and a total of 130 employees. No matter the size, being the police chief of any department may be more stressful than ever—especially with once-routine calls reaching boiling points, like that rolling disturbance near the border with Norwalk. It seemed like a run-of-the-mill police matter. Until it suddenly turned into something more complicated. Koskinas was driving that police cruiser with another member of his command staff riding shotgun. The man and the woman were arguing, and, in Koskinas's view, it could have gotten physical had the cops not rolled up.[2]

> **Koskinas:** I get out. The other officer gets out. I go to the girl. We separate them, and before we can even say what we're going to do for you, right away it turns into "These white cops don't understand it. Don't tell them anything. They're not here to help us. They're here to f— with us." Both were mid to late twenties. So here's where the story gets complicated. I'm speaking to the woman, and she really comes around. I'm like, "Hey, listen, ma'am. I'm here to help you." The next thing I know, I look over my shoulder, and the other cop that's with me is trying to pat down the pockets of the guy she was arguing with. He had cargo pants, and his pockets were stuffed. So they get into it a little bit, not a shoving match but the guy starts arguing, saying, "You can't touch me . . . you can't search me . . . you can't do this you can't do that."
>
> Based on how we responded and why we responded, we would have had every right to check him. Keep in mind, the officer who is with me is an experienced guy with a command position in the department. He had come up through the ranks. He's a well-educated and levelheaded guy; but right away he backs off. He completely backs off! Turns out he doesn't want to get into the black-and-white issue. So we get the man's name, but nobody ends up getting arrested. Nothing happens, and we get them on their way. The girl goes one way and the guy goes another.
>
> But there was a moment there where it got heated between the black guy and the white cop. After we cut them loose, I get back into the car and I ask the officer, "What hap-

pened?" He says, "I go to pat him down and his pockets are sticking out and we got into it." He says, "I don't know what happened. I just backed off! I didn't want to get into this." So, to make a long story short, later we checked the guy out. He lives in Norwalk, so we checked with the Norwalk police, and it turns out the man we stopped is moving drugs around Norwalk.

Within twenty-four hours, a confidential informant comes back and says, "Your guy he missed a s—load of drugs that guy had in his pockets." The informant, who's black, says, "He is totally laughing at you guys because he played the racial card and it worked." This is a black informant working for the police, and he's telling us this. So do you see what I'm saying, how it comes full circle because you go from one extreme of good, genuine people who want to put color and bias aside so that everyone can work together, and then you have the other extreme where somebody takes advantage of racial tension, uses it to their advantage and inflames the situation?

Pegues: So people are using the race card?

Koskinas: People are using the race card because cops are at a point where they don't want to get in the middle of this. They don't want the complaint against them . . . that it's a minority-related issue and they are seen as either profiling or picking on somebody or not treating them the same. So they back off! We've created an environment where cops will back off to avoid the racial issues.

Pegues: That sounds a lot like what FBI director James Comey has been saying and others have told me about the "Ferguson effect."

Koskinas: Jeff, I can tell you that we have officers here who tell me that when they are running radar, if a car goes by that's speeding and they will see that it's a black male or black female, they'll just wait for the next car. They'll say "I don't want to deal with it." It's not a matter of picking on people. They just don't want to deal with it.

Pegues: Why?

Koskinas: It's not worth it, because it's going to turn into something other than speeding. And it's not every incident . . . but people just avoid it.

Koskinas says that while more than 98 percent of the town's population is white, and less than 2 percent is black, the minority population grows during the day when people come from surrounding towns to work in restaurants, supermarkets, or office jobs.

Pegues: Have you seen these conflicts building over time between police and African Americans?

Koskinas: I became a police officer in 1996. It was right on the heels of the Rodney King beating and the early stages of the Abner Louima case. What we're seeing now is similar to what we were seeing back in 1996. It certainly is cyclical, I think. A lot of it never went away. But because of September 11th, the real-estate bubble, and the burst of the bubble, it has always been there but it hasn't been in the forefront as much as it is currently. A lot of those things do play into it. It's not like these racial tensions went away.

Pegues: Do you think they will go away?

Koskinas: I think it will get better, and I think we don't have a choice but for it to get better. I think all sides want it to get better. Do I think it will ever go away? . . . I want to be an optimist and not a pessimist on this, but I think people will always have their perceptions, their views and their biases that we always have to work through.

Pegues: On both sides?

Koskinas: On both sides.

Pegues: Have you seen that bias in law enforcement?

Koskinas: I think individuals have biases and it is very hard to filter through them in our hiring process. I will say overall the majority, if not most, of police officers don't come to work bringing those biases. I think some guys can put it aside while they do their job, while others might not. If that makes any sense. We're all human beings, and it doesn't have to be a black-and-white thing. It could be about personality or what somebody is wearing—the way they wear religious clothing [for example]—that might set someone off. My biggest thing is, the minute we put on the blue uniform, it doesn't matter what those beliefs are. One of the first things I did when I became chief was change our letterhead [to add a motto]. I said, look, I don't want to put a mission statement. I don't want to put anything long on it. "With courage, honor, and integrity we protect the rights of all citizens," and we just left it there. Because that's what the goal is.

Implicit bias is in everybody. I think if everybody can look at themselves in the mirror—it doesn't have to be a black-or-white thing—it could be a financial thing. Something that happened in your life. It could be a bad breakup. I mean, they exist all over the place. I think better screening of who we are hiring is huge. And it's going to take time, and we've gotten a lot of these people out of the way. And because of the older us-against-them mentality, the police-against-the-public [mentality], has left. But I think better screening of people [with] real, thorough psychological exams. Real, thorough polygraph exams. Real, thorough background exams. Talking to their family. Going to their college room-mate, speaking to their college coaches. We spend probably about 100 to 150 hours doing a background check on some-body before we hire them, and sometimes, because it is so thorough, we spend 150 hours and never hire them.

So I think the training part is big, because you have to do something with the people we currently have. You can't just say, "Ah, one day they'll be gone and we'll just hire better now." I agree with DOJ that we've got to do training with the people we have. But equally important you got to say, where do we go from here? How does it get better, and when does it get better? I think incredible backgrounds and I think very thorough hiring is going to help the future. I will be long retired, but I'm hoping the people I'm hiring today make that difference.

I came over here when I was a kid in 1981, not knowing a word of English. So I know the feeling of being that out-sider looking in. If that makes any sense. I was that kid in fifth grade that didn't know anybody and didn't know how to communicate with anybody. So I think it gives me a little bit of a different perspective on life and understanding what it is to be on the other side of it a little bit. Skin color aside and everything else aside, it was a pretty humbling learning curve.

Pegues: Do you find yourself having to talk to some of your officers about walking in other people's shoes?

Koskinas: I try to do it on an individual basis, but I think we do a better job through training. Putting as much as we can into understanding racial-bias-motivated crime, understanding the sensitivity. We work very closely with the Anti-Defamation League. While we may be talking about black-and-white issues, there are times when swastikas show up in different places in town; that completely tears through different places in this community. So it's on many different levels—counseling the officers and speaking with them about it. But it does start at the top with the leadership. I have expectations, and they know what those expectations are; and a very big part of that is knowing that we treat everybody the same.

Pegues: Have there been incidents in Westport?

Koskinas: I'll use one extreme that happens far more often than the bad stuff. This is what the best part of it is, because we are in a good community and a good world, as far as I'm concerned. It is not uncommon to walk Main Street or go out to lunch or be somewhere in uniform, and there is either a black gentleman that's driving a truck or a black gentleman that is getting on the train in Westport. They will absolutely make a point of coming up to me, not knowing that I'm the chief, and say, "Hey, look, between you and me, I thank you for what you guys do. I don't think there is anything personal. Thanks a lot for what you do, and I'm so glad you're out here. Let's put this black-and-white thing aside." We're getting it from both sides, the very wealthy getting on the train. But it's also the truck driver who will get out and shake my hand and say, "Thanks a lot, man . . . you're doing a good job. . . . I know it's not everybody." It happens so often, and that's really what makes you get up every morning and say, you know what? This is a good job. This isn't so bad.

Pegues: The other day you said that we have reached a boiling point. What did you mean by that?

Koskinas: I never speak for 100 percent of law enforcement, but one of the things that's been a boiling point. . . . Let's go back to Ferguson [and] Michael Brown . . . "hands up, don't shoot" . . . Black Lives Matter—the whole thing. Our government officials jumped on board, from our president to our attorney general. Completely. [They said,] this is wrong. This should have never happened. They did it without ever looking at a full investigation. One hadn't even been conducted.

Then we inflame the community, only to find out that Ferguson did its investigation; the state did its investigation; the Department of Justice did its investigation; and they find no wrongdoing on the part of that officer. But the same people that inflamed this whole thing, meaning the president, meaning the attorney general, Al Sharpton . . . where were they when that announcement was made? Where were they to say this was a terrible thing that happened and we do need to work better on relations—and [yet] that white officer didn't do anything wrong? And so every cop that puts the uniform on is thinking twice and saying, "I didn't come to work to kill somebody . . . a white person or black person. But I'm going to be tried, judged, and everything else before I even get a chance to be investigated."

Pegues: But the Department of Justice report afterward, which concluded that Ferguson's police department had become a revenue stream for the city and blacks were being unfairly stopped and penalized . . . how do you respond to that?

Koskinas: I also believe the DOJ report and all of this stuff was going on in that community. But [what] police officers saw, was [that] this white cop that got into a confrontation—he defended his life, and basically he got hung out to dry. I read the [DOJ] report closely, and I saw those things that you said. [I did it] to educate myself, if not for anything else, and said, "You know what? There was a lot of wrong going on there." Whatever the reasons, were there was a lot of wrong. Unfortunately, it all came out during that terrible incident. Now, as a community you would think the mayor, the police chief, and all those people should have been working toward those goals before it ever got to the Michael Brown thing. I think it is important for the police chief and the department heads to say, "I need to work on these relationships . . . to have these relationships with the black community, as small as it may be in Westport, while things are good." We need to have a relationship, and we need to understand each other. We need to understand each other's goals, so—god forbid—that terrible thing does happen, that's when you cash in on those relationships. I don't think in Ferguson those relationships existed, and I don't think people made the effort to have those relationships with the minority community.

Pegues: If we're at this boiling point, where do we go from here?

Koskinas: I think education is a huge part of it. I'm not a guy that liked school, so I don't want to push it that way. I think training for police officers. I have done two things recently. For instance, once the cops started getting shot in Dallas and St. Louis, I went out and spent quite a bit of money from asset forfeiture, which is money seized from our criminal activities, and bought the latest and greatest ballistic shields for the guys. Vests that will stop rifle rounds and stuff like that, to give the guys the reinforcement that I care, the community cares, the town cares, and we're going to give you the best equipment. And, god forbid, [if] something goes wrong, [we're prepared] for you to protect yourself, which ultimately gives you a better chance to protect the public. But that has an effect on the guys.

As far as training, for the twenty years that I've been here, we shoot four times a year. We're very proficient at what we do. I was on the SWAT team, where I shot every month. The guys on the SWAT team shoot once or twice a month right now. But we shoot at paper targets, and it is great when you are shooting at paper targets. It doesn't bring out any stress or your preconceptions about people. So one of the things we've instituted is a shooting program that is computer-based—real firearms. But you get put into situations, and how you react either escalates or de-escalates the situation. It does it with Asian victims; it does it with Asian suspects; it does it with black suspects. So in moments of stress, when you either think it is you or them, in a moment of training, it's so realistic [that] we'll be able to work through things and say, "Would you have done the same thing if that was a car full of white people? Would you have done the same thing—if you're black—if that was a car full of Jewish people? What are you afraid of? What are your preconceptions? Let's work through them."

It's real easy to just pull up a target and just shoot at it. It doesn't move. It's got no emotions; it's got nothing. This is far more realistic. If you overreact, the situation is going to get real ugly real fast. If you're good at diffusing situations, the system plays out with a shooting depending on how you handle it. Or it turns out you either recovered a gun or it wasn't a real gun—it was just a lighter or a wallet. So I think the cops need to have better training and situational awareness. Not just shooting at a paper target.

Pegues: Where does this training happen?

Koskinas: We partnered with five other local police departments. We're putting out quite a bit of money to do it. This is one of many programs, and I'm not saying this will solve anybody's problems, but this is just one more thing—where we're able to make this as real as possible and find our strengths and weaknesses in a time of stress. When it is almost the real thing.

Pegues: Some of the officers have body cameras. You told me about 80 percent?

Koskinas: It's a voluntary thing. We encourage it to the point that there are reward systems to wearing it. But what's happened is more and more cops are getting involved in situations—and not necessarily racially motivated situations—but people are figuring out that the cameras are working to their benefit. I don't have a single incident where somebody is coming in and saying, "Watch the camera and you'll see how bad this guy is treating me." But I have multiple incidents where people are coming in complaining about the officer. We'll go see the video, and they'll walk away without filing a complaint. Time and time again.

"Hey, Mr. Smith—you sure that's how it happened?"

"That's how it happened. The cop was this and this . . ."

"Okay, can we take a few minutes and just watch what happens, because it is recorded? Here you go. I watched it but I don't see a problem and maybe you can pinpoint where the problem is."

And they see it, and the eyes get bigger, and the jaw drops farther, and you get the—"Oh I'm sorry. It must have been that I was upset." And I get it. Sometimes it's not that easy, and you have to dig further.

Pegues: There are a lot of unions against body cameras. But it sounds like the cameras are helping the good cops.

Koskinas: Jeff, we are in a society where people have cameras at their house. Most people, either because of their kids or liability issues, have dashcams. Most taxi and limo services have them, and just regular citizens who have cameras running in their cars. So my message is [that] you're being recorded anyway. You've taken a public job, you're in a public place most of the time. If other people are recording you, why wouldn't you want your side recorded as representation of what really happened? Because when someone records you, and they want to use it to their benefit, they are going to cut that clip where you look like a complete jerk, because they are not showing the five to ten seconds before it or the five to ten seconds after, where you are tending to them. They are going to show the five seconds where you raise your voice and may have said the wrong thing—but nothing about what led up to it and how you handled it afterwards. So why, why would we ever as police officers put ourselves in that position?

Pegues: What about de-escalation techniques. Do you think the onus is on the people police are confronting?

Koskinas: There's both extremes. I'll be honest with you. I got pulled over a few days ago . . . my brake light was out. It's a police car—it's a department car, but it's unmarked. Nobody would know that it's a police car. I live in Fairfield—my heart was beating like a thousand times a minute, feeling like I did something wrong. I've now been a cop for twenty years. I'm a police chief! I saw the light behind me, and my heart is racing. So I get it! I absolutely get it!

So you got both extremes. People who don't know how to act, who get upset; and the officers don't know what's going on in their life at that moment. But a much smaller percentage of that is people that lure you right in. They could be white, black . . . they play into it, and they're going to get this cop worked up, and they are really good at it. It's a different mentality. A good, seasoned, well-trained, well-sought-after cop through background checks and stuff like that—shame on him if he can't see through that. It should be, "Hey, this person is really nervous; I should help him out. Let's see what I can do to minimize this so that we can leave; even if they get a ticket, they left here with a good experience." There's a good individual experience where they say, "Look, the guy gave me a ticket, but he was a gentleman he worked through it. He attended to my needs and he explained what was going on. It wasn't a robot, it was a human being talking to me." If we're true professionals and we say this is real profession, then you better be able to work through it.

Pegues: How do you get black males to like the cops?

Koskinas: It's very hard, because if their parents don't trust the police and every encounter they have with the police is either a parent getting in trouble or complaining about the police or not doing the right thing—how do we get those kids to trust the police? How do we get those kids to trust the police when all they see are police arresting their parents or at times mistreating their parents? I'm not saying police are perfect; but because of the environment, the police are always there. People are fighting, whether it's alcohol abuse or drug abuse. The father is absentee, and the police are always doing something that is not perceived as a good thing. How does that kid grow up and love the police? If you have an answer, I'd love to hear it.

Pegues: So do you think it's going to take twenty years for law enforcement to reform?

Koskinas: I don't think I can put a time line on this, because you just don't know the next thing that is going to inflame things. We just don't know it. But I think the training from DOJ for the cops we currently have is a must. . . . But it is equally important to do better screening of people we are hiring.

At the end of our interview, Koskinas sent me an e-mail. He thanked me for taking the time to interview him—which I found surprising. Another surprise was the quote he included at the bottom of the e-mail. It was not the department motto, but it could have been. Koskinas called it one of his favorite quotes. It was classic Maya Angelou: "I've learned that people will forget what you said, people will forget what you did, but people will never forget how you made them feel."[3]

CHAPTER FIFTEEN

DALLAS

On July 7, 2013, just hours before the shooting of the Dallas police officers, President Obama posted the following message on Facebook:

> All Americans should be deeply troubled by the fatal shootings of Alton Sterling in Baton Rouge, Louisiana[,] and Philando Castile in Falcon Heights, Minnesota. We've seen such tragedies far too many times, and our hearts go out to the families and communities who've suffered such a painful loss.
>
> Although I am constrained in commenting on the particular facts of these cases, I am encouraged that the US Department of Justice has opened a civil rights investigation in Baton Rouge, and I have full confidence in their professionalism and their ability to conduct a thoughtful, thorough, and fair inquiry.
>
> But regardless of the outcome of such investigations, what's clear is that these fatal shootings are not isolated incidents. They are symptomatic of the broader challenges within our criminal justice system, the racial disparities that appear across the system year after year, and the resulting lack of trust that exists between law enforcement and too many of the communities they serve.
>
> To admit we've got a serious problem in no way contradicts our respect and appreciation for the vast majority of police officers who put their lives on the line to protect us every single day. It is to say that, as a nation, we can and must do better to institute the best practices that reduce the appearance or reality of racial bias in law enforcement.
>
> That's why, two years ago, I set up a Task Force on 21st Century Policing that convened police officers, community leaders, and activists. Together, they came up with detailed recommendations on how

to improve community policing. So even as officials continue to look into this week's tragic shootings, we also need communities to address the underlying fissures that lead to these incidents, and to implement those ideas that can make a difference. That's how we'll keep our communities safe. And that's how we can start restoring confidence that all people in this great nation are equal before the law.

In the meantime, all Americans should recognize the anger, frustration, and grief that so many Americans are feeling—feelings that are being expressed in peaceful protests and vigils. Michelle and I share those feelings. Rather than fall into a predictable pattern of division and political posturing, let's reflect on what we can do better. Let's come together as a nation, and keep faith with one another, in order to ensure a future where all of our children know that their lives matter.[1]

Four days after the ambush on police in Dallas, the president of the International Association of Chiefs of Police, Terrence Cunningham, was asking for a meeting at the White House. He and other IACP executives pressed the president's advisors to clear time in his schedule to meet with them. The law enforcement community was hurting after Dallas. The death of the five officers in the ambush attack had rattled police officers across the country and reaffirmed what many believed—that they had targets on their backs. The rhetoric had become too heated and Cunningham, for one, was worried that the clock was ticking and that there could be other crazed people out there gunning for cops. He believed that rhetoric created the conditions for a tragedy like Dallas to happen in the first place.[2]

Cunningham: After Dallas, myself and Vince Talucci (IACP executive director), and a couple of other people from IACP staff, we sat down and said this has got to stop. The president had made some comments on his Facebook page when he landed in Poland as he was traveling, that were less than supportive of the police; and, from my position, kind of presupposed guilt on the part of the police in the Philando Castile and Alton Sterling shootings, even though the investigations were really in the infantile stages. So we sent a letter to our contact at the White House and said we need to talk to him.

They've got to tamp down on this rhetoric. Quite frankly, we felt like it was getting so out of control, and that's why Dallas had happened. So the person at the White House was very upset and said, "I can't believe that you don't think that the president was supportive and that the president hasn't been supportive." But he said, "Look, I can't get you a meeting with the president." So we said, "Who can?" He gave us three names of people and [we] said, "Look, if we don't meet with the president, then we are going to release the letter to the press and say that we had asked for the meeting with the president." Then, by Sunday evening, at around 11 p.m., we got an e-mail back from the president's general counsel, Neil Eggleston, who said okay, we've got a meeting set for Monday in the White House, but it's not going to be just IACP. Some of the other partners are going to be there, and both the president and the vice president will be there also.

A meeting had been set with a group Cunningham called the "Big Nine." It was a gathering of several sheriff's organizations, major city chiefs, and the Fraternal Order of Police. Cunningham says they met in the Roosevelt Room at the White House.

Cunningham: We chatted a bit and then the door opens and it was the president of the United States, and he says, hey look, I know I've said some things that have made the police feel like I'm less than supportive of them. In some cases, I know the police feel like I'm actually waging war on the police, and I don't understand that, and I don't understand what I've said [to give that impression]. I really want to have an open and honest dialogue.

Pegues: He admitted to making statements that were contrary to the interest of police officers, or that had upset police officers?

Cunningham: He said that he understood that the police felt that way from his comments. So I told him, that as somebody who really supports reform, believes in the 21st Century Task Force report, [and] made it one of my presidential initiatives to get out and to try to operationalize police legitimacy and procedural justice, it's demoralizing to me when I hear the president say things that presuppose guilt in some of these high-profile use-of-force cases. Just let the investigation run its course, and whatever it is, it is. But I said to him that, you know, we really need to let these investigations run their course; and he said, you know, I've got to push back. I think we should look at the transcripts, that's what he said. You know I'm very careful with my words and I don't think I've really said anything that was—that would presuppose guilt; and I said, "Look, Mr. President, you're a brilliant man. You're a constitutional scholar," I said. "I don't think we have to look at the transcripts. I think that you know you can think about some of the things that just happened recently—the Facebook page, the comments you made in Poland—and you can see how officers would feel that you're not being supportive of them at all. In fact, you're crossing the line, and that you're presupposing guilt in some of these cases." He didn't really respond to it; he just kind of let it hang out there. And then I also raised the fact that he doesn't call the families of law enforcement when the officers are killed.

Cunningham describes a brutally honest discussion between the country's law enforcement leadership and the president. The frustration had been building for some time, and Cunningham felt that it was important to maximize the time he and the others had with the president. Among the rank and file, the commander in chief's popularity had reached new lows. The whispers expressing disgust had grown louder, and police chiefs like Cunningham were feeling the pressure to change the dynamic. Cops even felt that the president was treating the families of fallen officers differently than the families of African Americans shot by police. That was another sore subject Cunningham brought up and pinned it on a case in March 2016, when a Virginia state trooper was shot and killed during a training exercise in Roanoke, Virginia.[3]

Cunningham: Somebody said, you know we're right here in the president's backyard, wouldn't it be nice if the president reached out to the widow and contacted the family? We sent an e-mail to our contact at the White House, and said, "Hey, this came up—any chance the president could reach out to the family? It would mean a lot to us." Nothing. Never hear a word. And so I used that as an example. "I understand you call the families when we have these high-profile use-of-force cases, but you don't call the families of law enforcement." He said, well, you know, I write a handwritten note to every family in law enforcement, and then they can hold on to it. I said, that's great, I appreciate that; but it would be nice if you could reach out to them and make the telephone call.

Cunningham and the other law enforcement officials were airing their grievances. The anger had really started to build in police officers two years earlier when they felt that President Obama and then attorney general Eric Holder took sides in Ferguson.

Cunningham: You know, it was actually Tom Manger, the president of Major Cities Chiefs. Tom's a really smart guy, very thoughtful, and as they went around the table, Tom said to him, "You know, one of the missteps that I like to point out is Ferguson. You had the sitting attorney general in the streets of Ferguson saying that Darren Wilson was going to be indicted."

Pegues: Wait a second. So you guys were bringing up all of the bad blood?

Cunningham: Yes, and I have to be honest with you, he was taking it, and he wasn't like defensive, he would push back occasionally. When I made my comments, I immediately went into the plan that IACP had to renew the good culture and root out the bad culture. Because I think one of the places where we really fail as a profession [is that] they're just not holding people accountable, and they are allowing that bad culture to just regenerate itself. Over and over again. We talked about recruitment and retention . . . all that stuff. But it was a very open and honest conversation.

As he continued telling me about this meeting between the president and the Big Nine, Cunningham mentioned that about two and a half hours in, the president got up to leave. But then he came back and sat down, and Cunningham says he addressed the president again.

> **Cunningham:** You know, he and I had just had an interaction. What I said to him was look—I admit there are bad cops, there's bad policing. If you want your police department to reflect the community they serve, do you think that there's racism and implicit bias in any community? Absolutely there is. And is it going to seep into a police department? Sure! But it's our job as police executives to root it out and to hold those people accountable. Then of course the whole idea of everything being laid at the feet of the police. You know every ill that society has. We don't know what to do with it, so we'll give them mental illness, untreated substance abuse, homelessness, joblessness. We say, the police will figure it out! He turned to me, and that's when he said to me, "It's a nonstarter if the police don't at least acknowledge that historically there's been a problem. And that the police, whether it's because of federal [or] state laws, the police had to enforce things that were very distasteful, at a minimum."

That statement still rings in Cunningham's mind. And it continued to resonate with him long after that meeting with the president had ended. In a lot of ways, the session with the president that day cleared the air. But if there was a moment when it felt like there had been a breakthrough, it was fleeting. The very next day, Cunningham was sitting just feet away from the fallen officers' family members in the audience when the president delivered the eulogy during a service for the five police officers killed by the Dallas gunman.

> **Cunningham:** We were there early, and the security was unbelievable because the two presidents were going to be there. I'm watching the little kids climbing on the parents' laps, and,

you know, I'm thinking to myself that there's got to be more that I can do—that we can do as a profession, that we can do as an association—to try and protect our officers and to try and help these communities heal. Then the president comes out and he speaks.

President Obama's speech that day honored the fallen officers:

Like police officers across the country, these men and their families shared a commitment to something larger than themselves. They weren't looking for their names to be up in lights. They'd tell you the pay was decent but wouldn't make you rich. They could have told you about the stress and long shifts, and they'd probably agree with Chief Brown when he said that cops don't expect to hear the words "thank you" very often, especially from those who need them the most.[4]

But the speech also touched on the police shootings that occurred that tragic week.

With an open heart, police departments will acknowledge that, just like the rest of us, they are not perfect; that insisting we do better to root out racial bias is not an attack on cops, but an effort to live up to our highest ideals. And I understand these protests—I see them, they can be messy. Sometimes they can be hijacked by an irresponsible few. Police can get hurt. Protestors can get hurt. They can be frustrating. But even those who dislike the phrase "Black Lives Matter," surely we should be able to hear the pain of Alton Sterling's family. We should—when we hear a friend describe him by saying that "Whatever he cooked, he cooked enough for every-body," that should sound familiar to us, that maybe he wasn't so different than us, so that we can, yes, insist that his life matters. Just as we should hear the students and coworkers describe their affec-tion for Philando Castile as a gentle soul—"Mr. Rogers with dread-locks," they called him—and know that his life mattered to a whole lot of people of all races, of all ages, and that we have to do what we can, without putting officers' lives at risk, but do better to prevent another life like his from being lost.

Cunningham was angered by these latter comments.

Cunningham: He started out really, really well; and then he took a right hand turn and all of a sudden I realized that he's not talking to the Dallas community, he's talking to the nation. Then he starts to talk about Philando Castile. And he talks about how everyone described him as Mr. Dreadlocks, and he starts . . . making it seem like he's a really good person. I don't know whether he was or he wasn't, but the investigation wasn't complete and we just talked about this the day before. There were some other things in his speech where I was just like "Really!?"

Then when I got up to walk out, there was a reporter from the *LA Times* and she was waiting for me. She says, I know you were at the meeting with the president yesterday and I know you heard what he had to say today, but before you respond, did you know that he called both the Castile and the Sterling family from Air Force One on his way here? And I'm thinking to myself, we just talked about this the day before, he's coming here for the memorial service for the five Dallas officers. And I just felt that it was disrespectful. If he's going to call the families, fine, but, you know, I thought the timing was wrong. So, I told her and I said there were some things in the speech that bothered me, and so she printed it in the *LA Times*.

The paper printed Cunningham's comments the next day. The same day, the IACP president, other law enforcement officials, community activists, Black Lives Matter, and the Reverend Al Sharpton were due to meet at the White House in the Eisenhower Room. White House officials were waking up to Cunningham's criticism of the president's speech in Dallas. The *LA Times* article reported that Cunningham said, "He did it again today."[5] President Obama had mentioned Philando Castile and Alton Sterling during the officers' service; but Cunningham wanted him to keep the focus on the police.

Cunningham: The president opened it up, and before it started someone from his staff said, "Just so you know, you are going to be sitting next to the president today." And I said, "Oh, okay." And she said, "Oh, by the way, he saw your comments in the *LA Times*." So he came in and he was very pleasant and he was clearly all business. He said, "I got this meeting slotted for four hours, and we're going to stay here until everybody has an opportunity to be heard; if you're going to move your flights, contact my staff and somebody is going to do it for you. I'm going to start with Chuck Ramsey and Laurie Robinson, the two co-chairs from the task force." So Chuck talked about how the task force report didn't go far enough that there were things they needed to get to but didn't have the time. Laurie reiterated the same.

And the president took it back and said, "You know, there's no shrinking violets here, and I know everyone will speak up, and I'm not going to call on anyone, but there's one person who has said some things privately and then said some things publicly, and, you know, I want to give him an opportunity to be heard." And he turned it over to me. There were probably fifty or sixty people there. Clearly he was using the Socratic method to draw out ideas. He wasn't currying favor to law enforcement, but he wasn't backing down either. I think he did a great job of kind of mediating—trying to extract what he needed to from people, and he called a couple of people out when they said things . . . is that really factually true?

Cunningham says that that meeting was a turning point. But there was still a lot of work to be done. Five days later, a gunman shot and killed three officers in Baton Rouge, Louisiana.[6] Police had been on high alert after Dallas, warning of ambush-style attacks. This was eleven days of anguish for police and their families. They feared it was just a matter of time before there would be another attack on police. The tone of the debate was more important than ever. Looking back, Cunningham thought that the meeting at the White House the day after the Dallas memorial was a turning point.

Pegues: [It was a turning point] for the president?

Cunningham: If you look at his comments prior to Dallas, and
then you look at what he said after Dallas, and then you
look at what he said after Baton Rouge. . . . His comments
got stronger and stronger toward law enforcement, and then
he released that open letter to law enforcement after Baton
Rouge, where he just sent something out to say how much he
supported law enforcement. I wish it had gotten more play.
I'm mean, I heard from so many people saying it's too little,
too late . . . he's trying to save his legacy. Look, I don't know
what he was trying to do; but, you know what, and one of
the conversations I had with him is that he is going to have
a very strong advocacy voice when he leaves office, and we
need his help to try to move this issue. And one of the things
we've always called for at IACP is a national commission on
criminal justice. This isn't just a police issue, and we need
his help with that; and he acknowledged that. That that was
something he could have done with an executive order, but
he didn't. And now he realizes that's something that's really
needed. But it's too late to do it.

In the wake of the tragedies in Dallas and Baton Rouge, President Obama penned a letter to the men and women of America's
law enforcement community. The president's letter was shared with
officers around the country.[7]

THE WHITE HOUSE
WASHINGTON
July 18, 2016

To the brave members of our Nation's law enforcement community:
Every day, you confront danger so it does not find our families,
carry burdens so they do not fall to us, and courageously meet test
after test to keep us safe. Like Dallas officer Lorne Ahrens, who
bought dinner for a homeless man the night before he died, you
perform good deeds beyond the call of duty and out of the spot-
light. Time and again, you make the split-second decisions that

could mean life or death for you and many others in harm's way. You endure the tense minutes and long hours over lifetimes of service.

Every day, you accept this responsibility and you see your colleagues do their difficult, dangerous jobs with equal valor. I want you to know that the American people see it, too. We recognize it, we respect it, we appreciate it, and we depend on you. And just as your tight-knit law enforcement family feels the recent losses to your core, our Nation grieves alongside you. Any attack on police is an unjustified attack on all of us.

I've spent a lot of time with law enforcement over the past couple of weeks. I know that you take each of these tragedies personally, and that each is as devastating as a loss in the family. Sunday's shooting in Baton Rouge was no different. Together, we mourn Montrell Jackson, Matthew Gerald, and Brad Garafola. Each was a husband. Each was a father. Each was a proud member of his community. And each fallen officer is one too many. Last week, I met with the families of the Dallas officers who were killed, and I called the families of those who were killed in the line of duty yesterday in Baton Rouge. I let them know how deeply we ache for the loss of their loved ones.

Some are trying to use this moment to divide police and the communities you serve. I reject those efforts, for they do not reflect the reality of our Nation. Officer Jackson knew this too, when just days ago he asked us to keep hatred from our hearts. Instead, he offered—to protestors and fellow police officers alike—a hug to anyone who saw him on the street. He offered himself as a fellow worshipper to anyone who sought to pray. Today, we offer our comfort and our prayers to his family, to the Geralds and the Garafolas, and to the tight-knit Baton Rouge law enforcement community.

As you continue to serve us in this tumultuous hour, we again recognize that we can no longer ask you to solve issues we refuse to address as a society. We should give you the resources you need to do your job, including our full-throated support. We must give you the tools you need to build and strengthen the bonds of trust with those you serve, and our best efforts to address the underlying challenges that contribute to crime and unrest.

As you continue to defend us with quiet dignity, we proclaim loudly our appreciation for the acts of service you perform as part of your daily routine. When you see civilians at risk, you don't see them as strangers. You see them as your own family, and you lay your life on the line for them. You put others' safety before your own, and you remind us that loving our country means loving one another. Even when some protest you, you protect them. What is more professional than that? What is more patriotic? What is a prouder example of our most basic freedoms—to speech, to assembly, to life, and to liberty? And at the end of the day, you have a right to go home to your family, just like anybody else.

Robert Kennedy, once our Nation's highest-ranking law enforcement official, lamented in the wake of unjust violence a country in which we look at our neighbors as people "with whom we share a city, but not a community." This is a time for us to reaffirm that what makes us special is that we are not only a country, but also a community. That is true whether you are black or white, whether you are rich or poor, whether you are a police officer or someone they protect and serve.

With that understanding—an understanding of the goodness and decency I have seen of our Nation not only in the past few weeks, but throughout my life—we will get through this difficult time together.

We will do it with the love and empathy of public servants like those we have lost in recent days. We will do it with the resilience of cities like Dallas that quickly came together to restore order and deepen unity and understanding. We will do it with the grace of loved ones who even in their grief have spoken out against vengeance toward police. We will do it with the good will of activists like those I have sat with in recent days, who have pledged to work together to reduce violence even as they voice their disappointments and fears.

As we bind up our wounds, we must come together to ensure that those who try to divide us do not succeed. We are at our best when we recognize our common humanity, set an example for our children of trust and responsibility, and honor the sacrifices of our bravest by coming together to be better.

Thank you for your courageous service. We have your backs.

Sincerely,
Barack Obama

The national Fraternal Order of Police shared the letter on its Facebook page and offered this comment to add greater context:

> The reason this letter has value is that we want and deserve to change the National Dialogue. The people of this country respect law enforcement. Now we continue to speak out about the issues that have helped create disconnects with members of the communities you work so hard to protect.
>
> We can and do provide the best quality law enforcement that we can but we cannot be held responsible for the social issues such as poverty, lack of mental health services, unemployment, and abject poverty. The work now is to assist our communities by continuing to recognize that we are but one spoke in the wheel and we will do our part. Now it's time for politicians and government to assist us in working in the communities we have always worked in to make life better for all Americans.[8]

Nationally, there was an air of cooperation and unity after the shootings of police officers in Dallas and in Baton Rouge. But it didn't last long. Less than a month later, more unrest and violence ripped through parts of another US city. This time it was Milwaukee, Wisconsin, that was in the crosshairs of angry crowds. Several stores were burned, rocks were thrown, and flames filled the sky. Once again, an officer-involved shooting sparked the chaos.[9]

Authorities say, it started when two officers stopped two people in a car. The men tried to run from police. One of them, a twenty-three-year-old, was armed with a handgun. The mayor of Milwaukee, Tom Barrett, said that the officer ordered the man to drop the gun; and when he didn't, the officer fired several times. During the violent protests, four police officers were injured, seventeen arrests were made overnight, and the National Guard was activated and was ready to deploy if needed. Later, police showed the media bodycam footage that they said was proof that the man who was shot and killed had a gun in his hands with twenty-three rounds. Such transparency is what many of the advocates for reform encourage, but that wasn't enough to calm angry residents. In response, thousands of people shared a photo of the twenty-four-year-old officer who fired the shots.

Some added threats: "Now y'all see his face if he's seen anywhere in the city drop him," was one such threatening post, according to the *Milwaukee Journal Sentinel.*[10] Another said, "we want blood like ya'll want it . . . eye for an eye. No more peace."

This was not necessarily unique to Milwaukee, though. It could have been anywhere in the United States, as tensions remain high, even at the time of this writing in early 2017. Whether you're talking to someone living in predominantly black communities or someone— like Dean Angelo—a voice for cops, you can see that this tension is pervasive.[11] Angelo, the president of the Fraternal Order of Police in Chicago, had been very open and candid about the tension between police and the black community.

> **Pegues:** What are your thoughts on [the tension], and how do you get over that—because that's at the heart of a lot of this.
>
> **Angelo:** Well, you know, I think a lot—I think initially a lot of it is generational, you know, where you have grown up in an environment or a family or in a household that didn't trust the police.
>
> **Pegues:** Why do you think that was?
>
> **Angelo:** Well, because of the enforcement, maybe. Because of the amount of crime around the area where you reside, where you grew up at, where your dad grew up.
>
> **Pegues:** In the '60s—I mean, you're saying generations. So you're saying police who enforce Jim Crow, for example, segregation, things like that? Because I think it is generational. I think you know there are still a lot of bad feelings in black families of all socioeconomic levels about law enforcement and its role in our lives.
>
> **Angelo:** Law enforcement and government in general. It's the government that pays you the food stamps to keep you unemployed and undereducated and set in the corner; and, historically, when you see the hoses or the police dogs at the demonstrations, then those are the cops, right? We had that Chicago Police Accountability Task Force report come out and say that we're all racist. But if you're African American and you're working in Englewood, you're stopping people

that look like you, are you racist? You're Hispanic, and you're working in Pilsen, which is all Hispanic, are you racist?

Pegues: Yeah, but is it—

Angelo: Don't take out all the variables.

Pegues: But do you become desensitized to who these people are, and you see them all in one way?

Angelo: Police, whether you're black or brown or white, you're in that blue uniform, you're a cop.

Pegues: But also, the other way. The cops see blacks the same way, could be a threat, probably a threat, you know, is that possible?

Angelo: Sure it is. Again, we're humans, and that's behavioral. When you are working in areas that are historically involved in criminal activity based on a geographical area that's populated by minority populations, you come to expect the element—the criminal element that comes from that population. That's where you work. That's where the crime is. That's where 80 percent of our homicides come from. Areas that are 70 percent or more minority, over 80 percent of the murders come from there. Over 80 percent of the gun arrests come from there. Over 80 percent or 74.5 to 75 percent of the narcotic arrests come from there.

So, when you have minority contact with the police, this is where the crime, the guns, the murders, and the dope is coming from. That's why in the Eleventh District, you've got 444 police officers assigned to it. It's a small geographical area. When you go to the Sixteenth District up on the far northwest side, which is near O'Hare Airport, you have 196 police officers that are controlling more than twice the geographical area of the Eleventh District because of the crime, the calls for service. So the deployment and the manpower goes to the areas where the criminal behavior occurs, and that's deployment based on the department. They send us there. Besides that, you lead in guns, gangs, and murders, so they send the gun teams, the gang teams, the narcotic teams, and the saturation teams, to the same area. So you're going to be overwhelmed with a police presence and you're going to have more contact with the police, because they're trying to keep a lid on that. And it could be by design, but that's where your contact comes from, and it could be suppressive, it could be overbearing, and it could be—and it obviously is being looked at like you are only f—ing with us. And I get it. But that's where they're sending me. This is my job. And do some people get mother-f—ed or put on the wall, "Let me see that f—ing ID"?

Pegues: Harassed?

Angelo: Yeah. Does it happen? Sure, it's going to happen. Is it by design? No. Will a body camera on me not mother-f— you? Sure, it won't, it better. You know, I tell these guys, if you're bringing a camera to the party, don't be the idiot in the corner with the lampshade on your head, because you brought the camera, and you're acting the fool.

So will [body cameras] adjust our approach and our behavior and our demeanor? Definitely. But will it capture [suspects, too]? Yes. And that, I think, it's going to be the equalizer—not that guys are overwhelmingly excited about getting body cameras, but I think that this is going to be something that will not only show people what we do, and what we confront, but it will also be a realization and an instrument of realization for our guys and girls to say "stop" [bad behavior].

That behavior needs to be adjusted. If [higher-ups] don't adjust my behavior [as an officer], that's on them—the department. If they don't take me to task, then I can get away with it, which is a problem for our whole discipline thing, that we're being looked at [for in the first place]. We have complaints against police officers that are five or six years old. There's two of them that have been adjudicated, and it could be verbal abuse. Guess what? "I [a dirty cop] mother-f—ed fifty other people between then and now, but you never said anything, so . . . ?" If you don't have the discipline [enforced] . . . close to the incident, it loses its impact. . . . So you need to adjust my behavior. If you don't, then don't expect me to do it because everything's fine to me. So if [the racist behavior] goes on, and now people get pissed. . . . Depending on my demeanor, it sets a barometer. *You know what? These cops are a—holes.* [or] *These guys are pretty good guys.*

So is there some room for people to get involved with, you know, oversight and transparency and all these other things? Definitely. But there's also that element of our society that most people have no idea is right next door. And that's what we're here for, you know, that's what we're supposed to be trying to eliminate, or to put where they belong—and they belong in the penitentiary. Can we make sure they stay there? No. That's not our job. We build a case. We testify, then we go away. And that's our job, you know, and it's a tough job. It's a good job; but it's done for the right reason, and it's got to stay that way, you know. We need this blue line. We need that. And God forbid it ever goes away, because then it's on, you know, and in some of our neighborhoods, it's on.

Angelo says that even with some of the conflict between police and the black community, the majority of the people who live in the tough neighborhoods that Chicago police officers patrol want the officers there to protect them.

Angelo: And that's my fear when I talk to people about the summer, when I talk to people about the uptick, when I talk to people about the suppressive police scene, legislation and tactics, and ideas that people are having out there that don't know what we do. Sheriff David Clark from Milwaukee County, who is very outspoken, likens fighting crime to surgery. And we have a death at the hands of a surgeon or in the operating room, and we all sit around and we start telling him what to do. Too much anesthesia, not enough anesthesia, too many nurses, not enough nurses, too many instruments, not enough instruments—we'll fix it. We don't know what they do. If we impact that operating room, more people are going to die, because we don't know what [surgeons] do. They don't want to know what we do. Don't want to get in the car. Don't want to learn. Don't want to ride along.

Pegues: Are you optimistic about the future of policing in Chicago?

Angelo: . . . I just worry about what it looks like going forward. When I met with the department on December 30th, they handed me a stack of paperwork, and they said, these are all going online in two days. *Why?* "*We're trying to get ahead of the DOJ.*" *Too late . . . they're here.* How can you get ahead of [the DOJ]? They're already here. Let them, let them figure out what we need. Let them do their job. They've done it in California, in Ohio, in Missouri, in Florida, in Louisiana, you know? Let them do it. They've even done the whole island of Puerto Rico. Let them tell us. They're subject-matter experts. They have people that have been around, they know this process; they're looking from the outside in; let them tell you.

Pegues: You trust them more than the politicians?

Angelo: I want them to tell us what we need, because if the city and the department doesn't do what they say, the [DOJ] will sue them.

Pegues: That's right.

Angelo: More training, more cops, more supervisors, more equipment. When I went [to Washington to meet with DOJ officials], I gave them our contract book, and I gave them some videos that we did, and I said, *You know, we had to bargain for four hundred cars to be bought on an annual basis, put it in our contract.* They go, *why?* I go, *I don't know, why you here to ask me?* You've got fourteen police officers to every one supervisor, largest gap or ratio, and you have a major department in the country. Why? Ask 'em. I can't fix that. I can only point it out as issues and as reasons why things are the way they are here. It's the Chicago Police Department. Welcome to [the] Chicago Police Department.

You know, in your cars, the floor is falling apart, the computers don't work, they said it's operational error. We got guys whose cars have wires that go through the roof. We're the bad guy? It's all this finger-pointing, it's unreal. But we're an easy target. Now we've gotten in everybody's crosshairs. It's our fault. It's not our fault. We've done nothing. [But] we do what any other union does: we try to keep our people employed. You can't go from no disciplinary history to *you're fired.* Why? Well because, you know, he came in drunk that day, he was late that day, his car's off, tags on his car are wrong, and, you know, all that other s—. You can't do that. You should have wrote him up when he was drunk. You should have written him up when he was late. You should have written him up when his license was expired. You can't use that now and throw every flag in the football game at him and say he's gotta go. No, he goes back to work. If you want to set a foundation for separation, build your foundation. When you don't, that's what we're here for. . . . So it's an uphill battle, but we'll be okay. We'll get through it. How will it look when we're done? I don't know. I don't know. You know, we just want to keep everybody safe. We want to keep everybody employed; and, you know, if the department finds that there's people that just cannot play by the rules, then they need to do what they need to do to remove them. Don't look for me to find them. That's not my job. You know, do we realize that some people shouldn't be cops? Yeah. Some people shouldn't be priests. Some people shouldn't be teachers. Some people shouldn't be politicians.

Pegues: Is the quality what it used to be? The quality of the hire?

Angelo: I think that some people are getting to the point where they wonder, why would I want to be a cop? Forget it. I'll go find something else to do.

CHAPTER SIXTEEN

TREAT PEOPLE AS YOU
WANT TO BE TREATED

San Francisco 49rs quarterback Colin Kaepernick continued his stand against police brutality by sitting down during the US national anthem. Just over a week away from the 2016 season-opening game against the Los Angeles Rams, some members of the Santa Clara Police Department were planning a protest of their own.[1] The union representing the police officers released a statement saying that some of its members may not work at 49rs games as a result of Kaepernick's comments and actions.

The board of directors of the Santa Clara Police Officers' Association called Kaepernick's criticism of police, "inappropriate workplace behavior."[2] "The board of directors of the Santa Clara Police Officers' Association has a duty to protect its members and work to make all of their working environments free of harassing behavior," the union wrote in the letter, according to KNTV.

Kaepernick began his protest to highlight what he believes is the systemic oppression of black people and people of color. The twenty-eight-year-old refused to stand with his teammates during "The Star-Spangled Banner," saying, "To me, this is bigger than football and it would be selfish on my part to look the other way. There are bodies in the street and people getting paid leave and getting away with murder."[3] His words and his stance won him both praise and scorn. It had also drawn the young millionaire into the center of the firestorm surrounding policing. News organizations covered the story and its implications around the clock. The tension in America increased. There were fleeting moments of peace and harmony between communities and police, then violent protests or comments by prominent officials, celebrities, or politicians would bring the pain and hurt to the surface once again.

But in Philadelphia's Nineteenth Police District, people were laughing, interacting, and smiling on a sunny summer day in one of the city's predominantly black neighborhoods. It was happening in a place where most would not expect to see a celebratory atmosphere. The sign above the door was not always viewed as welcoming. It read "Commitment to Excellence," and it was framed by two blue-and-black-colored police badges. Black and blue were coming together below the sign as residents milled about—not in protest—but simply to enjoy what had become a tradition in the "19th."

Summer Fun Day is an easy way for police officers to interact with members of the community. Back in the day, you'd see beat cops who were on a first-name basis with residents in the neighborhoods, and the residents knew them. Nowadays, a more frenetic pace of policing led to fewer opportunities to simply get to know one another. As one officer put it in a video recording the event, Summer Fun Day was an effort to earn the community's trust.[4]

"The main thing that we need in order to help fight crime and to make the community feel safe," says officer Ryan Mundrick of the Philadelphia PD, "is to have the community first have faith in us and enjoy our company; and show them that, you know, we also have a vested interest in their community."[5] It sounds simple enough.

Captain Joe Bologna is the commander of the Nineteenth District. He is easygoing and passionate about what he's doing and how police officers' interactions with the community are portrayed.[6] Bologna is Philly through and through. He is also white and sensitive about how the relationship between the black community and police is portrayed.

> **Bologna:** It's definitely important; and if it's not portrayed the right way—that could be bad. You see what happens when we don't give people a voice. Even if we don't understand that voice or we don't agree with that voice. When people are clammed up—we've seen the tragedies that occur. But, you know, we don't have problems with people venting their frus-

tration. At least they are releasing energy. It's like when you are going to a disturbent's house, you know the one you've got to be most careful of is the one in the background that's not saying anything. That's who you got to watch out for. The other folks are venting, and they are frustrated, which is normal . . . that's what's great about this country.

Pegues: How long have you been on the force?

Bologna: Next April, I'll have twenty-seven years on.

Pegues: If you had a platform to tell the rest of the country what really needs to change in terms of police-community relations, what do you think it would be?

Bologna: I just think everything we do needs to revolve as a team. The police can't operate independently of the community they serve, because it's a losing battle. The closer you are with the community, the less crime you're going to have. I don't care if the community is mostly white or mostly black, Hispanic, whatever. It's all about relationships; it's almost that simple. And I'm not saying it is easy to do. It's all about communication. You know what I always say about communication? It's the easiest and the hardest thing to do. We can say we're communicating, but we're really not. But I think that's it. And you have to develop relationships. And it takes time. It doesn't develop overnight. But you have to be real. You know when somebody is phony. You can fool somebody for a little bit, but after a little bit the way you are is really going to come out. The relationships take time. You think you do x, y, z and it works out? No!

But it's like when we run events—and I got a formula for events, your planning gives you your outcome. Event plus response equals outcome. That's my formula for when we run the bike patrol. I know what event I have. My response and my plan is going to dictate the outcome I want. So as a police district, I know the outcome I want. I want to make sure my community—they might not necessarily agree with everything we're going to do, and that's okay. But they are going to know that we are here to support them and protect them. You know, we're protectors of the community, not oppressors of the community. The only way to do that is daily interaction with the community. You have to be available to them. Is there one specific formula? No. Everybody is going to have their own. I've got my own little twist, because whatever we do has my personality behind it. Most of my community here is black. But I never looked at it that way. They are people. They're my people. I'm responsible for the safety and welfare of my folks in my district.

Pegues: Do you think there are some officers who look at them as perps, unfortunately?

Bologna: Yeah. Come on . . . they do.

Pegues: Why do you think that happens?

Bologna: I think because that's their whole mind-set. They are not seeing a different angle to it all the time.

Bologna says that what his officers often see are kids going down the wrong road at a young age.

Bologna: You can see where the problem lies, and in your head you say—*oh, man, this kid is going to have problems.* We try to get them diverted and get them the help that we can.

Pegues: But what do you see in these young kids where you see a red flag that pops up?

Bologna: They are doing what they have to [do to] survive out there. I don't think a lot of them are bad kids; I don't think they have any discipline in their lives. A lot of them, their older grand-moms and aunts are the parents they have. So what do kids naturally do? They want to be part of something—right. But they don't have a family structure, so they start running with the gangs. Maybe they're not Bloods or Crips, but they are like a block gang. So, from the time the sun comes up to the time the sun goes down, they are on the street by themselves. Nobody to show them some guidance. They're committing burglaries, and they are doing this and they are doing that. It's just a vicious cycle, because there is no family structure. Maybe you and I were lucky—we had a parent who smacked you and kicked you in your butt. A lot of these kids don't have that. Some of their grandparents that I talk to, they are too old they don't have the energy. And it just starts a vicious cycle.

Pegues: How is the morale [on the force] these days?

Bologna: I haven't seen a drop-off in morale whatsoever; and you know morale's a tough thing to gauge. Morale's always in a fluctuating state, so I look at the performance—what they're doing. I gauge how they are interacting with folks.

Pegues: Well, how do they feel about the public they are serving, [what] with everything that has happened nationally?

Bologna: I could speak in general; and I can speak about Philadelphia, which I think we have no problems whatsoever. I mean *major* problems. You're always going to have some isolated folks that just don't like the police because they don't like the police. Because of how we've always interacted with the community and stuff, we haven't slacked off whatsoever. I mean, we have this whole community tie, especially with the 19th. I've been here for four years; I haven't seen no [negative] effect, really. Have we had some discussions with the community about certain issues? Oh yeah. And I thought that was positive. They asked us to go to the church and speak to some of the young kids. A lot more requests for us to show up at meetings and stuff like that with the community where it's a positive interaction.

Pegues: You think that kind of interaction actually works?

Bologna: Anytime we get to interact with the community when we're not just responding to jobs is positive. Because, remember, most of what we do, we're responding from one bad situation to another. They're not calling us just to say hello. They're calling us because they have a problem, right? They either were a victim, or they need assistance to stop ongoing disputes in their home. . . . Even the best people, they call us at the worst time—because something is wrong. So any opportunity we get to interact with the folks on an even level, like it's just a regular meeting—like when I have my captain's meetings and our public service area meetings— I always have police officers there. Because now they get to meet folks and not in an adversarial position. You got folks coming, and they are coming because they want to come; so everybody is on the same level. They might have issues at the meeting, but we can discuss that. We always have breakout sessions after the meetings where they put a face behind the badge. And that's big for me. That's what I like to call it. Our face-to-face interaction. You put a name behind that badge, you put a face behind that badge other than it just being a uniform. Now you're a human being.

Pegues: How do you stay so positive? You have a high-stress job. Why are you so comfortable among black folks?

Bologna: This is what I do. And in my opinion there is no better time to be in the police profession than right now. We're involved in change—changing the way the community maybe views us, where we can both understand certain things. Most of us took this job to make a difference. So why would you be negative? It's easy to be negative; but this is what I do. This is what I love to do. When you love what you do, brother, it's easy to be positive. Even in tough times.

Pegues: You're the type of guy who, for some reason, makes everybody feel comfortable. How do you do it?

Bologna: I think a lot has to do with my background; and I give a lot of credit to my grandfather, a very famous boxer in the city of Philadelphia. His boxing name was Teddy Baldwin, and he was one of the top fifty boxers of Philadelphia history. He's at the top of that list. His real name is the same as mine. I'm actually named after my grandfather. Everybody knows him as Teddy Baldwin. He was boxing in the 1930s and '40s.[7] The first time he got a fight—it was hard for Italians back in that day to get fights—and he fought a guy named Teddy Baldwin. He was an Irish guy, and they are sitting in the locker room, and the guy said "that was the last fight." My grandfather did a number on him or whatever. So my grandfather, being the kind of guy he was, seizes the opportunity. He says, "You mind if I use your name to get some fights?" And the guy says, "Yeah, sure." So most people don't even know my grandfather's real name. Anyway—now fast-forward. So when I was a kid, we lived with my grandparents, and my grandfather would go everywhere in the city—every neighborhood. And I would go with him. He and Joe Frasier were very good friends. He actually helped Frasier a lot. So I've been in Frasier's gym a lot, and you're talking at a young age in the '70's and early '80's. I was in different parts of the city when the city was still kind of segregated. Black folks living over here, and there was still the influx of Hispanics in the east division. But it was all open to us because of my grandfather. So I got to meet all kinds of people. That's why everybody laughs at my taste for food. All the ladies out here love giving me greens. They want me to evaluate their greens. But I've been eating greens since I was six years old. My grandfather used to make them at home. He loved eating them! My grandfather always told me, Joe, you treat people the way they treat you. Don't matter what color they are or what religion they are. And this is a man that grew up in a different time period.

So, I always looked at things a little differently, and then I started playing ball and traveling all over the place and meeting different people. I've always looked at things that way. It's just the way I am. That was the way I was brought up. In my family, it's just the way we are. We treat everybody with respect, and I don't care what they look like, who they pray to. It's just how I am. Don't get me wrong. I'm no saint. There are some folks—if they're a s—head, they are a s—head. But I think a lot has to do with that. And maybe I had parents and grandparents that thought differently, that understood struggles just like everybody else.

Pegues: Do you think that's important? Relating to people's struggles?

Bologna: Well, yeah. I can relate to everybody else. It's common ground. I can understand folks. How discrimination affects people in all different types of ways. It's one of the reasons why I became a police officer. One—because I never liked bullies, mind you. I don't like seeing other human beings being taken advantage of, brother—honestly, and I don't care who they are. And this gave me that opportunity to do that. There are some folks that are good people. We're there to protect them because they just can't protect themselves. You've got to like people, and I love people. I ask a lot of questions, and it drives my wife crazy! She goes, "Joe, you can talk to a paper bag." On a plane, I always get the aisle seat so I can talk to people. I love it. I'm very interested in people. I'm very interested in what makes them tick. I do that to my cops when I'm talking to them. And I keep reminding them why they do what they do.

Pegues: Are you doing that more these days?

Bologna: Well, you know, I felt myself doing it more because of all the pressures they were under. We put a lot of time into the community. You know how it is; it takes a lot of time to build a relationship with the community, and just a second to ruin it. For over four years, we've really been building confidence with the community. You don't do that overnight. It takes time, and I wanted to make sure—no matter what was going on around the country or even here—that we were still going to act professionally and do what was the right thing to do, no matter what the circumstances. We know taking this job that you're going to be second-guessed. It's part of the business. But some of us who've been on the job for a while, we're used to it. Here in the 19th I got a lot of the young guys and girls—the commissioner likes sending me the new guys and girls because we train them up right. So I need to get in their heads. Police work is not about intimidation. Police work is all mental—okay? You need the right frame of mind. You need to be in the right frame of mind to deal with, maybe, difficult people sometimes. When cops are maybe struggling with why they took this job or something, it's my job as the police captain to get in their heads and see if someone needs individual attention. I have help—my clergy is great, I got some real community members. It's a mental game; my job as a police captain is to make sure I'm in their heads in a positive way. It would be easy for them just to say, oh, I'm not doing my job, and the community don't appreciate us, and all this nonsense they might be hearing—

which is so far from the truth. I believe that's part of my job. It isn't all about locking up the bad guys. . . . It's about giving the community the policing they want, they need, and they deserve. Also, to do it as professionally as possible. Are we going to mess up? You bet we're going to mess up. But you know what I'm going to tell you, Jeff, when you're dealing with the community and they know your heart's in the right place and you got their backs, when you screw up, they're not going to throw sand in your face. They're going to give you that opportunity to explain what happened, or they are going to give you the benefit of the doubt. But if you treat your folks, and I can't help but call this district "my folks," because they are. When you treat your community—and this can be generalized across the country, because I believe this— if you treat your community like crap . . . okay, well, guess what—when you screw up, you know what they're going to do? They're going to kick you in the face, okay? And trust me, our police officers are going to make mistakes. They are, and it's part of the learning process. I hate to say it; it's not perfect—they are going to make mistakes. However, when your community knows that you have their best interest in hand and 99 percent of the time you are there to help them and protect them, when you mess up they are going to give you the benefit of the doubt.

Pegues: How many officers do you have under your command?

Bologna: I got about 240; and supervisors, there are about thirty.

Pegues: Do you think there's enough training?

Bologna: Well, you can never have enough training. One of the big things we do is get the most updated training for our officers as possible. I think we do a really good job for a department this size, with our responsibilities, to make sure we have enough officers on the street every day and all of that. We're really into reality-based training. We've been doing that for the last three years now. We really ramped that up, and the folks love it. We do a lot of our own training in house—like in the districts. Every two weeks, we do what we like to call "fat day" training. Where all the squads are working on the same day. And we do daily training at roll call. We do a lot of tactical training; we do community intervention, de-escalation, a lot of it at the district level. It's just about being creative. A lot of it is seeing what the needs are. When former police commissioner Charles Ramsey got here, training ramped up. What I see happening sometimes is when money gets tight, training is the first thing to get cut. But that would be the last thing I would cut. The better trained the officers, the greater impact they are going to make with the community. You cut that training out, and you know what's going to happen? Now your internal-affairs complaints are going to go up. Maybe use of force is going to go up. You're going to be paying for it in the long run anyway.

Use of force had been an issue for the Philadelphia Police Department. In 2013, the Department of Justice Office of Community Oriented Policing Services (COPS Office) examined the department's deadly force policies and practices. That year, there had been a drop in violent crime and assaults against police, but the number of fatal officer-involved shootings was on the rise. The review found policy, training, and operational deficiencies. But it also revealed an undercurrent of "significant strife between the community and [the police] department" and recommended that there be a reform of its deadly force practices.[8]

CHAPTER SEVENTEEN
CODE OF SILENCE

"The police need to know who they work for—the community. The authority that they have belongs to the people."

That quote is right at the top of Chicago's Police Accountability Task Force Report. It was the prevailing sentiment during a community forum at Sullivan High School. There's no mistaking the message the report is sending.[1]

The perception of the Chicago Police Department is of an organization that lacks leadership, a moral compass, and discipline. For years, cops were getting out of line without paying the price. The task force concluded that the lack of accountability was at the core of what was rotten in the CPD.[2]

Going back years, and continuing to the present day, CPD has missed opportunities to make accountability an organizational priority. Currently, neither the non-disciplinary interventions available nor the disciplinary system are functioning.

The public has lost faith in the oversight system. Every stage of investigations and discipline is plagued by serious structural and procedural flaws that make real accountability nearly impossible. The collective bargaining agreements provide an unfair advantage to officers, and the investigating agencies are under-resourced, lack true independence and are not held accountable for their work. Even where misconduct is found to have occurred, officers are frequently able to avoid meaningful consequences due to an opaque, drawn out and unscrutinized disciplinary process.

Complaints go uninvestigated. From 2011 [to] 2015, 40% of complaints filed were not investigated by IPRA or BIA.

Arbitrators reduce or void disciplinary recommendations. In 2015, arbitrators reduced disciplinary recommendations in 56.4% of cases and eliminated any discipline in 16.1% of cases. In total, arbitrators reduced or eliminated discipline in 73% of cases.

No risk management regarding lawsuits. There continues to be an unacceptably high number of lawsuits filed against the City and individual police officers every year. Despite this persistent problem, which results in the outlay of tens of millions of dollars every year, CPD does not employ a systematic tool for evaluating risk issues identified in lawsuits.

High number of CPD officers with significant CRs. The enduring issue of CPD officers acquiring a large number of Complaint Registers ("CRs") remains a problem that must be addressed immediately. Any one of these metrics in isolation is troubling, but taken together, the only conclusion that can be reached is that there is no serious embrace by CPD leadership of the need to make accountability a core value. These statistics give real credibility to the widespread perception that there is a deeply entrenched code of silence supported not just by individual officers, but by the very institution itself. The absence of accountability benefits only the problem officer and undermines officers who came into the job for the right reasons and remain dedicated to serving and protecting.[3]

As troubling as the findings of the accountability task force are, amazingly, there's more. According to the *Chicago Tribune*, of more than four hundred police shootings between 2007 and 2015, only two were found to be unjustified.[4] Furthermore, the Citizens Police Data Report found that there were more than twenty-eight thousand abuse complaints and more than $500 million in legal settlements paid to victims of police misconduct.[5]

It was going to take years to turn this troubled police department around. But some neighborhoods in Chicago didn't have time to wait. The city was in the midst of a deadly wave of violence that wasn't showing signs of slowing down. A record number of people were dying on the city's streets, and local television stations were reporting that it had been two decades since Chicago had seen that many murders in a year.

In 2016, the nation's third largest city was ranking first in murder rates. Its 487 homicides were way ahead of New York's 222 and Los Angeles's 176.[6] With four months left in the year, Chicago was also close to topping the previous year's total of 490 murders.[7] In a news release, police pinned part of the blame for the violence on repeat gun offenders:

> The City of Chicago, like many major cities throughout the United States, continues to be challenged with violent crime committed by repeat offenders using illegal guns. As we close out the month of August, this fact is underscored by a data analysis recently conducted by the University of Chicago that shows nearly 40 percent of those arrested for homicide in 2015 had prior arrests for gun crimes. "The historical cycle of violence we have seen in some communities must come to an end," said CPD Superintendent Eddie Johnson. "Repeat gun offenders who drive the violence on our streets should not be there in the first place and it is time to change the laws to ensure these violent offenders are held accountable for their crimes."
>
> The month of August saw 90 murders, 384 shooting incidents, and 472 shooting victims. Yet the increase in violence in Chicago has not affected all communities equally. Six police districts are flat or down in murders in 2016, while five districts on the South and West Sides of the city account for a majority of the increase.
>
> We continue our efforts to stem the violence and keep communities safe. This year, murder arrests are up over 18% for the month of August compared to the same time in 2015, while gun arrests year to date are up nearly 5% compared to the same period in 2015. Additionally, guns seized both by officers and through gun turn-in programs, so far in 2016 have increased by nearly 22% compared to last year—that's 5,900 guns—nearly one illegal gun off city streets every 59 minutes.
>
> CPD has also made significant efforts in striking at the heart of gang operations and putting repeat offenders on notice that their actions will not go without consequence. During the month of August several enforcement missions have targeted over 200 offenders throughout the city who contribute to the cycle of violence in some neighborhoods. The majority of these individuals are documented gang members and on the Department's Strategic Subject List (SSL) which calculates the propensity of an individual to be an offender or victim of gun violence.

During the month of August, Superintendent Johnson hosted over a dozen police chiefs from throughout the United States to a conference focused on the increase of violent crime scene across a number of major cities. This initial discussion helped frame an ongoing conversation between the nation's law enforcement leaders, including one hosted in Washington, DC, on how to effectively reduce crime while protecting the civil liberties of the communities we serve.[8]

Would they be able to do it? That's currently an unanswered question in cities across America. If you take away "Broken Window"–style police tactics like stop and frisk, will police be able reduce crime? Dean Angelo, the president of the Fraternal Order of Police, says that politicians are putting handcuffs on cops with some of the initiatives baked into reform. Crime, he says, is already getting out of hand. What he views as anti-police legislation are the laws that he insists will make it easier for people to file complaints against cops. It is a tool that he predicts targets of police investigations will abuse, which will put more pressure on cops.[9]

> **Angelo:** . . . Right now with the city council legislation they want to pass, or the anti-police legislation down in Springfield, they are going to, more or less, release the hounds. I'm working in Englewood every day. I'm stopping all these guys every day, because I've got to keep these families from getting shot. And I don't care about getting complaints. Make your accusation; I'm not doing anything wrong. Here's my body camera, you can watch me. These guys are going to have IPRA on speed dial.

IPRA was the Independent Police Review Authority, which is charged with investigating complaints against police.

> **Angelo:** Now [if] they're on speed dial, I'm getting five complaints, fifteen complaints—five, ten, fifteen, twenty, I could be getting thirty, forty complaints a week, if not more.
> **Pegues:** So the number of complaints are going to go up?

Angelo: So what's going to happen? My sergeant has to handle those complaints. He's going to say *Dean, get the f— out of that area. What are you doing?* I'm rousting, man, I'm trying to get them off the corner. *Are you locking them up?* No, I'm just breaking their business 'cause if I park my squad car here, there ain't nobody buying here. If I park my squad car here? Nobody's buying. If I can run back and forth between handling my calls for service, between getting the in-progress calls, or the calls for backup, and come back here, and disturb their business, they ain't making no money. You ain't making any money, you're gonna move into a different box, but it ain't going to be my box, and these people are safe.

[But] if you keep the complaints on my file forever, these guys will have IPRA on speed dial, and they will eventually get that sergeant to say *Stay out of that f—in' box. I'm sick of doing these bulls—complaints.* Well, what happens? Give them a corner. You give them the block. You give them the community. It's over. You are restricting proactive policing by having people who don't realize the adverse impact [this legislation] is going to have on the safety of the communities that they represent. This is their neighborhood.

Pegues: Well, why isn't the new police superintendent speaking up and saying that? Or is he—?

Angelo: Politics. This is a very political environment.

Pegues: So the reforms that they're recommending, you're saying [they] are going to lead to more crime because they're putting handcuffs on police?

Angelo: In a nutshell. I told them if they designed this street stop document that was originally proposed in Senate Bill 1304,[10] I said, you're going to just eliminate people from being, you know—

Pegues: Stopped?

Angelo: Searched, or approached by the police, because it's going to be ridiculous.

Pegues: More paperwork?

Angelo: But I've got so much other stuff to do and now if this is

fifteen minutes for these five, fifteen minutes for that five, I
don't have the time to do it, because I'm running like an idiot
out here. We're doing thirty jobs a day besides this. Twenty to
thirty jobs—you got another one! Jesus Christ! . . . So we got
all that going on, and we got to come back and roust these
guys. And now I've got to drop ten pages of paper—two-sided
for each one of these guys. So when people [who] don't know
what we do, try to impact what we do, [it] turns into becoming
a problem. You don't have police officers anywhere saying that
this is a good idea. And the politicians are running on that anti-
police platform to stay in office, but they're going to increase
the problems in their own communities. Then what happens
when it's law? When you restrict these protections against BS
allegations against police, or you want their complaint history to
last forever? [Say] I'm going to get promoted—I want to go to a
specialized unit. I want to be considered for merits, although a
union doesn't like merit at all. We want a rank order, you know?
But how am I going to be considered for merit when I'm getting
twenty complaints a month? That never goes away.

Pegues: I get what you're saying, but the image that the public
remembers is Laquan McDonald being shot, how many
times? Sixteen times?

Angelo: Mmm-hmm.

Pegues: Or Michael Brown being shot and killed. Or Eric Garner
being arrested in the way that he was. So can you understand
why people in the community would be outraged by tactics
like that?

Angelo: I can understand why people in the community could be
outraged by mistreatment . . .

Pegues: Sixteen shots, and he was walking, he was walking away, I
mean how does that get out of control?

Angelo says the shooting may not have happened had Van Dyke
and the other officers who responded to the scene had Tasers.

Angelo: There's no Tasers. People have been asking for Tasers for
the last ten, fifteen minutes.

Pegues: Van Dyke couldn't find a Taser?

Angelo: They're in the building. They're in the station. Nobody checked them out.

Pegues: So those officers didn't have . . .

Angelo: Supervisors are supposed to have them. Was that supervisor trained? Now before the DOJ started coming, people were putting in for training for Tasers, [but] they couldn't get in the class. *Well, we don't have any openings. We don't know when the next one is gonna be available. We'll get back to you. Call back next month.* Now everybody is going for Taser training. It's a little late.

Pegues: Yeah, why didn't they have them before? Was it a money issue?

Angelo: They had them. They're in the building.

As we continue to discuss the shooting of Laquan McDonald, Angelo—the president of Chicago's Fraternal Order of Police, admits that doesn't recall anyone flagging the McDonald shooting to the FOP as anything unusual the night that it happened.

Pegues: It didn't stand out?

Angelo: No, nothing came to us.

Pegues: Why wouldn't that stand out? Is that part of the problem? Sadly, something like that doesn't stand out anymore?

Angelo: I think that if that situation [the McDonald shooting] was addressed [by the city and the police department] as being problematic in 2014, things would be different right now.

Pegues: Had they addressed it early on?

Angelo: Yeah, I think if you have an incident, that the best thing you can do is address it. And not try to politicize it, or not try to cover it up.

Pegues: Did that ever happen when you were on the beat? Honestly, where there was this effort to cover something up? *Hey, this is what happened, let's all stick to the story?* Did that ever happen? Honestly?

Angelo: In my career, no.

Pegues: . . . Did you hear about it happening with other people?

Angelo: You know what, if you—if there was a goof in your circle, you stay away from him. My dad said, *Keep your eyes open, your ears open, your mouth shut, and your hands in your own pockets, and you won't have too many problems.*

Pegues: Did you say that to your son who's an officer?

Angelo: I told my son.

Pegues: But then "mouth shut," isn't that what the code of silence is?

Angelo: No, it is—it's not silence. It is listening, not talking. Learn by observing, learn by hearing. You don't learn by gabbin', you know. You need to watch people that are good and listen to how they talk. Watch how they behave and read what they write, so that you can at some point in your career become that guy, become that productive person, become the person that's compassionate to people, that doesn't say, *Hey, a—hole, where you goin'?* all the time. There's a time you do that, but it's not to everybody. It's not every traffic stop. So, there's a way to treat people, and you don't learn that by talking, and by trying to out-talk or quick-talk people. You shut up and learn. But in my career as a union rep, you know, you have people that need to have—which is what discipline is designed for—to have their behaviors adjusted.

Pegues: Like Van Dyke?

Angelo: No, not like Van Dyke. Jason Van Dyke. Jason's background has, I think, they say eighteen complaints against him.

Van Dyke had twenty complaints against him, including allegations of misconduct.[11] There are twelve thousand officers in CPD, and 402 have twenty or more complaints apiece. Van Dyke's twenty complaints didn't result in discipline.[12]

Pegues: Is that a lot?

Angelo: Not in a fifteen-year career working in some of the worst places of the city and one of the worst cities in the country.

Pegues: "The worst cities in the country" . . . ?

Angelo: Chicago's violence and shootings. We have taken, every year we take more guns off the street than Los Angeles and New York combined.[13] For those young kids growing up there, you know, we're pretty prepared for this. We go to work cognizant of where we're going. Some of these young kids are growing up in those communities, my god, how do you survive through that? You become so desensitized so early that—it's a shame that you've got kids, and I think I mentioned this, that you've got kids that can describe what size round that was they just heard from the gunshot in the background. You've got families, when we had the high-rise projects and, you know, subsidized housing units like Cabrini Green and on South Federal, and, you know, all the different projects—you had families that were putting mattresses on the floor [or] up against the window so if a round came through, it would miss someone, it would go over them. . . . So, most people have no idea what goes on in the city of Chicago, no idea.

People, and I told this to the Senate subcommittee [when] we were talking about body cameras, you know, I said, *You are going to be subjected to an element of our society that you have no idea exists.* It's like, welcome to the show! Don't edit these things. You want to see what we do, see what we do. Get some popcorn. It'll be the best movie you can see—but you know what's the scariest part of it? It's real. Nobody's going to go take the makeup off. It's not one of those exploding, you know, little pops when somebody gets shot. This is real blood, that's real brains, that's the real thing, those are real victims that, four commercials later, you don't have your bad guy. So, I think, and I told them, *You're going to come away from these videos with a whole new sense of appreciation of who these girls and guys are in blue uniforms. And what they do, and how compassionate they are, how professional they are, and how good they are at what they raised their hand to do, because you don't know what happens.*

I'm trying to get all these elected officials to do ride-alongs with our guys. They won't do it. They lose their narrative that we're the bad guy. They lose their narrative that we're quick to box people. We don't want to box anybody. We don't want to shoot anybody. We want to go to work, wave to the kids, make sure they go to school, make sure they come home, make sure that guy doesn't choke out his wife, make sure that guy doesn't take that little lady's purse, make sure that these kids on the train don't get punched and robbed for their cell phone, and go home. That's all we want to do. We don't want to come here and box and fight and shoot. But there are times that you have to. Most of what we do is determinant of the behavior of the people that's in front of us. They comply, it's over. Drop the knife, it's done. Don't go for the gun, it's over. Get your hands off her throat, it's over. Put your hands behind your back, it's over. But no. Nobody wants to go to jail. Nobody wants to drop their gun. Nobody wants to stop beating their wife.

You know, and these are obviously generalities, but you know, you have people out there—and I say this a lot—why does that guy rape that twelve-year-old kid? Why does he get that nine-year-old kid in a basement and sexually abuse him? Because he's a pedophile, that's what they do. That's his lot in life. Now, can he be cured? Some say yes; some say no. But I can't cure him. So don't get surprised when the pedophile rapes somebody that's a kid. Don't get surprised when a stick-up guy robs you, 'cause it's a stick-up guy. That's what he's there for. He wakes up in the morning, he starts thinking, *Who am I—where am I going to go to stick somebody up?* When a kid that's a purse snatcher comes out and he's not in school and he's roughed around, what's he looking for? He's looking for somebody that's a victim that he can snatch without any sort of fight. Get her. Grab it. And go. Same thing with a rapist. Same thing with someone who's trying to get money for his narcotics. *Who can I hit for money to fill my arm?* That's what they do, so that's why we're at work. That's what we face every day. And it's not like, *Excuse me, sir, are you—are you a junkie, are you going to rob that lady?* I don't know who you are. So when

I come up to you and I say, "Let me see your ID"—*Why?*—"Because I asked for it." You do it so you identify yourself, and now it starts. So it escalates sometimes, but it should not escalate based on me; and sometimes it does, because I go, "This mother—er, I said, I want your ID!" *Well, wait a minute, I'm not a junkie, I'm a college kid. I'm going to school.* "Why you mother—in' me now?" *I just asked why do you want to see my ID?* . . . So we have sometimes the inability to address people the way we should. Does that happen? Yeah, it happens.

Pegues: How do you . . .

Angelo: But when we ask fifteen people for their IDs, and all fifteen go "F— you, man; I ain't showing you my ID," it's like, "I'm done! Give me your f—ing ID," and guess what? Now you're in a college, kid, sorry. But you can't go back and say that; but the other ones, we've got to make sure that we conduct ourselves in a way that initially you'd get the courtesy. Initially you get the respect. But I can tell you what, it's gotten to the point where there is no respect. Everybody's like "F— you, I ain't gonna show you no ID!" And it could be on . . . on film. The part when you said, "F— you, pig," is edited [out]. On YouTube, you see me or hear me [say] "F— you, motherf—er, let me see that ID." That's what you see. Now I'm looking at five days' suspension, and now I'm going to get written up. Now I'm going to be a YouTube sensation; and now, guess what? Keep your f—in' ID, go get your dope, I'm done.

CHAPTER EIGHTEEN

TRAIN TO KILL

J a'Mal Green—for one—was still leading the march toward what he believed would be lasting reform. But Officer Jason Van Dyke's actions the night he shot Laquan McDonald are this unforgettable horror stamped in his mind.[1]

> **Green:** You see Jason Van Dyke just unloading his clip, and he was going to reload, and his partner had to stop him from reloading. What is in Jason Van Dyke that makes you want to shoot someone that many times? If that was a white kid, would he have shot that kid at all? Probably not.
>
> **Pegues:** You don't think so?
>
> **Green:** No.
>
> **Pegues:** Why do you say that?
>
> **Green:** Not a lot of white kids are getting killed by police. And then you look at who's killing the black kids . . . they are either white or sometimes Hispanic. The problem is, they go into our neighborhood and they automatically think we are criminals. They automatically think everyone is a thug. They think everyone's a threat. They are afraid of black people.
>
> **Pegues:** Is there a lack of respect in the black community for cops? Because that's what cops think. That black people don't respect the badge.
>
> **Green:** I disagree. Because if somebody does something to us, who are we going call? We are going to call police and ask them to help. The CPD culture is to train to kill and to always be against us instead of actually helping us. So when they are arriving on the scene and, say, this is happening—they are

already ready. They already got their hands on their guns. The attitude is not to help. It's, *What's going on? I'm fixing to Tase you or shoot you.* And so the problem is [that] they are trained to kill and not to help. That's in the training, and that needs to change.

I did an interview with the BBC the other day. You look at the police in London that don't even have weapons. They can't do anything that will bring them into a bad situation. They have to handle things a certain way. In Chicago, you have trigger-happy cops. You have cops walking around with PTSD. You got cops that have just been on the force so long and seen so many things that they just, mentally, they are not ready to handle these situations how they really should be, because they've seen so many things. So they act a certain way.

Pegues: Do you hate the cops?

Green: No. I think there are good cops. I have family on the force. I know some great cops that have helped me in the past. I just think that there are a bunch of cops that are shaping the culture. The bad are making the whole culture look bad. Jason Van Dyke made the whole department look bad. . . . So at the same time we have to figure out a way to rid these bad cops that—we need a better system to deal with the complaints. There have been sixty thousand complaints filed in the last five years against officers in the Southwest Side and North Side. Ninety-six percent of those complaints were not investigated, so the majority [of] officers you see walking around are walking around with twenty to twenty-five complaints. No discipline, nothing happened to them; no investigations—and then they kill somebody. Now you're looking at, *Oh, shoot—this officer had twenty-five complaints. We should have investigated that.* Because then this officer shouldn't have been on the street. Like Jason Van Dyke.

Pegues: Do you think the task force recommendations are going to make a difference?

Green: I don't know. What should have happened immediately is a change in police culture and millions of dollars of economic development to change these urban communities. Millions of dollars in programs.

. . .

Pegues: Do black folks have to change too?

Green: Definitely, but I'll put more blame on our people when they are living in the same conditions as white people. And a lot of these people . . . most of these people, a lot of their reasons are systemic.

Pegues: That's not an excuse?

Green: No, it's not an excuse. People downtown look at it as an excuse, because they don't have to live here. But let's figure out how we can do a switch. Let them live in our neighborhood for a year, and then we'll live in theirs. I think you'll start seeing more killings of drug dealers still in the same place—and they'll be white.

Just days after Alton Sterling and Philando Castile were shot by police, Green organized a protest at the Taste of Chicago. He was arrested and charged with attempting to disarm an officer, two counts of aggravated battery of a peace officer, and two counts of aggravated battery in a public place. He was also charged with two misdemeanor counts of resisting or obstructing an officer. The young activist was all of a sudden facing felony charges that could land him behind bars for years. The police department he'd spent months railing against had thrown Green in jail.

CHAPTER NINETEEN

THE MAGIC WAND

Sunday, September 25, 2016, capped another emotional week for the nation and law enforcement. There were two more police shootings of black men. One in Tulsa—in which the man who was killed was unarmed—and one in Charlotte as well. Both sparked protests, anger, and again calls for reform.

The protests in Charlotte were violent after Keith Lamont Scott was shot and killed by police. Police say he refused to drop a gun when he was confronted by officers. But the dashcam video was inconclusive, as even the Charlotte-Mecklenburg police chief acknowledged after seeing the footage. The video did not contain "absolute, definitive evidence that would confirm that a person was pointing a gun," Chief Kerr Putney said.[1] Putney initially refused to release the videotape to clear up any confusion about what happened, as Scott's family insisted that he was holding a book and not a gun. After five days of protests—which saw demonstrators roughing up reporters, setting fires, and smashing downtown windows, and even a murder was committed in the middle of a demonstration—the police chief relented. Putney decided to release the video, perhaps with the prospect of more unrest to come.

Two years after Ferguson, Charlotte had not heeded the lessons of other cities that had experienced similar unrest. As much transparency as possible, without compromising a case, was among the keys to easing the tension between police and community, especially in the aftermath of a police shooting. The unrest in Charlotte was yet another sign that departments across the country still required guidance in navigating minefields during a crisis that threatened to rupture the peace between police and the communities they served. At the time, Washington's Police Executive Research Forum (PERF) was helping agencies prepare best practices to avoid the massive figurative potholes.

Leading the Connecticut Avenue think tank was Chuck Wexler. PERF's executive director was widely respected in law enforcement circles for being able to work with police chiefs from across the nation to come up with solutions. Wexler was an MIT grad with hands-on law enforcement experience; he had worked in the Boston Police Department, and over the last two decades at PERF he had helped departments of all sizes develop best policies and practices. Now Wexler and Kevin Morison, the director of program management for PERF, are trying to sort through what has been plaguing law enforcement for the last couple of years—even though the problems have been bubbling under the surface a lot longer than that.[2]

Wexler was raised in a suburb of Boston. But while he was in graduate school in Florida, he turned on the television to find that the problems had been under the surface in Boston all along. He recalls watching CBS News and seeing Walter Cronkite reporting from the steps of a high school in South Boston that was the scene of the latest strife over desegregation.[3]

> **Wexler:** So he's covering the desegregation of Boston schools. You know how our perceptions change? That was a part of Boston I did not know. South Boston was where they had enormous violence and pushback, and that's when I started in the police department, and I worked in that area of the desegregation of the schools. I investigated racially motivated crime. We couldn't even call it "racial incidents," we had to call it "community disorders." We needed a euphemism. People didn't want to say that it was a racial incident. We had to say "that's a community disorder." And how you define that really was important. Like African Americans might think, this is a racial incident. A black family moving into a predominantly white area would have their tires slashed and racial epithets put on their house, and the report from police would come in as "vandalism." Clearly, if you were that family living in that house, it wasn't vandalism; it was a concerted effort to get you not to live there.

Pegues: It was hate.

Wexler: Right. So our unit would look at those incidents and reclassify them as "community disorders," and that meant it would get a higher priority. And then we worked with the state attorney general in Massachusetts, because local prosecutors wanted to treat these crimes as just vandalism. We asked Barney Frank, who was a Boston city council member and later a state representative, to support a state civil rights law, to allow the Massachusetts attorney general to get injunctive relief for these victims of racial violence, because the local courts weren't going to do anything with a minor vandalism claim.

And sometimes, what would happen is that after people kept slashing a man's tires, he'd pick up a baseball bat, because he was fed up with having his house and car vandalized. And when the police arrived, who do you think they were going to arrest? The kid slashing the tires who had disappeared, or the man with the baseball bat? So we had to get involved in that and ask, "Whoa, wait a minute, why does this guy have a baseball bat?" You would pick up a bat too if you felt threatened, if someone kept slashing your tires and spraypainting your house, and the police aren't doing anything.

Pegues: Since you brought that up, it reminds me that my grandfather integrated a white neighborhood in the Birmingham, Alabama, area. He had guns at the time, because the sentiment in the black community was that the police will not come to protect us. And so that goes to "where does this tension come from?" Well, it's just decades of feeling targeted by police rather than protected by police. I bring that up to talk about the future. How do you move forward and get beyond this? How does that happen across the country, in your opinion?

Wexler: There's not monolithic thinking on that subject, within law enforcement or within the community. Kevin and I are working on a project for Baltimore and Chicago. Both cities have violent crime issues and Department of Justice investigations. We're working with Kevin Davis [Baltimore police commissioner] and Eddie Johnson [Chicago police superintendent]. You have people living in these communities who suffer from the lion's share of crime. There is drug dealing and gang violence, and the residents perceive that the cops are just not stopping the crime.

Pegues: The cops are giving up?

Wexler: They're being more cautious. Think about it: you're a cop in Baltimore, and you saw how six officers got involved in a street stop, and all of a sudden they're charged with serious crimes, including attempted murder. Or you're in Chicago and you have to fill out a two-page report when you stop someone. It's difficult to be a cop right now and know exactly what is expected of you.

Pegues: That's what Dean Angelo [president of the Chicago FOP] said, by the way.

Wexler: A reasonable cop has a little more concern about what he does. There are some cops who use this as an excuse to do nothing. They say, "See, I told you. See that cop who was running around making all those arrests? See what happened to him?" But even the officers who always try to do the right thing are more cautious. They are wondering, "Am I going to be supported in this political environment?" That's the challenge in Baltimore and Chicago. That's what we're working on now. Residents in very challenged, high-crime neighborhoods are saying that they just don't see the police anymore; the police aren't stopping.

In Chicago, arrests were down in 2016 by 28 percent.[4] Police were making fewer stops, being less proactive than they had been in the past, and it was not a phenomenon unique to Chicago. It's just that Chicago was getting all of the attention. DOJ reports and police-shooting videos had changed the perception of police officers in the public eye.

Wexler understood why cops were pulling back from being proactive. To explain what's behind it, he pointed to the Baltimore Department of Justice report, which found that 44 percent of police stops occurred in predominantly African American neighborhoods with just 11 percent of the city's population. Officers felt that they were being unfairly painted as racist when they were simply patrolling where they were told to patrol and doing what they were ordered and trained to do.

Wexler: When I worked in Boston, there was a woman who literally called 911 every day to say there were kids hanging out on her corner. The cops would get the call, go to the location, and tell the kids to move. And the kids think, "Why are the police hassling us? We live here!" But the police were responding to citizen calls. So community perceptions can frame how you view the police. James Baldwin said in *Nobody Knows My Name* that the police could hand out candy to the kids in some neighborhoods and they would still be viewed as an occupying army.

I think what's happened today is that people living in some of these communities want better police *and* more police, because their problems are real. They don't want their kids to have to walk past drug dealers, but they also don't want their nineteen-year-old son who works the night shift getting stopped by the police each time he comes home from work. So it's complicated as to how the police sort out the law-abiding people who live in that area versus those who are creating havoc. It goes back to James Baldwin and *Nobody Knows My Name.*

Pegues: How do you solve the problem? Is this going to take generations of police officers?

Wexler: I don't have an easy answer for you, but take a look at Los Angeles. PERF was hired to help LA select a new police chief after Bernard Parks. LA had a very contentious relationship with the black community back then, and the LAPD was viewed in a very negative way. And while it is still has challenges, I think the LAPD is one department that has been transformational on the issue of race. In South Central LA, instead of "hooking and booking," as they used to do, now they are engaging. Los Angeles had extreme problems, from

Rodney King and the riots to the Rampart scandal and more. You had some huge issues, and LAPD has managed to address them.

Pegues: So how do you find the right balance?

Wexler: If you had a magic wand, what you would ask for is true community policing, where the police officer in a given neighborhood knows the community, and knows what the community wants and needs. So if people are coming into the neighborhood to commit crimes, the officer can differentiate them from the guy I was talking about who's working the night shift and comes home and is doing nothing wrong. What do you think, Kevin?

Morison: The promise of community policing back in the 1990s was that we would get that very thing: community understanding and engagement. In fact, in Chicago we built the community policing model on the concepts of geographically defined police beats and beat integrity. We weren't going to send officers who were assigned to one beat answering calls here, there, and everywhere. They were supposed to stay on their assigned beat, so they could figure out who were the good folks in the community and the not-so-good folks. That was the promise of it. But while it sounded good on paper, it became a challenge to maintain that kind of program.

Wexler: That was the CAPS program.

Morison: Yes. When we started CAPS, the Chicago Alternative Policing Strategy, we had five prototype districts. One of them was in the Englewood community on the South Side, which was one of the toughest neighborhoods then, and still is. There was a commander named Ronnie Watson who went on to become police chief in Cambridge, Massachusetts. He could get the community and the police together and challenge the community. "If there's crime going on, that's on us," he would say. "If there's litter in the streets and houses that aren't kept up, that's on you. You've got to work on that."

There was cheering in these meetings, and people saying, "You're right, Commander. We've got to go do that." And there was a real sense then —this was 1994—that, wow, we're bringing police and the community together around the common goal.

Pegues: Is that happening now, or is it realistic for that to happen now, given the number of officers you have in Chicago? They don't have enough officers to keep them on one beat in one neighborhood.

Wexler: Well, they have a lot of cops in Chicago. I think one of the problems is that before you can do community policing with cops, you have to figure out a way to get to them to feel that their needs are being met. I think cops today are feeling defensive and angry.

Pegues: But is it justified? Their job is to protect and serve. This is a public service they are doing. Is it justified for them to feel that way?

Wexler: Whether it's justified is a different question, but it's the reality. It's hard to generalize when you have eight hundred thousand individual police officers in the country, but by and large it is the sentiment out there, that the cops feel like they are being heavily criticized. So they are a bit defensive and cautious. So now it's a little tricky for a police chief to just tell his officers, "I want you to go back into the communities and do community policing." I think something has to happen before you do that.

Pegues: What could happen to ease the feelings of hurt? It's like a marriage with the therapist in the middle. How do you bridge that gap?

Wexler: I don't know exactly, but it has to start with people—police and residents—talking with one another.

Pegues: So bring law enforcement and some sort of black leadership together?

Wexler: Dallas police chief David Brown has figured out a way to make this happen. He has taken steps that reflect the work PERF is doing to curtail the questionable uses of force that break down trust between police and communities.

For example, having a strict policy against shooting at cars, unless someone in the car is shooting back at them. If you have a white police officer who shoots a black teenager in a stolen car—and that exact scenario has happened many times—you know, that's a terrible thing. No matter how good your relationship is with the community, when that happens, the community asks, "You killed a seventeen-year-old kid over a stolen car?"

So there are certain things police departments can do to improve police-community relationships. In 2016, PERF released "Thirty Guiding Principles on Use of Force," and not shooting at vehicles is one of those thirty principles. Another is a concept called "proportionality," or the notion that the police response should be proportional to the threat faced.

Again, Chief David Brown in Dallas recognized this when it comes to foot chases, which often begin over some minor thing, like shoplifting. The officer chases the kid, the kid makes a furtive movement, and the officer ends up shooting because he thinks the kid has a gun, but he doesn't. Dallas adopted a policy that restricts foot chases, because that response isn't always proportional if the underlying offense is minimal, and it was putting officers and citizens in dangerous encounters.

So there are things that police departments can do, in terms of policy and training, that will reduce these kinds of bad incidents. These changes will have an impact on the community's view of the police, and they will make both cops and community members safer. The really substantive changes that police agencies need to make are in their policies and their training. All it takes is one police officer to act in a way that causes the public to ask, "Was that use of force really necessary?" and the police are back to square one in terms of building trust. Sound policies and good training help protect against that.

And remember, it's not always deadly-force encounters that cause concern in the community. There have been some other incidents that we have watched on TV that have shocked all of us. Like the police officer in McKinney, Texas. There was a reported disturbance at a pool party, everybody was in bathing suits, and he takes out his gun! Or the situation, also in Texas, with Sandra Bland, whose vehicle was stopped for a traffic violation and the cop asked her to put out her cigarette. When she didn't put out her cigarette, the officer goes "hands-on," and the entire encounter is captured on a dashcam and then shown on TV. People watch that, and they're appalled. The public intuitively understands the concept of proportionality. It's images like this that break down trust, and not just in one community, but in cities across the country.

And it is hurting the policing profession. PERF recently hosted a meeting with about four dozen departments, looking at recruiting and hiring of police officers. This is about the processes needed to attract and retain high-quality officers for the twenty-first century. We're talking about police officers seeing their job as being guardians, not just warriors, and that means attracting different people to the profession. Issues of use of force and police-community relations have affected the mix of people you want to recruit. You want a diverse workforce and people with a wider range of skills, especially communications skills, people skills, [and] problem solving skills, to help communities.

But I was recently in a room with eighty-five prospective police chiefs, many of them up-and-coming police leaders and people of color, and I asked them, "How many of you would like your kid to be a police officer?" And none of them raised their hands. Zero. Most people are reluctant to have their children join the profession in the current environment. I was speaking at Princeton recently and asked the students there how many of them would want to become police officers when they graduated. None of them raised their hands. So who will be tomorrow's police officers?

Morison: And that is unusual, because traditionally, a top recruiting tool for law enforcement was fathers, aunts, uncles, and other family members who were officers, who would encourage the next generation to join the profession.

Back to the broader question about building relationships of trust between police and communities, I think the needle that police chiefs are trying to thread is how to acknowledge the hurt, the pain, and the anger in the community, especially African American communities, without making your cops feel like you're selling them out or accusing them of being racist or unfair.

Wexler: In Chicago, a recent task force report essentially characterized the police department's actions as racist. It doesn't say that every officer on the department is racist, but that's how many cops view it. Who wants to be called a racist?

Morison: One of the very first recommendations in that report is that the department acknowledge its racially biased past.

Pegues: And that has been overlooked. I think that is a big part of going forward. It's a reconciliation process. I think that's a really important part of this. I think there are a lot of people who feel that there is a segment of the population that doesn't want to acknowledge that this is happening, even with all of the video recordings of these incidents.

Wexler: One of the hardest things I've ever done involved work with a large Midwest police department. They wanted to look at the issue of race within the department itself. So I sat down and organized a number of roundtable sessions with officers. The white officers felt [that] we were making more of something than we should. The black officers felt [that] we weren't dealing with the real issues. So they looked at the same issue from extremely different perspectives.

There was a *New York Times* article whose premise was that within police departments, officers don't talk about race. They talk about issues of race in the community, but officers don't talk about it inside the department. And that was the case in that city. They just didn't talk about race in the department, and this would get manifested in various ways.

For example, a white commander would be put in charge of the narcotics unit. He'd go in and transfer out three black individuals and transfer in his buddies, who happened to be white. So for the cops, especially the African American cops, they thought it was all about race. But from the commander's point of view, he just wanted to have his own trusted colleagues in this unit—people he had worked with in the past.

Or you'd have an arrest on some minor thing, like a young

African American kid who was mouthing off to the police. A black commander would come to the scene and say, "What do you have here?" And the white officer says, "This kid called me [an obscenity]." And the black commander says, "That's all? Take the handcuffs off; you can't arrest somebody for calling you a name." And the white officer would walk away in a huff, thinking the young man was being released because he was black. But in reality, he was being released because it was a trivial thing to begin with.

So white and black officers carry around this baggage, these perceptions, and then something would happen, and all of a sudden racial tensions would flare up. Our work in this city didn't exactly "solve" anything, but it did have a long-range impact on making people aware of how their actions are perceived and how they affect others in the workplace.

This is the whole concept of implicit bias, which agencies now teach on a regular basis to recruits and veteran officers. The idea is that everyone has implicit biases that they carry around; they're unavoidable. But you can deal with them if you understand them. I think it's much more effective than the "cultural diversity" training that many agencies used in the past. Implicit bias training recognizes that white and black people bring their history and their perceptions to work. If you can acknowledge and better understand those issues, it makes you more sensitive to the nuances of life.

It's not easy, because even well-intentioned people can say the wrong thing. I've seen people do this to Chuck Ramsey [former Philadelphia police commissioner]. They come up and say, "You know, you're one of the best black police chiefs in the country." The person thinks they are giving him a compliment. I'm watching Chuck's face. He responds, "Thank you very much!" But the guy walks away, and Chuck rolls his eyes.

So as we look to bridge the divide and bring together police and communities, especially communities of color, we have to start with perceptions, with acknowledging [that] we all have biases, and then moving forward with better communications, understanding, and mutual respect.

But do people want to acknowledge the real issues? Is there a way to get back to a climate in which both community and police are working together and share the same goals with a sense of understanding? Those are the some of the important questions going forward for law enforcement leaders and community leaders, with 2017 beginning a new year and perhaps a new chapter in this conflict.

CHAPTER TWENTY
"BROKEN WINDOWS IS NOT BROKEN"

At exactly the wrong time, some of this country's brightest minds in law enforcement are walking away. Charles Ramsey is one of them. He is the former commissioner of the Philadelphia Police Department, and he ran the Metropolitan Police Department in Washington, DC. Ramsey, who is a Chicago native, is widely respected for implementing policing reforms, and he is also adept at being able to put his finger on the pulse of the community in order to find the right balance between its needs and fighting crime. They are qualities President Obama no doubt saw in Ramsey when he appointed him to serve as co-chair of the President's Task Force on 21st Century Policing.

Looking in from the outside, the public doesn't often view its police departments as think tanks, or labs where ideas are discussed and eventually transferred from paper to the city streets. But the best police chiefs are essentially strategists who are constantly thinking of ways to make the job safer and communities better. Like a football coach plots the next play with x's and o's, a police chief must make the right move to get a win against crime. But, of course, the stakes are a lot higher. If you're a police chief and you don't deploy your resources properly, someone can get killed. If you're not seeing trends and heeding the warnings, it could cost someone his or her life. It may be one of your officers or someone in one of the neighborhoods you're trying to protect. The unpredictability of crime and of community unrest is now pushing law enforcement leaders across the country to evolve and to adjust to changing trends and demographics. The police chiefs who are successful don't go with the flow but instead come up with detailed plans and training to lead the men and women under their command into the future.

In New York City, that meant making a clean break with the past. How ironic that the police department that pioneered "Broken Windows"–style tactics now blazes a trail in another direction. As the debate over policing erupts in cities across America, the NYPD is breaking new ground.

Its leader knew that the time for change had come, and he acknowledged it, which is important. While some in law enforcement denigrated the Black Lives Matter movement, New York City police commissioner William Bratton seemed to be listening to its message. He may not have agreed entirely with the message, but he did not dismiss BLM or lash out at it as some fringe movement; instead, Bratton's actions and public statements seemed to empathize with what Black Lives Matter stood for and what it meant as an extension of what blacks all across the country were feeling about law enforcement.

In an appearance on the CBS News program *Face the Nation* a few days after five police officers were shot in Dallas, Bratton was able to succinctly put into words what may be the key to moving forward for departments across the country:

BRATTON: This is a time of great pressure on our officers.

There's always pressure on American police officers, danger. But the good news is that American police, the American police profession is a strong profession that has been going through profound changes over the last 20 years, constant improvement in their training, constant improvement in use of force, continuing efforts in recent years to teach our officers de-escalation techniques, and also the idea of trying to see the community and have the community see them.

Policing is a shared responsibility. It's all about dialogue. It's all about understanding each other, seeing each other, hearing each other. Remember, police officers come from the community. We don't bring them in from Mars. They come from the communities they police.

And over the years, increasingly, we have had much more diversity in policing, Muslim officers, increasing numbers of African-American officers, Latino officers. And that's a good thing, because the community wants to see that. And that's part of the way we bridge the divide that currently exists police and community, a divide that's been closing and a divide that we hope over time, and certainly here in New York—and I can speak for our efforts here the last several years, myself and Mayor de Blasio, not only to bridge the divide, but to close it.

And I think it can be done. I'm ever the optimist on this issue.

[HOST JOHN] DICKERSON: Commissioner Bratton, as someone who had police officers killed in a similar incident to the kind of [*sic*] that happened in Dallas, did you see this coming, given the level of tension and debate?

BRATTON: We did not. I will speak for myself that we have had a relatively peaceful two years in New York since that horrific murder of Detectives Liu and Ramos, that the communities did come together. We have been engaging in dialogue.

I have had close to 600 meetings since that murder[,] with community leaders, community activists. And we have had a relative—relatively long period of stability in New York City. We increased the training of our personnel. We're increasing our de-escalation techniques.

And it's been a time of healing. So, did we see it coming? No. But, in policing, that—you always plan for the worst, hope for the best. Dallas was beyond anybody's ability to speculate about or even think about . . .

Not only did Bratton allude to a "time of healing," but he also mentioned the community meetings he'd participated in and the dialogue with residents and community leaders. From what I had heard about him, communication was a hallmark of Bratton-run police departments, dating back to the 1990s, when he was brought in by Mayor Rudy Giuliani as New York City's police commissioner. While Giuliani has always had a troubled relationship with the black community, Bratton, even in the Giuliani years at city hall, was respected in the black community. In addition, cops admired him because he was known for rewarding them with the resources they needed to do the job. Former police officers interviewed in the book *Giuliani: Flawed or Flawless?* said that Bratton was a true commander who brought strong and decisive leadership to the department.[1] While in the same book, the Reverend Al Sharpton noted that Bratton, through his leadership, set a tone that brought discipline to the ranks.[2]

According to Sharpton, "the tone Bratton set was that the police community is not going to get away with barbaric and over-the-line actions." Sharpton was quoted as saying, "I don't always agree with Bratton, but he had standards and the police knew it."

Bratton was part of the tip of the spear in the early '80s, with police tactics that, according to the numbers, made New York City safer. But over time those tactics drove a wedge between communities of color and the police. It was an unintended consequence of the style of policing he was advocating. But Bratton didn't double down on those tactics in the wake of Eric Garner's death in 2014; instead, the veteran cop found a way to drive down crime while at the same time tossing out stop and frisk.

Bratton believes that public safety is a shared responsibility; and when he submitted his retirement letter to New York mayor Bill de Blasio in late 2016, he wrote about what he called his department's core reform.[3] He was now relying on neighborhood-based policing initiatives with something that he had called his Neighborhood Policing Plan. He touted it as a "fundamental redesign of the way our precincts and police service areas conduct patrol." Under his plan, he wrote, "the precincts have been sectored to reflect neighborhood boundaries, and each sector is patrolled by a team of officers who work that sector exclusively."

Bratton also said that he had created a new position, "neighborhood coordination officer or NCO, to work closely with the residents and businesses, with two NCOs permanently assigned to each sector." These so-called NCOs were his twist on community policing. In some ways, one could argue, it was all public relations, but it was effective. By October 2016, he promised to have this Neighborhood Policing Plan in place in more than half of the patrol precincts. Bratton pledged that he was dedicating more resources to communities and responding to their needs. And perhaps most importantly, he wrote, "we are bringing the cops and the citizens of New York City closer together, with substantial benefits for both crime fighting and quality of life." The New York City police commissioner was addressing the community's needs and essentially telling the public, "we work for you, and I am doing exactly what you are asking us to do." It seemed to be working and the NYPD had the numbers to show it. In his letter to De Blasio, Bratton wrote:

> In the first two years of your term, index crime decreased 5.7 percent and has gone down 2.5 percent so far this year. Your years in office have seen the lowest murder total since 1957 and the fewest robberies, burglaries, and auto thefts since the mid-1960s. Even as crime continues to drop, arrests, criminal summonses, and Terry stops are all down as well, and by very considerable margins. Precision policing has achieved results that exceed anything obtained by over-reliance on street stops and indiscriminate enforcement. It fulfilled the vision you and I shared: that we could maintain safety in our city with far fewer interventions on the street.

Based on the data, the NYPD had demonstrated that you could scrap stop and frisk and still drive down crime.[4]

Still, Bratton did not back down when it came to defending "Broken Windows" policing. In his final days in office, his department released a scathing rebuttal to an inspector general report that was critical of "Broken Windows." The report titled "An Analysis of Quality-of-Life Summonses, Quality-of-Life Misdemeanor Arrests, and Felony Crime in New York City, 2010–2015" was published over the summer of 2016 and concluded that there was "no empirical evidence demonstrating a clear and direct link between an increase in summons and misdemeanor arrest activity and a related drop in crime."[5]

Here's what the report found:

> Between 2010 and 2015, quality-of-life enforcement rates—and in particular, quality-of-life summons rates—have dramatically declined, but there has been no commensurate increase in felony

crime. While the stagnant or declining felony crime rates observed in this six-year time frame may be attributable to NYPD's other disorder reduction strategies or other factors, OIG-NYPD finds no evidence to suggest that crime control can be directly attributed to quality-of-life summonses and misdemeanor arrests. This finding should not be over-generalized to preclude the use of summonses and misdemeanor arrests for the purpose of targeted crime and disorder reduction, but given the costs of summons and misdemeanor arrest activity, the lack of a demonstrable direct link suggests that NYPD needs to carefully evaluate how quality-of-life summonses and misdemeanor arrests fit into its overall strategy for disorder reduction and crime control.

According to the inspector general investigation, between 2010 and 2015 the NYPD issued 1,839,414 quality-of-life summonses for public urination, disorderly conduct, drinking alcohol in public, and possession of small amounts of marijuana. "Issuing summonses and making misdemeanor arrests are not cost free," the report's authors wrote. "The cost is paid in police time, in an increase in the number of people brought into the criminal justice system and, at times, in a fraying of the relationship between the police and the communities they serve."

That report was calling into question the bedrock of what Bratton had built his career on; the IG report was harpooning what the commissioner believed to be true and key to his crime-fighting strategies over his thirty-five-year career leading six different police departments across the country. He fired back with his rebuttal titled "Broken Windows Is Not Broken." In an NYPD press release, Bratton was quoted arguing against the idea that "Broken Windows" policing is racially discriminatory:

"Going back as far as 1978, in the streets of the Fenway, I have seen community complaints about quality of life conditions dominate conversations between the community and the police," said Police Commissioner William J. Bratton. "The NYPD's Neighborhood Coordination Officer Program re-affirms what I learned all those years ago, that neighborhood residents expect action on the part of the police regarding lesser crimes and signs of disorder. Enforcement targeting these conditions has become known as 'quality-of-life' policing, and it has been frequently disparaged as a vehicle of oppression that creates racially disparate outcomes. That could not be further from the truth. This type of policing is an essential tool of community engagement and trust building, most often in direct response to community concerns. Quality of life policing will remain a key strategy for the NYPD."

- QOL enforcement in minority communities closely reflects complaints made *from* those very diverse communities through both 311 and 911 calls, as well as community meetings and public opinion polls.
- The police department has no reason to ignore these calls for service, and, in fact, has a duty to respond.
- In the era of quality-of-life policing in New York City (past 21 years), both city and state prison populations have fallen from previous highs, by 49 percent and 27 percent, respectively. QOL policing is not filling jails.
- The NYPD has scaled back on misdemeanor arrests, down 80,000 at the end of 2015 from their high in 2012 (and another –6.7% YTD through August 2016). It has also scaled back on summonses, down 300,000 at year-end 2015 from their high in 2005 (and another –9% YTD through 2016).
- The OIG report also fails to consider a number of prior studies that evaluated the effect of QOL enforcement on felony crime in NYC, including: Harcourt and Ludwig in 2006; and Rosenfeld, Fornango and Rengifo in 2007. Additionally, the OIG report also:
- Omits fieldwork in which QOL enforcement was witnessed, resulting in very little contact with the NYPD in preparing the study. (Had this been done, OIG would have had exposure to the many levels of discretion exercised by officers while on patrol, which are not documented, or considered, anywhere in the OIG report.)
- Selects precincts as population samples. (With populations that often exceed 100,000, precincts do not provide a framework for meaningful comparisons. Street blocks and census tracts are typically more appropriate.)
- Omits fluctuations in population regarding time of day, zoning, etc.

Beyond the NYPD's own comprehensive review and subsequent rejection of the OIG report, two independent eminent criminologists, Richard Rosenfeld and David Weisburd, have also roundly criticized the report, citing: problems with its research and statistical methodology; the lack of consideration for officer discretion; and the omission of the 16 years prior to 2010—when misdemeanor arrests strongly correlated to the largest crime decline in New York City history. These criminologists have also determined the analysis contained in the report is not strong enough to support its conclusions.

The OIG has issued a report using questionable methodology and has reached unsupported conclusions challenging a police strategy that has been central to the city's efforts to promote public safety while also enhancing trust and public confidence in the police department. This report perpetuates misunderstandings about a police strategy that is critical to the well-being of New York City and has played a central role in creating the safest big city in America.[6]

In August 2016, the NYPD released its end-of-summer crime summary. It touted decreases in every category. A press release reported the following:

There were 1,610 fewer crimes reported during the months of June, July and August 2016, or a 5% decrease, compared with the same period in 2015. This also marks a 73% decrease, or 73,463 fewer crimes, compared with the same period in 1994—the initial year Compstat was implemented under Police Commissioner William J. Bratton's first tenure leading the NYPD.

For the month of August 2016, each category of index crime experienced a decrease—resulting in 957 fewer total index crimes reported, or a 9% reduction, compared with August 2015. Murder is down one crime, or –2.9% for the month of August 2016, compared with August 2015. Also for the month of August 2016: rape is down 10 crimes, or –6.7%; robbery is down 247 crimes, or –15%; felonious assault is down 162 crimes, or –7.6%; burglary is down 289 crimes, or –20%; grand larceny is down 224 crimes, or –5.4%; and grand larceny auto is down 23 crimes, or –3.3%.[7]

The press release also noted that it was Commissioner Bratton's final crime briefing, and it put the numbers into perspective—especially when you compare them to his first year leading the department.

> "For context, there were 1,946 murders in 1993. There were 352 murders in 2015. In calculating the annual reduction in murders over the ensuing two decades, it can be inferred that approximately 28,800 fewer murders have occurred in New York City since Commissioner Bratton first implemented Compstat with the late Jack Maple in 1994. Detractors said it couldn't be done. We have further reduced violence and serious crime across this city, yet again," said Police Commissioner William J. Bratton. "The tremendous focus on a small group of criminals has resulted in these unprecedented declines in crime—as violence has increased in other American cities significantly. To the men and women of this Department, thank you for what you do every day to make this the safest big city in America."[8]

Meanwhile, one of the city's tabloids issued a rare apology. The headline on August 8, 2016, read, "We Were Wrong: Ending Stop and Frisk Did Not End Stopping Crime."[9]

> Three years ago this month Manhattan Federal Judge Shira Scheindlin ruled unconstitutional the NYPD's program of stopping, questioning and sometimes frisking people suspected of criminality. The third anniversary of Scheindlin's ruling—August 12—presents an opportune moment to evaluate its consequences on the city after the passage of a reasonable amount of time. While her findings remain as flawed today as they were then, New York has come through to a brighter day.

Three years earlier, the article predicated a "rising body count from an increase in murders" without stop and frisk.[10] Now they were acknowledging that they were wrong.

> The NYPD began scaling back stops under [Commissioner Ray] Kelly before Scheindlin's decision and accelerated the trend

under Commissioner Bill Bratton. As a result, the number of stops reported by cops fell 97% from a high of 685,700 in 2011 to 22,900 in 2015. Not only did crime fail to rise, New York hit record lows. . . . there can be little doubt that the NYPD's increasing reliance on so-called precision policing—knowing whom to target, when and where—has played a key role.

They admitted that their fears were baseless and that the facts were clear. Stop and frisk was not a necessary tactic to drive down crime. With this new approach New York was safer and there weren't as many heated clashes between police and the minority community. Would New York police policies be replicated in other cities and towns across the country once again, as they were three decades earlier? On September 18, 2016, William Bratton walked away from the police department he loves—likely for the final time. Because he had once again orchestrated a major tactical shift in policing on the biggest stage of all, he left on top, widely regarded as one of the best police commissioners this country had ever seen.

CHAPTER TWENTY-ONE

"SIXTEEN SHOTS AND A COVER-UP!"

In the fall of 2016, Chicago was still searching for a solution to its crime hell. It was trapped in this never-ending cycle of violence that did not show any signs of letting up.

According to the Brennan Center, which analyzed crime data from the thirty largest cities, in 2015 murder across the country increased by 14 percent, with just three cities accounting for half of that increase.[1] Baltimore, Chicago, and Washington, DC, were driving the crime numbers higher across the country. But, according to the Brennan Center's forecasts, Baltimore and Washington were slated to see decreases in 2016. Baltimore would be down by 9.7 percent; and Washington, DC, down 12.7 percent. But Chicago would be among the cities projected to see violent crime rise. The Brennan Center study called Chicago an outlier, where crime rose significantly in 2015 and would continue to do so. And it found that no other large city was expected to see the same type of increase in violence. The report concluded, "The causes are still unclear, but some theories include higher concentrations of poverty, increased gang activity, and fewer police officers."[2] The authors of the Brennan Center study were able to surmise that "cities with long-term socio-economic problems (high poverty, unemployment, and racial segregation) are more prone to short-term spikes in crime, and that the spikes are created by as-of-yet unidentified local factors, rather than any sort of national characteristic."[3]

Every city's crime spike is unique. What appeared to be playing a role in Chicago's uptick in violence was the lack of trust between the black community and not only the police but also city leadership. More than two years after the Laquan McDonald shooting, the relationship was still troubled. The mayor and the city's police superintendent had attempted to build bridges to the community and had taken steps to reform the police department, but wholesale change on both counts was still a long way off.

In October 2016, Mayor Rahm Emanuel succeeded in winning the city council's support for his version of oversight of the Chicago Police Department. According to the *Chicago Tribune*, a new Civilian Office of Police Accountability would be created.[4] It would replace the troubled Independent Police Review Authority. IPRA, as it is called in Chicago, failed on so many counts to hold police officers responsible for misconduct. That was at the core of some of the complaints about police in the city. The bad police officers were giving the good ones a black eye because the bad ones weren't being held accountable. This goes back to the Police Accountability Task Force Report, which found that there was no accountability. A high number of police officers were getting large numbers of complaints from citizens.[5] Between 2007 and 2015, over 1,500 CPD officers had ten or more complaint registers (CRs). Sixty-five of those officers had thirty or more. Furthermore, the report cautioned that these statistics reflected only the complaint histories about which the task force was made aware. The reality was, unfortunately, that there was no way of knowing whether those numbers reflected the actual numbers of complaints. Were some of the complaints ignored or lost? To summarize, there was no accountability among the police, and over time that eats away at community trust. The task force report authors said that the data on complaints, "give real credibility to the widespread perception that there is a deeply entrenched code of silence supported not just by individual officers, but by the very institution itself."

With Mayor Emanuel's backing, the new agency that had won city council support would have greater power to investigate alleged police abuse and the use of deadly force than had been granted to the previous task force.

As the *Chicago Tribune* wrote, the Civilian Office of Police Accountability would also be able to offer recommended changes to both police policy and procedure in the police department. Additionally, the new agency would create a new position: deputy inspector general. This individual would "audit the new police accountability system and identify patterns and practices that violate constitutional rights. That person will be picked by the inspector general, who is appointed by the mayor."[6] The *Tribune* continued, indicating that Emanuel had hoped to pass the police oversight ordinance months earlier but kept having to put off the vote because he didn't have the support he needed. He had to give up ground and accept changes, including a minimum funding level, so if the mayor didn't like what was happening he couldn't gut the power of the new police investigations agency or the new watchdog.

The vote on the ordinance that established the new police watchdog was also telling. The reporters for the *Tribune* wrote that it essentially came down along racial lines, with one of the mayor's allies, Ald. Walter Burnett Jr., saying, "We can holler and scream, we can march, we can protest, we can hate folks and all of those things, but at the end of the day, we try to get things done. . . . Did everybody get 100 percent of everything that they wanted? No." But the representatives of largely white neighborhoods in Chicago voted against the measure. A lot of police officers reportedly live in those areas. According to the *Tribune*, Southwest Side Ald. Michael Zalewski has cops in his ward who gave him an earful about the vote. The cops he heard from didn't feel like they were getting a fair shake. "The rank-and-file police officers that I represent were not supportive, and they made that very clear to me," Zalewski said.[7]

There was resistance to reform in some Chicago neighborhoods. In others, the activists kept trying to push for changes. Several months had passed since Ja'Mal Green and I had talked. He was still leading some of the protests in Chicago. Still calling for reform. As I mentioned in an earlier chapter, one protest had taken place during the annual Taste of Chicago over the summer. It was in response to the police shootings in Minnesota and Louisiana. According to local news reports, there were about two hundred demonstrators leaving the event when an officer saw Green climb a fence. After ordering the activist to get down, prosecutors say an officer was threatened by Green, who allegedly said he was, "going to beat his ass."[8] The protest was allowed to continue but later there was another confrontation when Green allegedly grabbed the duty belt of a police captain. Prosecutors say it was about an inch away from the officer's revolver. When a police lieutenant yanked Green's arm away and attempted to arrest him, Green reportedly said, "You're going to get it—I'm going to have your badge."

The activist was arrested and charged with a combination of felonies and misdemeanors: attempting to disarm an officer, two counts of aggravated battery of a peace officer, two counts of aggravated battery in a public place, as well as resisting or obstructing an officer. Bond was set at about $350,000. Family members argued that the bond was set too high. But relatives and Green's supporters were able to raise the money. He did end up spending time behind bars, and in an interview with me he insisted that his arrest was in retaliation for the protests he led and helped organize against the mayor and the police.[9]

> **Green:** Definitely they're still holding it over my head for a little while.
> **Pegues:** Do you think they were retaliating against you for something?
> **Green:** Definitely. Definitely.
> **Pegues:** Oh, really?
> **Green:** Pure politics. No evidence of nothing. So, pure politics.
> **Pegues:** Do you expect them to drop the charges?
> **Green:** Definitely. Nothing can stick. There's no evidence, so nothing can stick.
> **Pegues:** Have you talked to Police Superintendent Eddie Johnson since your arrest?
> **Green:** We talk all the time. He's doing what he can—so we'll see what happens.
> **Pegues:** How did they treat you in jail?
> **Green:** The first two days, it wasn't the best treatment in the city. But when I got to the county, it was fine. I had a room with a TV. I was in solitary confinement, and they gave me good food and my own phone.
> **Pegues:** They took care of you?
> **Green:** They took care of me when I was inside, but at the police

station I was still under CPD, so they weren't giving me food or taking care of me.

Pegues: Has your position on the cops changed at all, or is it much the same?

Green: They're still pretty bad. There have been no dramatic changes in the CPD. [Superintendent] Eddie [Johnson] has done a better job than the last two police superintendents, I give him that, in handling these police shootings and being transparent. But other than that, nobody has made any radical changes to the [system] protecting officers. You know you got the FOP that needs to be dismantled. You know, everything is still protecting the officers; and there is still no accountability, so we haven't moved in that direction yet. When we start moving in that direction, then we'll start getting some real change.

Pegues: What about on the streets? Are you seeing more cops in the streets talking to people?

Green: No.

Pegues: No?

Green: None of that! Nope! Nope . . . no changes . . . there's no community policing.

The path forward in Chicago is long. The city has been taking steps to bring the police and the community together, but the process has been slow and still there are people who believe their voices aren't being heard or have been silenced. Instead of celebrating a victory during that city council meeting, which saw the passage of an important pillar of police oversight, Mayor Emanuel's critics were still beating him over the head with his Achilles' heel. A woman stood up in the crowd of onlookers and yelled, "Sixteen shots and a cover-up! We will never forget."[10] CPD's failure at transparency following the shooting of Laquan McDonald almost exactly two years earlier was still haunting the city of Chicago.

CHAPTER TWENTY-TWO
COMING CLEAN

Every time there's progress in breaking down the barriers between neighborhoods and the police, something happens to derail the discussion. Late in 2016, Terence Crutcher, an unarmed black man, was shot and killed by a police officer. There was another incident in Charlotte, when Keith Scott was shot and killed by a police officer. But within days after the police shootings, the nation's attention turned to other things. The presidential campaign drowned out everything else in the news. Clinton v. Trump was the first "reality TV" presidential campaign. The American people were drawn to their television screens by a candidate who kept tripping over the controversy surrounding her private e-mail server and questions about her integrity, and her opponent, who repeatedly insulted women, blacks, and Hispanics with statements that usually defied the facts.

So many issues became casualties of "Campaign 2016," including the conflict between police and the black community. The American public and politicians may have been distracted by other things, but law enforcement was plugging away at evolving: tweaking tactics, working to hire more people, improving the screening of applicants, holding the bad cops accountable, while also reaching out to the community. Meanwhile, Americans seemed to be gaining more respect for the police. Were the reforms taking hold and changing perceptions? Perhaps, or maybe it was because police shootings weren't in the headlines every day, or people were slowly becoming numb to the images or already forgetting. The data was clearly showing that Americans' respect for police had surged.[1] According to a Gallup poll, 76 percent of Americans said that they had "a great deal" of respect for the police in their area. That was a significant spike over the year before. According to the Gallup poll from 2015, just 52 percent of Americans responded that they had confidence in the police. That number marked a twenty-two-year low for the poll. The last time confidence in police was that low, it was in 1993, just as four white Los Angeles police officers were on trial for violating the civil rights of Rodney King. In 2015, there were similar signs of stress for law enforcement. Police actions against black men in Ferguson, Missouri; Staten Island, New York, and North Charleston, South Carolina, were viewed as contributing factors to the decline in confidence.

In 2016, with the Gallup poll signaling a fresh start, commanders were encouraged that maybe police and community relations had turned a corner. They were encouraged that perhaps the unrest would be dying down as communities of color witnessed concrete changes in police departments. For example, there were steps being taken to improve community policing in dozens of cities. Sure, there were still many who weren't seeing a difference. Remember, Ja'Mal Green told me that he hadn't noticed any major shifts toward community policing in Chicago. The changes would take time to sink in and spread, but commanders across the country largely saw the value in establishing relationships with residents before trouble started brewing. It wasn't about flooding neighborhoods with cops walking beats—although that could make a difference, too—it was more about getting to know people on city blocks. Throwing a football around with a young kid in the neighborhood or just jumping rope with the children in the neighborhood. Anything that established common ground and bridged the gap. It's the small things that would really pay off during the tough times, when the police really needed community support.

Those relationships also pay off when police are trying to solve crimes. The more police reached out in the good times, the more likely they were to get a tip during the bad times. I've heard it said numerous times over the years: policing a community is a shared responsibility. Officers have to work hand in hand with the people they are trying to protect. Too often the relationship has become strained over the years, and there have been more disagreements than consensus.

Accountability is also key to repairing the rift. Take Chicago, for example, where the bad cops have tarnished the badge even though most of the cops on the force are doing the right thing. The Chicago Police Data Project discovered that complaints are disproportionately filed against a small subset of the Chicago Police Department. "Repeat officers," it says, "those with 10 or more complaints—make up about 10% of the force but receive 30% of all complaints."[2] Accountability has not been a part of CPD culture, and it took a court battle to get some measure of transparency and for the public to get a closer look at what was really happening and how the police were treating black residents.

In the fall of 2016, news organizations got their hands on spreadsheets covering complaints against police that were filed between 1967 and 2001.[3] They showed that there were 134,683 records of complaints against 18,907 officers. According to the *Chicago Sun-Times*, in 87 percent of the complaints, no action was taken to discipline the officer.[4] In just 13 percent of the cases there were reprimands, suspensions, and firings. During that period, just 553 complaints ended in a firing or "separation." That's less than half of 1 percent of the total complaints filed.

The city tried to keep the so-called complaint registers secret but after a lengthy court battle was compelled to make them public. When the records were made public, it was clear that a lot of the bad behavior was aimed at the black community. The Chicago Police Data Project found that black Chicagoans filed 61 percent of all complaints in the database, but made up only 25 percent of sustained complaints. In contrast, white Chicagoans—who filed 21 percent of total complaints—account for 58 percent of sustained complaints.

The revealing statistics found in this data raises an important question. Should cities and police departments have to be compelled to release data on complaints? For there to be positive reform, most of the police officials I've interviewed support transparency. If there is a shooting, show the public the body-camera footage and identify the officer involved. Police unions may not agree, but the consensus among law enforcement these days is that the public has a right to know.

To that end, body cameras are a game changer for police officers. A Pew Research Center survey in 2016 found that about eight in ten blacks and a larger share of whites favor the use of body cameras by police to record encounters with citizens.[5] In addition, the survey found that majorities of both races also believe that the use of so-called body cams would prompt officers to act more appropriately when dealing with the public. While many rank-and-file police officers did not welcome having to work with the cameras and the unions fought them, it turns out that the cameras are clearing cops who are doing their jobs the right way. In Cleveland, I was told that the officers are now thrilled to have them because they are working in their favor. In Washington, DC, interim police chief Peter Newsham told me that his officers embraced the technology.[6] "They wanted their side of the story to be told," he said. Newsham believes the community wants the cameras because, "they want to see how our police are interacting with folks out there in the community." Newsham and other police chiefs, commissioners, and superintendents have begun to turn the mirror back on themselves, realizing that for the good of their communities, there needed to be change.

Part of that change involved treating people in the communities they served with respect and dignity. I recall what Foti Koskinas, the police chief in Westport, Connecticut, told me during our interview. He said that it was important to him that his officers cared about making sure the people they interacted with had a "good experience."[7] While that's not always possible, in most instances it is. Some officers, he says, should stop acting like robots. Show the community that you are a human being. "Hey, this person is really nervous; I should help him out. Let's see what I can do to minimize this so that we can leave— even if they get a ticket—they left here with a good experience."

Koskinas was among those in law enforcement who were smart and dedicated to the future of policing. I could see the changes happening in his department, and there would be more dramatic shifts in approach ahead. By the fall of 2016 as the election neared the finish line, men and women applying to be cops, veteran rank-and-file officers, commanders, and the FBI director were pushing forward with reform. They were reinforcing positive narratives for change and also confronting some of the hardest realities. Another Gallup poll over the summer asked Americans to offer solutions for solving deadly shootings.[8] When they were asked what was the single most important thing that could be done to reduce the number of deadly encounters between black men and police, the answer was, over-whelmingly, improve relations, communication, and understanding.

Whether you are trying to improve a marriage, kick a bad habit, or stop overspending, in order to make a positive change, you first have to admit that there is a problem. While there were elements of policing opposed to and fighting against the calls for change, law enforcement's most vocal leaders had, for the most part, gotten on board and come together on the issue. But one of the most important elements of those changes had largely been overlooked.

In mid-October 2016, at a gathering of law enforcement personnel in San Diego, California, a prominent voice in the business made a speech that significantly signaled a dramatic change in tone. His statements were provocative by design. They were intended to get people to notice and to spark a conversation. At the time, Chief Terrence Cunningham, president of the International Association of Chiefs of Police, had come to the end of his term leading the organization, but before he walked off into the sunset, he was going to deliver an explosive speech.

I had first met Cunningham three months earlier, after the 2016 shooting attack on police in Dallas, Texas. I introduced myself to him in the green room before we were both set to appear on *Face the Nation*. He was in uniform and very comfortable in the role of peacemaker. Later that morning, when he was asked by host John Dickerson to respond to comments by Rudy Giuliani, in which the former mayor roundly criticized the black community and called the Black Lives Matter movement racist, Cunningham chose a different approach. He discussed the path forward and some of the needed reforms. As we were leaving the set, he also mentioned something that stood out to me. He acknowledged that while the majority of police commanders wanted to make changes and reform, there were some who denied that there was a problem. That, he admitted, was troubling.

Ultimately, Cunningham came to believe that he had to make a bold statement—that he had to do something to jump-start the conversations between black and blue. The images of the families of the fallen cops at that memorial service in Dallas had really stuck with him. He says he kept thinking then, "we got to do something."[9] He understood that being a cop was a dangerous job and that the officers needed to be protected. But he feared that there were, "a hundred people like the killer in Dallas, sitting in their basement, waiting for the spark that is going to set them off." In my interview, he told me that he had growing concerns that his words could be a spark. He felt that it was important to rein in the rhetoric and get others to fall in line. He had also taken the president's words to heart. President Obama pressed him and law enforcement in general to at least acknowledge that, historically, some police departments had brutally enforced the laws of the land with force—sometimes deadly force.

Over a period of several weeks, Cunningham had come to the realization that he had to say something to change the trajectory of the debate. Just weeks before the International Association of Chiefs of Police (IACP) convention in San Diego, a survey by Pew Research Center served a clear reminder of the challenges police faced. In late 2016, there remained stark differences in how whites and blacks perceived the police:[10]

> Only about a third of blacks but roughly three-quarters of whites say police in their communities do an excellent or good job in using the appropriate force on suspects, treating all racial and ethnic minorities equally and holding officers accountable when misconduct occurs. Roughly half of all blacks say local police do an excellent or good job combating crime—a view held by about eight-in-ten whites.
>
> Blacks and whites also differ over the root causes of the fatal incidents between police and blacks in recent years. Even before the recent lethal encounters between police and black men in Tulsa and Charlotte, the survey found that blacks are 25 percentage points more likely than whites to say the deaths of blacks during encounters with police in recent years are signs of a broader societal problem and not merely isolated incidents.
>
> Confidence in local police is considerably lower among blacks. Just 14% of blacks say they have a lot of confidence in their local police, and 41% say they have some confidence. By comparison, about four-in-ten whites (42%) say they have a lot of confidence in their local police, and another 39% say they have some confidence.[11]

The deep racial tensions still exist in terms of how law enforcement is perceived, and it goes beyond what has happened over the last several years—it goes back generations in the black community. Cunningham was especially moved by the story of Austin Callaway.[12] In 1940, Callaway, who was black, was accused of attempted assault on a white woman. He was arrested and taken to jail in LaGrange, Georgia, where he would never get the opportunity to prove his innocence.

On the night of his arrest, six white men wearing masks and armed with at least one gun reportedly forced the jailer to open Callaway's cell. The men then reportedly took Callaway and drove him eight miles out of town, where they shot him in the head and arms and left him to die. Callaway's killers were never brought to justice.

Cunningham says the current police chief of LaGrange brought the case to his attention because to this day it is "a stain on the community."[13] But "the police had never acknowledged it," he says, "never mind apologized for it." Cunningham has learned that the history of mistrust runs deep, and he knew that the IACP would have to play an important role in bridging the divide. To finally solve this emotional issue and break through some of the barriers that have stopped the progress, police chiefs across the country would have to confront history. It was at the heart of any successful reform, and yet most people did not want to touch it. On October 17, 2016, Cunningham addressed it head-on with what can only be described as a stunning apology:

> I would like to take a moment to address a significant and fundamental issue confronting our profession, particularly within the United States. Clearly, this is a challenging time for policing. Events over the past several years have caused many to question the actions of our officers and has tragically undermined the trust that the public must and should have in their police departments. At times such as this, it is our role as leaders to assess the situation and take the steps necessary to move forward.
>
> This morning, I would like to address one issue that I believe will help both our profession and our communities. The history of the law enforcement profession is replete with examples of bravery, self-sacrifice, and service to the community. At its core, policing is a noble profession made up of women and men who are sworn to place themselves between the innocent and those who seek to do them harm.

Over the years, thousands of police officers have laid down their lives for their fellow citizens while hundreds of thousands more have been injured while protecting their communities. The nation owes all of these officers, as well as those who are still on patrol today, an enormous debt of gratitude.

At the same time, however, it is also clear that the history of policing has also had darker periods.

There have been times when law enforcement officers, because of the laws enacted by federal, state, and local governments, have been the face of oppression to far too many of our fellow citizens. In the past, the laws adopted by our society have required police officers to perform many unpalatable tasks, such as ensuring legalized discrimination or even denying the basic rights of citizenship to many of our fellow Americans.

While this is no longer the case, this dark side of our shared history has created a generational—almost inherited—mistrust between many communities of color and their law enforcement agencies that serve them.

Many officers who do not share this common heritage often struggle to comprehend the reasons behind this historic mistrust. As a result, they are often unable to bridge this gap and connect with some segments of their communities.

While we obviously cannot change the past, it is also clear that we must change the future. We must move forward together to build a shared understanding. We must forge a path that allows us to move beyond our history and identify common solutions to better protect our communities.

For our part, the first step in this process is for the law enforcement and the IACP to acknowledge and apologize for the actions of the past and the role that our profession has played in society's historical mistreatment of communities of color.

At the same time, those who denounce the police must also acknowledge that today's officers are not to blame for the injustices of the past. If either side in this debate fails to acknowledge these fundamental truths, we will be unable to move past them.

Overcoming this historic mistrust requires that we must move forward together in an atmosphere of mutual respect. All members of our society must realize that we have a mutual obligation to work together to ensure fairness, dignity, security, and justice.

It is my hope that, by working together, we can break this historic cycle of mistrust and build a better and safer future for us all.[14]

Although Cunningham received a standing ovation for the speech from the police chiefs who were in the audience, the speech itself received mixed reviews from officers across the country.

Pegues: Why did you think any apology was important?

Cunningham: You know, I honestly believe it's no different than when you're having an argument with your wife—particularly when you've done something wrong. You got to start with an apology so you can get by it, so that you can start to talk about the issues. And move on and heal the relationship. If we don't have those open and honest conversations, how do you expect to build trust? . . . My god, it has taken us generations to get there; it may take us generations to get out of it—but we got to start somewhere.[15]

In the weeks since he delivered that speech, Cunningham has received hate mail and telephone calls laced with profanity, including the n-word.[16] Five people resigned from the IACP—although the IACP leadership had expected more defections. It was a chance, Cunningham says, the leadership was willing to take. "We said, you know what, if those people are the 'knuckle draggers,' and they can't get it, well, then go ahead and resign."[17]

Some of the hate mail came from cops who, Cunningham says, had no qualms about identifying themselves. There were others who wanted to make a more public pronouncement against the speech. In an online publication called "Law Officer," someone identified only as "Deputy Matt" called Cunningham's statement "white cop guilt":

This man most definitely does NOT speak for law enforcement as a whole. The Atrocities he speaks of, the enforcement of Jim Crow laws, the blatant abuse of people of color, those things happened more than a decade before I was even born, and more than 30 years before I became a cop. I do not have to apologize for something I did not do. It is entirely possible for me to acknowledge that something bad happened, that something was done wrong, without my needing to accept blame for it. Expecting modern law enforcement to apologize for things done 50 years ago is the same as expecting white people to apologize for slavery. It is liberal minded, SJW bull crap![18]

FBI director James Comey preceded Cunningham at that IACP event in San Diego. In his speech, "The True Heart of American Law Enforcement," he appealed for leadership during this "uniquely difficult time in American law enforcement."[19] He likened the moment to an ocean with dangerous riptides. Referring to the police chiefs in the audience, he said:

> Your patrol officers, your deputies, your detectives, your agents face challenges that those who came before them could hardly imagine. There is water rushing in and water rushing out, and your people are standing where these unpredictable currents meet. They are being pulled in different directions. They are being pulled by the communities they serve, by their colleagues, by expectations, by their leaders, by the media.
>
> There is a very real chance of drowning in the currents. There is a need for leadership in the middle of those riptides. There is a need for people to stand tall, plant their feet, speak the truth, and calm the waters.[20]

AFTERWORD

On November 8, 2016, the American people elected Donald J. Trump as the forty-fifth president of the United States. He had received the endorsement of law enforcement organizations across the country that had felt that Hillary Clinton had cozied up to the Mothers of the Movement—mothers who'd lost children to police or gun violence—and Black Lives Matter. Trump had also campaigned with a pledge to bring back stop and frisk policies and restoring law and order. Both policies are a signal to black Americans that the new president would not pursue solutions that bridge the divide between police and communities of color.

It is unclear where the issue goes next. While confidence in police is growing, all of that can be reversed if police departments fail to make positive changes. As I have mentioned in this book, such change is definitely in the air. Several major cities have approved measures to bolster oversight of law enforcement. The common dominator in many of the police-involved shootings is that oversight must be improved. Civilian-run police commissions have been established as communities create a structure for oversight. Denver's independent monitor, Nicholas Mitchell, says that "there's a recognition that to help fix the issues in policing, we need not only to be focused on the few bad apples but to identify problems with the barrel itself."[1] The National Association of Civilian Oversight of Law Enforcement says there are 114 oversight agencies as of this writing in 2016.

Terrence Cunningham, president of IACP, says that while the report from the President's Task Force on 21st Century Policing was a good effort, he and others didn't think it went far enough.[2] The IACP had been pushing for something that sounds a lot like a new deal for law enforcement. Cunningham believes that the nation needed a national commission on criminal justice—something similar to

Lyndon Johnson's President's Commission on Law Enforcement and Administration of Justice. President Johnson announced his plans for the commission in March 1965 in a letter to Congress.[3] In it, he wrote, "Law enforcement cannot succeed without the sustained—and informed—interest of all citizens. . . . The people will get observance of the law and enforcement of the law if they want it, insist on it, and participate in it."

It seems to me that Johnson was calling for the public to participate in making law enforcement better. The commission ultimately led to the establishment of new norms in policing.[4] It saw the importance of family, the school system, and job creation as key to helping law enforcement. There was also a realization that there was inherent unfairness in the dispensation of justice and that the system often punished the poor. The commission recognized the importance of improving communications and increasing trust between law enforcement and the communities they serve. At the time, the recommendations were forward-thinking, and the commission even led to the establishment of the 911 system.[5] Perhaps the time is right for the next commission that will once and for all lead policing into the future.

ACKNOWLEDGMENTS

Looking back now, it all seems like a blur. I started this project in the fall of 2015 when, on a whim, I decided to shop around to see if there was any interest in my book idea. I'd been heavily involved in reporting on police shootings and rising crime in cities across America. The time was right, in my opinion, for a book that told both sides of the story.

I could not have finished this project without the assistance of dozens of people. First and foremost, to my family, I love you all! To my wife, Tareaz, your support makes a real difference. To my daughters, Jordyn and Peyton, thank you for the joy you bring to my life each and every day. Also, thanks to Mom and Dad; my big brother, Joseph E. Pegues III; Stephanie Powers Pegues; Gabrielle; Zara; Ron; Valerie; Philip; Tiffany; Dorothy Poellnitz; Joseph E. Pegues Sr.; Louise Pegues; Lloyd Moore; Stephanie Moore; Ashley Moore; Karen; Celestine; Casey; Carlos; and Morgan.

To my CBS News family, David Rhodes, Ingrid Ciprian-Matthews, Al Ortiz, Steve Capus, Scott Pelley, Bob Schieffer, Norah O'Donnell, Gail King, Charlie Rose, Kim Godwin, Bob Orr, Ryan Kadro, Chris Isham, Ward Sloan, Mosheh David Oinounou, Chris Licht, Caroline Horn, Chloe Arensberg, Andres Triay, Katie Ross Dominick, Julia Kimani Burnham, Allyson Ross Taylor, Kate Rydell, Mary Walsh, Paula Reid, Duncan McKenna, Nick Fineman, Pat Milton, Len Tepper, Julianna Goldman, Alturo Rhymes, Diana Miller, Terri Stewart, Crystal Johns, Tony Furlow, Caitlin Conant, John Dickerson, Mary Hager, Julia Boccagno, and the entire CBS News Washington Bureau, thank you!

My agents, the legendary Richard Liebner and Peter Goldberg, have helped to guide my career. Thank you to my friends at Prometheus Books, who took a chance on me, including Steven L. Mitchell, Jade Zora Scibilia, Cheryl Quimba, Hanna Etu, Mark Hall,

Bruce Carle, Catherine Roberts-Abel, and Laura Shelley. I also want to acknowledge all of the people who have been on my team for years or decades: Christopher Carmichael, Chuck Murray, Mark Edwards, Gregg Burger, Justin Carmichael, Beth Carmichael, KC, Richard Burns, Elizabeth Murphy Burns, Todd Bloom, Kristin Bloom, JR Rodriguez, Cindy Rodriguez, Ron Hosko, Chuck Wexler, Charles Ramsey, Terrence Cunningham, Sarah Guy, Foti Koskinas, Bahiyyah Muhammad, Howard Kleiman, Raoul Davis, Leticia Gomez, Jacquie Pirnie, MB, Cat McKenzie, Rick Martin, Ducis Rodgers, Janet Leissner, Shefali Razdan Duggal, Molly Fay, Arles Hendershott, Vince Tirola, Barbara Tirola, Randy Walker, Terry Hoeppner, Shawn Watson, Pat Narduzzi, Hugh Morgan, Dr. Robert Vogel, Miami University, Miami University Football, Laddie Lawrence, Staples High School, Staples High School Football, and Staples High School Track.

NOTES

CHAPTER ONE: REFORM IS IN THE AIR

1. Max Ehrenfreund and Denise Lu, "More People Were Killed Last Year than in 2014, and No One's Sure Why," *Washington Post,* January 27, 2016, https://www.washingtonpost.com/graphics/national/2015 -homicides/?tid=a_inl (accessed June 2, 2016).

2. Michael S. Schmidt and Matt Apuzzo, "FBI Chief Links Scrutiny of Police with Rise in Violent Crime," *New York Times,* October 23, 2015, http://www.nytimes.com/2015/10/24/us/politics/fbi-chief-links-scrutiny -of-police-with-rise-in-violent-crime.html (accessed June 2, 2016).

3. FBI Director James Comey, in interview with the author and National Press Corps, October 22, 2015.

4. Eric Tucker, "Overhaul Prompting Early Release of Thousands of Prisoners," *Associated Press,* October 11, 2015, http://www.pbs.org/ newshour/rundown/sentencing-overhaul-prompting-early-release -thousands-federal-drug-prisoners/ (accessed June 2, 2016).

5. Justin Worland, "What Happened When California Released 30,000 Prisoners," *Time,* October 7, 2015, http://time.com/4065359/ california-prison-release-department-of-justice/ (accessed June 3, 2016).

6. FBI Director James Comey, in interview with the author and National Press Corps, October 22, 2015.

7. Monica Davey and Mitch Smith, "Murder Rates Rising Sharply in Many U.S. Cities," *New York Times,* August 31, 2015, https://www.nytimes .com/2015/09/01/us/murder-rates-rising-sharply-in-many-us-cities.html ?action=click&contentCollection=U.S.&module=RelatedCoverage&region =EndOfArticle&pgtype=article (accessed January 21, 2017).

8. Alexandra Sifferlin, "Heroin Use in the US Reaches Epidemic Levels," *Time,* July 7, 2015, http://time.com/3946904/heroin-epidemic/ (accessed June 2, 2016).

9. Joseph Goldstein, "Judge Rejects New York's Stop-and-Frisk Policy," *New York Times,* August 12, 2013, http://www.nytimes.com/2013/

08/13/nyregion/stop-and-frisk-practice-violated-rights-judge-rules.html (accessed June 3, 2016).

10. "Stop-and-Frisk Data," New York Civil Liberties Union, http://www.nyclu.org/content/stop-and-frisk-data (accessed June 2, 2016).

11. FBI National Press Office, "2015: Crime in the United States," https://ucr.fbi.gov/crime-in-the-u.s/2015/crime-in-the-US-2015 (accessed June 2, 2016).

12. FBI National Press Office, "FBI Releases Preliminary Semiannual Crime Statistics for 2015," press release, January 19, 2016, https://www.fbi.gov/news/pressrel/press-releases/fbi-releases-preliminary-semiannual-crime-statistics-for-2015 (accessed June 2, 2016).

13. Lauren-Brooke "L.B." Eisen and James Cullen, "Update: Changes in State Imprisonment Rates," Brennan Center For Justice, June 7, 2016, https://www.brennancenter.org/analysis/update-changes-state-imprisonment-rates (accessed June 15, 2016).

14. Comey, interview.

15. Giovanni Russonello, "Race Relations Are at Lowest Point in Obama Presidency, Poll Finds," *New York Times,* July 13, 2016, http://www.nytimes.com/2016/07/14/us/most-americans-hold-grim-view-of-race-relations-poll-finds.html (accessed July 15, 2016).

16. Sarah Dutton, Jennifer DePinto, Fred Backus, and Anthony Salvanto, "Negative Views of Race Relations Reach All-Time High—CBS/NYT Poll," CBS News, July 13, 2006, http://www.cbsnews.com/news/negative-views-of-race-relations-reach-all-time-high-cbsnyt-poll/ (accessed January 11, 2017).

17. Benjamin Mueller and Al Baker, "2 N.Y.P.D. Officers Killed in Brooklyn Ambush; Suspect Commits Suicide," *New York Times,* December 20, 2014, https://www.nytimes.com/2014/12/21/nyregion/two-police-officers-shot-in-their-patrol-car-in-brooklyn.html (accessed January 21, 2017).

18. Ed Hornick, "Holder 'Nation of Cowards' Remarks Blasted, Praised," CNN, February 19, 2009, http://www.cnn.com/2009/POLITICS/02/19/holder.folo/ (accessed June 3, 2016).

19. FBI Director James Comey, "Hard Truths: Law Enforcement and Race," February 12, 2015, https://www.fbi.gov/news/speeches/hard-truths-law-enforcement-and-race (accessed January 11, 2017).

CHAPTER TWO: BROKEN WINDOWS

1. US Department of Justice, *Investigation of the Ferguson Police Department*, March 4, 2015, https://www.justice.gov/sites/default/files/opa/press-releases/attachments/2015/03/04/ferguson_police_department_report.pdf (accessed June 15, 2016).

2. US Department of Justice, *Investigation of the Baltimore City Police Department*, August 10, 2016, https://www.justice.gov/opa/file/883366/download (accessed November 2, 2016).

3. Jeff Pegues, "Former Baltimore Police Commissioner Breaks His Silence," CBS News, April 27, 2016, http://www.cbsnews.com/news/freddie-gray-former-baltimore-police-commissioner-anthony-batts-breaks-his-silence (accessed September 2, 2016).

4. US Census Bureau, "Welcome to Quick Facts," https://www.census.gov/quickfacts/table/INC110214/24510 (accessed August 3, 2016).

5. Department of Justice, *Investigation of the Baltimore City Police Department*.

6. Ibid.

7. Ibid.

8. George L. Kelling and James Q. Wilson, "Broken Windows: The Police and Neighborhood Safety," *Atlantic*, March 1982, http://www.theatlantic.com/magazine/archive/1982/03/broken-windows/304465/?single_page=true (accessed July 2, 2016).

9. "Stop and Frisk Facts," New York Civil Liberties Union http://www.nyclu.org/node/1598 (accessed July 3, 2016).

10. Victoria Bekiempis, "U.S. Prison Population Drops to Lowest Level since 2005," *Newsweek*, September 17, 2015, http://www.newsweek.com/prison-poplation-united-states-drug-offenses-police-reform-bureau-justice-372647 (accessed January 21, 2017).

11. Joel Rose, "Despite Laws and Lawsuits, Quota-Based Policing Lingers," NPR, April 4, 2015, http://www.npr.org/2015/04/04/395061810/despite-laws-and-lawsuits-quota-based-policing-lingers (accessed January 21, 2017).

12. Alicia Bannon, Mitali Nagrecha, and Rebekah Diller, "Criminal Justice Debt: Barrier to Reentry," (paper, Brennan Center for Justice, New York University School of Law, 2010), http://www.brennancenter.org/sites/default/files/legacy/Fees%20and%20Fines%20FINAL.pdf (accessed September 2, 2016).

13. Joel Achenbach, William Wan, Mark Berman, and Moriah

Balingit, "Five Dallas Police Officers Were Killed by a Lone Attacker, Authorities Say," *Washington Post*, July 8, 2016, https://www.washington post.com/news/morning-mix/wp/2016/07/08/like-a-little-war-snipers -shoot-11-police-officers-during-dallas-protest-march-killing-five/ (accessed January 12, 2017).

14. Bart Jansen, "3 Police Officers Fatally Shot in Baton Rouge; Dead Suspect Identified," *USA Today*, July 17, 2016, https://www.google.com/ amp/amp.usatoday.com/story/87218884/?client=safari (accessed January 12, 2017).

CHAPTER THREE: THREE DAYS AND SEVEN DEAD

1. Fox News, "Deafening Silence: Obama, 2016 Dems Mum on Recent Police Deaths," February 12, 2016, http://www.foxnews.com/ politics/2016/02/12/deafening-silence-obama-2016-dems-mum-on-recent -police-deaths.html (accessed January 21, 2017).

2. Terrance Cunningham, former president of the International Association of Chiefs of Police, in interview with the author, November 8, 2016.

3. CBS News, "Dallas Suspect Said He Wanted to Kill Whites," CBS News, July 8, 2016, http://www.cbsnews.com/news/dallas-shooting-suspect -kill-whites/ (accessed September 4, 2016).

4. "Afghan Tour Made Dallas Gunman a 'Hermit,' Family Says," CBS News, July 11, 2016, http://www.cbsnews.com/news/dallas-micah-johnson -family-military-service-army-afghanistan/ (accessed January 14, 2017).

5. Associated Press, "The Latest: Castile's Family Condemns Dallas Shootings," *Associated Press*, July 9, 2016, http://bigstory.ap.org/article/ fe19fddb6c7f4a4c84c3497693d02476/latest-dallas-police-man-photo -turned-self (accessed September 4, 2016).

6. Camilla Domonoske and Bill Chappell, "Minnesota Gov. Calls Traffic Stop Shooting 'Absolutely Appalling at All Levels,'" NPR, July 7, 2016, http://www.npr.org/sections/thetwo-way/2016/07/07/485066807/ police-stop-ends-in-black-mans-death-aftermath-is-livestreamed-online -video (accessed September 4, 2016).

7. Bill Chappell, "'We're Hurting,' Dallas Police Chief David Brown Says," NPR, July 8, 2016, http://www.npr.org/sections/thetwo-way/ 2016/07/08/485220431/were-hurting-dallas-police-chief-david-brown-says (accessed January 21, 2017).

8. Asiaha Butler, in interview with the author, May 28, 2016.

9. Patrick Gillespie, "U.S. Job Creation Weak, Even as Unemployment Rate Falls to 4.7%," CNN Money, June 3, 2016, http://money.cnn.com/2016/06/03/news/economy/us-economy-may-jobs-report/ (accessed January 14, 2016).

10. Chicago Tribune, "Crime in Chicagoland," *Chicago Tribune*, November 2–December 2, 2016, http://crime.chicagotribune.com/chicago/community/englewood (accessed October 4, 2016).

11. Steve Schmadeke, "Chicago Cop Asks That Charges over Laquan McDonald's Killing Be Dropped," January 10, 2017, *Chicago Tribune*, http://www.chicagotribune.com/news/laquanmcdonald/ct-laquan-mcdonald-jason-van-dyke-court-met-20170110-story.html (accessed January 14, 2017).

12. Ja'Mal Green, in interview with the author, May 30, 2016.

13. Mary Ann Ahern, "Mayor Goes Silent after Release of Laquan McDonald Shooting Video," NBC 5 Chicago, November 30, 2015, http://www.nbcchicago.com/blogs/ward-room/Mayor-Silent-After-Release-of-Laquan-McDonald-Shooting-Video-358892041.html (accessed September 5, 2016).

14. CNN, "Video Shows Cop Shoot Teen," CNN, November 2015, http://www.cnn.com/videos/us/2015/11/25/laquan-mcdonald-chicago-shooting-dashcam-video-orig-mg.cnn (accessed September 5, 2016).

15. "Rahm Emanuel Biography," *Biography*, last updated April 4, 2014, http://www.biography.com/people/rahm-emanuel-381074 (accessed September 8, 2016).

16. Bill Ruthhart, John Byrne and Hal Dardick, "Emanuel Apologizes for Laquan McDonald Police Shooting," *Chicago Tribune*, December 9, 2015, http://www.chicagotribune.com/news/local/politics/ct-rahm-emanuel-met-1209-20151209-story.html (accessed September 8, 2016).

17. Mayor Rahm Emanuel, author's transcript of speech to City Council of Chicago, December 9, 2015; footage available at "Mayor Rahm Emanuel Full Speech Dec 9, 2015 to City Council Police Accountability," YouTube video, 37:57, posted by "UWEN NEWS (Universal World Eye News)," December 10, 2015, https://www.youtube.com/watch?v=2bjANmm5qWY.

18. Green, interview with author.

CHAPTER FOUR: THIN BLUE LINE

1. Dean Angelo Sr., in interview with the author, May 27, 2016.

2. Jessica D'Onofrio, Leah Hope, and Eric Horng, "Police Union's Hiring of Jason Van Dyke as Janitor Sparks Anger," ABC7Chicago, March 31, 2016, http://abc7chicago.com/news/police-unions-hiring-of-jason-van-dyke-sparks-anger/1270140/ (accessed September 8, 2016).

3. Laura Podesta, "Chicago Crime: 66 Killed in 318 Shootings; 397 Total Victims Shot in May," ABC7Chicago, June 1, 2016, http://abc7chicago.com/news/chicago-crime-66-killed-in-318-shootings;-397-total-victims-shot-in-may/1366020/ (accessed October 2, 2016).

4. Jordan Fabian, "Obama, FBI Director Spar over the 'Ferguson Effect' on Police," November 1, 2015, The Hill, http://thehill.com/news/administration/258737-obama-fbi-director-spar-over-the-ferguson-effect-on-police (accessed January 14, 2017).

5. "A Weekend in Chicago," *New York Times*, June 1, 2016, http://www.nytimes.com/interactive/2016/06/04/us/chicago-shootings.html (accessed October 2, 2016).

CHAPTER FIVE: "SOMETHING IS HAPPENING IN AMERICA"

1. "FBI's Comey: Clinton 'Extremely Careless' about Emails, but Bureau Will Not Advise Criminal Charges," Fox News, July 5, 2016, http://www.foxnews.com/politics/2016/07/05/fbi-recommends-no-charges-to-be-filed-against-clinton.html (accessed January 21, 2017).

2. Emily Schultheis, "FBI Director to Congress: Still No Charges Recommended after Latest Clinton Emails Reviewed," CBS News, November 6, 2016, http://www.cbsnews.com/news/fbi-director-comey-congress-new-letter-hillary-clinton-emails-still-no-charges/ (accessed January 14, 2017).

3. FBI director James Comey, "Law Enforcement and the Communities We Serve: Tied Together in a Single Garment of Destiny" (speech, Sixteenth Street Baptist Church in Birmingham, Alabama, May 25, 2016).

4. John Archibald, "Birmingham Hits High-Crime Trifecta; Other Alabama Cities Struggle Too," Al.com, September 28, 2016, http://www.al.com/opinion/index.ssf/2016/09/birmingham_hits_high-crime_tri.html (accessed January 21, 2017).

5. Darrel W. Stephens, "Violent Crime Survey: Totals Midyear Comparison between 2016 and 2015," Major Cities Chiefs Association,

https://www.majorcitieschiefs.com/pdf/news/mcca_violent_crime_data
_midyear_20162015.pdf (accessed October 15, 2016).

6. Comey, "Law Enforcement and the Communities We Serve."

7. FBI press release, "FBI Releases 2015 Crime Statistics," September 26, 2016, https://www.fbi.gov/news/pressrel/press-releases/fbi-releases -2015-crime-statistics (accessed January 14, 2017).

8. Chicago Tribune, "Crime in Chicagoland," Crime Reports in Austin, November 2–December 2, 2016 (http://crime.chicagotribune .com/chicago/community/austin (accessed October 2, 2016).

9. Cook County Commissioner Richard Boykin, in interview with the author, May 29, 2016.

10. Chicago Police Accountability Task Force, *Recommendations for Reform: Restoring Trust between the Chicago Police and the Communities They Serve*, April 2016, https://chicagopatf.org/ (accessed November 2, 2016).

11. Ibid., p. 6.

12. Ibid., p. 4.

13. Ibid., p. 7.

14. Ibid.

15. Ibid., pp. 17–18.

16. Cook County commissioner Richard Boykin, in interview with the author, May 29, 2016.

CHAPTER SIX: LIVESTOCK

1. Jermont Montgomery, in interview with the author, May 28, 2016.

2. Derrick Blakley, "New Interim Supt. Johnson Says He's Never Witnessed Police Misconduct in 27 Years with CPD," CBS Chicago, March 29, 2016, http://chicago.cbslocal.com/2016/03/29/new-interim-supt-johnson -says-hes-never-witnessed-police-misconduct-in-27-years-with-cpd/ (accessed January 14, 2017).

3. Mark Konkol, "Top Cop Eddie Johnson Spins Tall Tales While Trying to Earn Chicago's Trust," DNAinfo, May 18, 2016, https://www .dnainfo.com/chicago/20160518/bronzeville/top-cop-eddie-johnson -spins-tall-tales-while-trying-earn-chicagos-trust (accessed June 3, 2016).

4. Tracy Siska, "This New Top Cop Is Wholly Unqualified to Reform CPD," Crain's Chicago Business, April 20, 2016, http://www.chicago business.com/article/20160420/OPINION/160419797/this-new-top-cop -is-wholly-unqualified-to-reform-cpd (accessed June 3, 2016).

5. Ja'Mal Green, in interview with the author, May 30, 2016; *United States v. Ian Furminger.*

6. Annie Sweeney, Jeremy Gorner, and Dan Hinkel, "Top Cop Seeks to Fire 7 Officers for Lying about Laquan McDonald Shooting," *Chicago Tribune,* August 18, 2016, http://www.chicagotribune.com/news/laquan mcdonald/ct-laquan-mcdonald-police-punished-met-20160818-story.html (accessed January 14, 2017).

CHAPTER SEVEN: GHOST SKINS

1. CBS News/Associated Press, "Chief: Miami Beach Police Sent Hundreds of Racist, Pornographic Emails," CBS News, May 15, 2015, http://www.cbsnews.com/news/miami-beach-police-sent-hundreds-of -racist-and-pornographic-emails-departments-chief-says/ (accessed October 15, 2016).

2. Ibid.

3. Ibid.

4. Ibid.

5. *United States v. Ian Furminger,* Case no. CR 14-0102 CRB, United States District Court, Northern District of California. Government's Opposition to Defendant Furminger's Motion for Bail Pending Appeal.

6. Ibid.

7. Ibid.

8. KTVU, "Former SF Cop Sentenced to More than 3 Years in Jail in Corruption Case," KTVU, February 23, 2015, http://www.ktvu.com/ news/4202408-story (accessed November 4, 2016).

9. Timothy Williams, "San Francisco Police Officers to Be Dismissed over Racist Texts," *New York Times,* April 3, 2015, http://www.nytimes .com/2015/04/04/us/san-francisco-police-officers-to-be-dismissed-over -racist-texts.html?_r=0 (accessed November 4, 2016).

10. Timothy Williams, "San Francisco Police Officers to Be Dismissed over Racist Texts," *New York Times,* April 3, 2015, https://www.nytimes .com/2015/04/04/us/san-francisco-police-officers-to-be-dismissed-over -racist-texts.html (accessed January 14, 2017).

11. Ibid.

12. Ibid.

13. US Department of Justice, COPS: Community Oriented Policing Services, *Collaborative Reform Initiative: An Assessment of the San Francisco*

Police Department, October 2016, https://ric-zai-inc.com/Publications/cops-w0817-pub.pdf (accessed November 2, 2016).

14. Census Quick Facts, http://www.census.gov/quickfacts/table/PST045216/00.

15. Ibid.

16. US Department of Justice, COPS: Community Oriented Policing Services, *Collaborative Reform Initiative: An Assessment of the San Francisco Police Department*, October 2016, https://ric-zai-inc.com/Publications/cops-w0817-pub.pdf (accessed November 2, 2016).

17. Ibid.

18. Ibid.

19. Derek Hawkins, "Flight Attendant to Black Female Doctor: 'We're Looking for Actual Physicians,'" *Washington Post*, October 14, 2016, https://www.washingtonpost.com/news/morning-mix/wp/2016/10/14/blatant-discrimination-black-female-doctor-says-flight-crew-questioned-her-credentials-during-medical-emergency/?tid=pm_national_pop_b (accessed November 2, 2016).

20. Michael E. Miller, "Cop Accused of Brutally Torturing Black Suspects Costs Chicago $5.5 Million," *Washington Post*, April 15, 2015, https://www.washingtonpost.com/news/morning-mix/wp/2015/04/15/closing-the-book-on-jon-burge-chicago-cop-accused-of-brutally-torturing-african-american-suspects/ (accessed November 2, 2016).

21. Ibid.

22. Ibid.

23. Unidentified police chief, interview (on condition of anonymity) with the author.

24. FBI Counterterrorism Division Intelligence Assessment, October 17, 2006, "White Supremacist Infiltration of Law Enforcement" (unclassified), http://s3.documentcloud.org/documents/402521/doc-26-white-supremacist-infiltration.pdf.; Kenya Downs, "FBI Warned of White Supremacists in Law Enforcement 10 Years Ago. Has Anything Changed?" *PBS NewsHour*, October 21, 2016, http://www.pbs.org/newshour/rundown/fbi-white-supremacists-in-law-enforcement/ (accessed November 2, 2016).

CHAPTER EIGHT: SIXTEEN SHOTS

1. Ja'Mal Green, in interview with the author, May 30, 2016.

2. Progress Illinois, "Report: Chicago's Youth Hit Hard by Unemploy-

ment," press release, January 26, 2016, http://progressillinois.com/news/content/2016/01/26/report-chicagos-youth-hit-hard-unemployment (accessed November 2, 2016).

3. Dean Angelo Sr., president of Chicago FOP, in interview with the author, May 27, 2016.

4. Ibid.

CHAPTER NINE: EXECUTIVE ORDER 13684

1. President's Task Force on 21st Century Policing, *The Final Report: The President's Task Force on 21st Century Policing* (Washington, DC: Office of Community Oriented Policing Services, May 2015), https://cops.usdoj.gov/pdf/taskforce/taskforce_finalreport.pdf (accessed November 4, 2016), pp. 9, 19, 31, 41, 51, and 61.

2. President's Task Force on 21st Century Policing, *The Final Report: The President's Task Force on 21st Century Policing* (Washington, DC: Office of Community Oriented Policing Services, May 2015), https://cops.usdoj.gov/pdf/taskforce/taskforce_finalreport.pdf (accessed November 4, 2016), pp. 9, 19, 31, 41, 51, and 61.

3. Ibid.

4. Ibid.

5. Ibid.

6. Ibid.

7. White House, "Remarks by the President after White House Convening on Building Community Trust," press release, July 13, 2016, https://www.whitehouse.gov/the-press-office/2016/07/13/remarks-president-after-white-house-convening-building-community-trust (accessed November 2, 2016).

8. Ibid.

9. Mike Rawlings, mayor of Dallas, Interview by John Dickerson, *Face the Nation*, CBS, July 10, 2016.

10. Sherrilyn Ifill, NAACP Legal Defense Fund, interview by John Dickerson, *Face the Nation*, CBS, July 10, 2016.

CHAPTER TEN: TRUTH AND RECONCILIATION

1. Desmond Tutu, "Truth and Reconciliation Commission, South Africa (TRC)," Encyclopedia Britannica, January 3, 2014, https://www .britannica.com/topic/Truth-and-Reconciliation-Commission-South-Africa (accessed November 2, 2016).

2. Chicago Police Accountability Task Force, April 2016, https:// chicagopatf.org/wp-content/uploads/2016/04/PATF_Final_Report _4_13_16-1.pdf (accessed January 21, 2017).

3. FBI director James Comey, "Hard Truths: Law Enforcement and Race," Georgetown University speech, February 12, 2015, https://www .fbi.gov/news/speeches/hard-truths-law-enforcement-and-race (accessed January 14, 2017).

4. Victor E. Kappeler, "A Brief History of Slavery and the Origins of American Policing," Eastern Kentucky University Police Studies Online, January 7, 2014, http://plsonline.eku.edu/insidelook/brief-history -slavery-and-origins-american-policing (accessed August 2, 2016).

5. K. B. Turner, D. Giacopassi, and M. Vandiver, "Ignoring the Past: Coverage of Slavery and Slave Patrols in Criminal Justice Texts," *Journal of Criminal Justice Education* 17, no. 1 (2006): 181–95.

6. Pew Research Poll, "King's Dream Remains an Elusive Goal; Many Americans See Racial Disparities," August 22, 2013, http://www.pew socialtrends.org/2013/08/22/kings-dream-remains-an-elusive-goal-many -americans-see-racial-disparities/ (accessed January 14, 2017).

7. Sam Roberts, "Race Equality Is Still a Work in Progress, Survey Finds," *New York Times*, August 22, 2016, http://www.nytimes.com/2013/ 08/23/us/americans-see-racial-equality-as-a-work-in-progress-pew-poll -finds.html (accessed September 1, 2016).

8. Pew Research Center, "Stark Racial Divisions in Reactions to Ferguson Police Shooting," Pew Research Center, August 18, 2014, http:// www.people-press.org/2014/08/18/stark-racial-divisions-in-reactions-to -ferguson-police-shooting/ (accessed November 1, 2016).

9. "McClatchy-Marist Poll," Marist Poll, July 28, 2015, https://marist poll.marist.edu/wp-content/misc/usapolls/us150722/2016July/Complete %20July%202015%20McClatchy_Marist%20Poll_2016_Tables.pdf (accessed November 2, 2016).

10. Bruce Drake, "Divide between Blacks and Whites on Police Runs Deep," April 28, 2015, Pew Research Center, http://www.pewresearch.org/ fact-tank/2015/04/28/blacks-whites-police/ (accessed November 2, 2016).

11. US Department of Justice, *Investigation of the Baltimore City Police Department*, August 10, 2016, https://www.justice.gov/opa/file/883386/download (accessed November 2, 2016), p. 32.

12. Ibid., p. 33.

13. Department of Justice, *Investigation of the Ferguson Police Department*, March 4, 2015, https://www.justice.gov/sites/default/files/opa/press-releases/attachments/2015/03/04/ferguson_police_department_report.pdf (accessed January 14, 2017).

14. Community activist Ray E. Kelly, interview by Jeff Pegues, *CBS Evening News*, CBS, August 10, 2016.

CHAPTER ELEVEN: FEAR OF THE BADGE

1. Alderman Christopher Taliaferro, in interview with the author, May 27, 2016.

2. Police Accountability Task Force, *Recommendations for Reform: Restoring Trust between Chicago Police and the Communities They Serve*, April 2016, http://chicagotonight.wttw.com/sites/default/files/article/file-attachments/PATF_Final_Report_4_13_16.pdf (accessed October 2, 2016), p. 10.

3. Chicago Police Department, "What Is CAPS," http://home.chicagopolice.org/get-involved-with-caps/how-caps-works/get-the-most-from-your-beat-meeting/ (accessed January 14, 2017).

CHAPTER TWELVE: POLICING SYSTEM IS BROKEN

1. Cook County Commissioner Richard Boykin, in interview with the author, May 29, 2016.

2. CBS News, "Prosecution Fails for the 4th Time in Freddie Gray Case," July 18, 2016, http://www.cbsnews.com/news/brian-rice-freddie-gray-trial-acquitted-baltimore/ (accessed January 17, 2017).

3. Author's transcript of Marilyn Mosby's press conference on July 27, 2016; footage available at "Marilyn Mosby Press Conference 7/27/16," YouTube video, 11:56, posted by "LesGrossman News," July, 27, 2016 https://www.youtube.com/watch?v=dQoRXO7cZLY.

4. Kimberly Kindy and Kimbriell Kelly, "Thousands Dead, Few Prosecuted," *Washington Post*, April 11, 2015, http://www.washington

post.com/sf/investigative/2015/04/11/thousands-dead-few-prosecuted/
?tid=a_inl (accessed January 16, 2017).

    5. Pete Williams and Jay O'Brien, "Baltimore Policeman's Decision
to Forego Jury Trial Paid Off, Experts Say," MSNBC, May 23, 2016, http://
www.msnbc.com/msnbc/baltimore-policemans-decision-forego-jury-trial
-paid-experts-say (accessed January 16, 2017).

    6. Philip Stinson Sr., professor at Bowling Green University, in
interview with the author, August 24, 2016.

    7. CNN.com, February 24, 2009, "Ex-Atlanta Officers Get Prison
Time for Cover-up in Deadly Raid," http://www.cnn.com/2009/CRIME/
02/24/atlanta.police/ (accessed January 17, 2017).

    8. Mark Berman, "Mistrial Declared in Case of South Carolina
Officer Who Shot Walter Scott after Traffic Stop," *Washington Post*, December 5, 2016 https://www.washingtonpost.com/news/post-nation/
wp/2016/12/05/mistrial-declared-in-case-of-south-carolina-officer-who
-shot-walter-scott-after-traffic-stop/?utm_term=.e67740274802 (accessed
January 19, 2017).

CHAPTER THIRTEEN: THE RECRUITS

    1. Tom Jackman, "Study Finds Police Officers Arrested 1,100 Times
per Year, or 3 per Day, Nationwide," *Washington Post*, June 22, 2016,
https://www.washingtonpost.com/news/true-crime/wp/2016/06/22/
study-finds-1100-police-officers-per-year-or-3-per-day-are-arrested
-nationwide/ (accessed August 22, 2016).

    2. Brian A. Reaves, "Census of State and Local Law Enforcement
Agencies, 2008," Bureau of Justice Statistics, July 26, 2011, http://www.bjs
.gov/index.cfm?ty=pbdetail&iid=2216 (accessed August 12, 2016).

    3. Jackman, "Study Finds Police Officers."

    4. Jeff Pegues, "Officers Wanted: Police Departments Struggle with
Recruiting," *CBS Evening News*, September 1, 2015, http://www.cbsnews
.com/news/officers-wanted-police-departments-struggle-with-recruiting/
(accessed November 1, 2016).

    5. Ibid.

    6. Stephanie Sanchez, "Arizona Law Enforcement Agencies Face
Officer Shortage," KAWC, December 15, 2015, http://kawc.org/post/
arizona-law-enforcement-agencies-face-officer-shortage (accessed
November 2, 2016).

7. US Department of Justice, *Hiring and Retention of State and Local Law Enforcement Officers, 2008–Statistical Tables*, by Brian A. Reaves, October 2012, https://www.bjs.gov/content/pub/pdf/hrslleo08st.pdf (accessed November 2, 2016), p. 14.

8. Adam Ferrise, "Cleveland Officer Who Shot Tamir Rice Had 'Dismal' Handgun Performance for Independence Police," Cleveland.com, November 22, 2016, http://www.cleveland.com/metro/index.ssf/2014/12/cleveland _police_officer_who_s.html (accessed December 18, 2016).

9. Ibid.

10. Ibid.

11. Ibid.

12. Christine Mai-Duc, "Cleveland Officer Who Killed Tamir Rice Had Been Deemed Unfit for Duty," *Los Angeles Times*, December 3, 2014, http://www.latimes.com/nation/nationnow/la-na-nn-cleveland-tamir-rice -timothy-loehmann-20141203-story.html (accessed January 17, 2017).

13. Ibid.

14. Ron Hosko, in interview with the author, July 27, 2016.

15. Ron Hosko retired from the FBI in 2014 after a thirty-year career. Law Enforcement Legal Defense Fund, "Board of Directors: Ron Hosko (Voting—April 2014–Present)," http://www.policedefense.org/board-of -directors/ (accessed January 19, 2017).

16. Hosko, interview.

17. Tom Dunkel, "The DC Police Department Tries to Solve a Difficult Case: How to Recruit New Cops," *Washington Post*, September 29, 2016, https://www.washingtonpost.com/lifestyle/magazine/the-dc-police -department-tries-to-solve-a-difficult-case-how-to-recruit-new-cops/2016/ 09/28/e62cbe56-75e8-11e6-8149-b8d05321db62_story.html?tid=sm_tw (accessed October 11, 2016).

18. Ibid.

19. President's Task Force on 21st Century Policing, *The Final Report: The President's Task Force on 21st Century Policing* (Washington, DC: Office of Community Oriented Policing Services, May 2015), https://cops.usdoj .gov/pdf/taskforce/taskforce_finalreport.pdf (accessed November 4, 2016), p. 51.

20. Ibid.

21. US Department of Justice, "Department of Justice Announces New Department-Wide Implicit Bias Training for Personnel," press release, June 27, 2016, https://www.justice.gov/opa/pr/department-justice-announces-new -department-wide-implicit-bias-training-personnel (accessed August 12, 2016).

22. Emanuella Grinberg, "4 Ways You Might Be Displaying Hidden Bias in Everyday Life," CNN.com, November 25, 2015, http://www.cnn.com/2015/11/24/living/implicit-bias-tests-feat/ (accessed January 17, 2017).

23. Philip Stinson Sr., professor at Bowling Green University, in interview with the author, August 24, 2016.

24. Hosko, interview.

25. Jeff Pegues, "Officers Wanted: Police Departments Struggle with Recruiting," CBS News, September 1, 2015, http://www.cbsnews.com/news/officers-wanted-police-departments-struggle-with-recruiting/ (accessed November 1, 2016).

CHAPTER FOURTEEN: THE RACE CARD

1. David Fink, "Housing Data Profile: Westport," *PSC Housing*, 2013, http://www.pschousing.org/housingprofiles2013/PSC_2013HsgProfile_Westport.pdf (accessed October 22, 2016).

2. Westport police chief Foti Koskinas, in interview with the author, October 7, 2016.

3. Bob Kelly, "Worth Repeating: More Than 5,000 Classic and Contemporary Quotes," 2003; the quote is attributed to Maya Angelou.

CHAPTER FIFTEEN: DALLAS

1. Barack Obama, Facebook post, July 7, 2016, 2:07 p.m., https://www.facebook.com/potus/posts/507884336068078 (accessed November 1, 2016).

2. Terrance Cunningham, former president of the International Association of Chiefs of Police, in interview with the author, November 8, 2016.

3. CBS/AP, "State Trooper, Suspect Killed in Shooting at Va. Bus Station," CBS News, March 31, 2016, http://www.cbsnews.com/news/greyhound-bus-station-shooting-in-richmond-virginia/ (accessed November 2, 2016).

4. Barack Obama, "Remarks by the President at Memorial Service for Fallen Dallas Police Officers," held at Morton H. Meyerson Symphony Center in Dallas, Texas, July 12, 2016, https://www.whitehouse.gov/the-press-office/2016/07/12/remarks-president-memorial-service-fallen-dallas-police-officers (accessed January 19, 2017).

5. Molly Hennessy-Fiske, "Obama in Dallas to Comfort a Nation in Mourning," *LA Times,* July 12, 2016, http://www.latimes.com/nation/la-live-updates-obama-speak-service-obama-in-dallas-this-is-the-most-1468357732-htmlstory.html (accessed January 17, 2017).

6. Steve Visser, "Baton Rouge Shooting: 3 Officers Dead; Shooter Was Missouri Man, Sources Say," CNN.com, July 18, 2016, http://www.cnn.com/2016/07/17/us/baton-route-police-shooting/ (accessed January 17, 2017).

7. President Barack Obama, in open letter to America's law enforcement community, July 19, 2016; text available at the White House, "Read President Obama's Open Letter to America's Law Enforcement Community," https://www.whitehouse.gov/blog/2016/07/19/read-president-obamas-open-letter-americas-law-enforcement-community (accessed January 19, 2017).

8. National Fraternal Order of Police, Facebook Post, July 18, 2016, https://www.facebook.com/NationalFraternalOrderofPolice/posts/1365234003490755 (accessed October 22, 2016).

9. Emanuella Grinberg and Thom Patterson, "Tensions High after Milwaukee Police Shooting," CNN, August 16, 2016, http://www.cnn.com/2016/08/14/us/milwaukee-violence-police-shooting/ (accessed October 22, 2016).

10. Ashley Luthern and Ellen Gabler, "Social Media Threats Intensify, Focus on Officer," *Milwaukee Journal Sentinel,* August 17, 2016, http://www.jsonline.com/story/news/crime/2016/08/16/social-media-threats-intensify-focus-officer/88874910/ (accessed January 17, 2017).

11. Dean Angelo Sr., president of Chicago FOP, in interview with the author, May 27, 2016.

CHAPTER SIXTEEN: TREAT PEOPLE AS YOU WANT TO BE TREATED

1. Ian Cull, "Santa Clara Police Union Threatens Boycott of 49ers Games over Kaepernick Protest, Police Chief Calls for Safety," NBC Bay Area, September 4, 2016, http://www.nbcbayarea.com/news/local/Santa-Clara-Police-Officers-Association-May-Boycott-Working-49ers-Games-392214541.html (accessed November 2, 2016).

2. CBS SF Bay Area, "Santa Clara Officers Condemn Kaepernick Protest, Threaten to Boycott Policing Levi's Stadium," CBS SF Bay Area, September 2, 2016, http://sanfrancisco.cbslocal.com/2016/09/02/

santa-clara-police-protest-colin-kaepernick-threaten-boycott-levis-stadium/ (accessed November 2, 2016).

3. Marissa Payne, "Colin Kaepernick Refuses to Stand for National Anthem to Protest Police Killings," *Washington Post*, August 27, 2016, https://www.washingtonpost.com/news/early-lead/wp/2016/08/27/ colin-kaepernick-refuses-to-stand-for-national-anthem-to-protest-police -killings/ (accessed October 22, 2016).

4. "Philadelphia Police Department 19th Police District Fun Day," YouTube video, 5:41, 19th District Commander Captain Joseph Bologna outlines efforts toward community policing, posted by "Philadelphia Police," August 1, 2016, https://www.youtube.com/watch?v=TTtOVopJUi0 (accessed December 27, 2016).

5. Ibid.

6. Captain Joseph Bologna, commander, Philadelphia Police Department, in interview with the author, September 15, 2016.

7. "Philly Boxing History: Boxers," Philly Boxing History, http:// phillyboxinghistory.com/boxers_page01.htm (accessed October 22, 2016).

8. George Fachner and Steven Carter, "Collaborative Reform Initiative: An Assessment of Deadly Force in the Philadelphia Police Department," 2013, US Department of Justice Office of Community Oriented Policing Services, https://ric-zai-inc.com/Publications/cops -w0753-pub.pdf (accessed January 18, 2017).

CHAPTER SEVENTEEN: CODE OF SILENCE

1. Police Accountability Task Force, *Recommendations for Reform: Restoring Trust between Chicago Police and the Communities They Serve*, April 2016, https://chicagopatf.org/wp-content/uploads/2016/04/PATF _Final_Report_4_13_16-1.pdf (accessed October 22, 2016), p. 1.

2. Ibid., p. 6.

3. Ibid., pp. 10–12.

4. Dan Hinkel and Jennifer Smith Richards, "Two Chicago Police Shootings into Vehicles Ruled Unjustified by Oversight Agency," *Chicago Tribune*, July 21, 2016, http://www.chicagotribune.com/news/local/ breaking/ct-ipra-shootings-rulings-met-20160721-story.html (accessed October 22, 2016).

5. Shane Shifflett, Alissa Scheller, Scilla Alecci, and Nicky Forster, "Police Abuse Complaints by Black Chicagoans Dismissed Nearly 99

Percent of the Time Investigators Rarely Sustain Allegations of Any Kind," *Huffington Post*, December 7, 2015, http://data.huffingtonpost .com/2015/12/chicago-officer-misconduct-allegations (accessed October 23, 2016).

6. NBC Chicago, "Chicago Has Recorded More Murders So Far This Year than NYC and LA Combined, Data Shows," NBC Chicago, September 6, 2016, http://www.nbcchicago.com/news/local/chicago-records-more -murders-than-new-york-los-angeles-combined-this-year-391771211.html (accessed November 2, 2016).

7. CBS Chicago, "Chicago Wrapping Up Most Violent Month in Nearly 20 Years," CBS Chicago, August 31, 2016, http://chicago.cbslocal .com/2016/08/31/chicago-wrapping-up-most-violent-month-in-nearly-20 -years/ (accessed September 21, 2016).

8. Chicago Police Department, "Chicago PD: August 2016 Crime Summary," press release, September 1, 2016.

9. Dean Angelo Sr., president of Chicago FOP, in interview with the author, May 27, 2016.

10. "Senate Bill 1304 Includes the 'Law Enforcement Body Worn Camera Act' and the 'Police & Community Relations Improvement Act,'" Illinois Police Benevolent and Protective Association, http://www.pbpa.org/ Portals/0/News/Senate%20Bill%201304.pdf (accessed October 22, 2016).

11. Eliott C. McLaughlin, "Chicago Officer Had History of Complaints before Laquan McDonald Shooting," CNN, November 26, 2015, http://www.cnn.com/2015/11/25/us/jason-van-dyke-previous-complaints -lawsuits/ (accessed October 1, 2016).

12. "Jason Van Dyke," Citizens Police Data Project, https://cpdb.co/ officer/jason-van-dyke/7655 (accessed November 2, 2016).

13. Progress Illinois, "Chicago Police Confiscate 2,800 Guns from City Streets Since January 1," press release, April 28, 2016, http://www .progressillinois.com/news/content/2016/04/28/chicago-police -confiscate-2800-guns-city-streets-january-1 (accessed November 2, 2016).

CHAPTER EIGHTEEN: TRAIN TO KILL

1. Ja'Mal Green, community activist, in interview with the author, May 29, 2016.

CHAPTER NINETEEN: THE MAGIC WAND

1. Ames Alexander and Mark Washburn, "CMPD Chief: Video Provides No 'Definitive' Evidence That Victim Pointed Gun before Officer Shot Him," *Charlotte Observer*, September 22, 2016, http://www.charlotteobserver.com/news/local/crime/article103380852.html (accessed November 2, 2016).

2. Chuck Wexler and Kevin Morison, Police Executive Research Forum, in interview with the author, September 12, 2016.

3. *CBS Evening News*, Vanderbilt Television Archive, January 7, 1975, https://tvnews.vanderbilt.edu/programs/236990 (accessed October 2, 2016).

4. Mick Dumke and Frank Main, "The Watchdogs: Arrests Down 28 Percent in Chicago This Year," *Chicago Sun-Times*, December 24, 2016, http://chicago.suntimes.com/news/the-watchdogs-arrests-down-25-percent-in-chicago-this-year/ (accessed January 18, 2017).

CHAPTER TWENTY: "BROKEN WINDOWS IS NOT BROKEN"

1. Deborah Hart Strober and Gerald S. Strober, *Giuliani: Flawed or Flawless? The Oral Biography* (Hoboken, NJ: Wiley, 2007), p. 172.

2. Ibid., p. 172.

3. William J. Bratton, in retirement letter to Mayor de Blasio, September 14, 2016.

4. Ibid.

5. "NYPD Responds to Deeply Flawed Inspector General's Quality-of-Life Report," *NYPD News*, September 7, 2016, http://nypdnews.com/2016/09/nypd-responds-to-deeply-flawed-inspector-generals-quality-of-life-report/ (accessed November 2, 2016).

6. NYPD, "NYPD Responds to Deeply Flawed Inspector General's Quality-of-Life Report," press release, September 7, 2016.

7. NYPD, "New York City Experiences Safest Summer in Modern History," press release, September 6, 2016.

8. Ibid.

9. "We Were Wrong: Ending Stop and Frisk Did Not End Stopping Crime," editorial, *New York Daily News*, August 8, 2016, http://www.nydailynews.com/opinion/wrong-ending-stop-frisk-not-stopping-crime-article-1.2740157 (accessed October 23, 2016).

10. Ibid.

CHAPTER TWENTY-ONE: "SIXTEEN SHOTS AND A COVER-UP!"

1. Matthew Friedman, Ames C. Grawert, and James Cullen, *Crime in 2016: A Preliminary Analysis*, Brennan Center for Criminal Justice, September 21, 2016, https://www.brennancenter.org/sites/default/files/publications/Crime_2016_Preliminary_Analysis.pdf (accessed October 15, 2016).

2. Ibid.

3. Ibid.

4. John Byrne and Hal Dardick, "Emanuel Wins Round on Police Reform, But Hard Work Remains on Thorny Issue," *Chicago Tribune*, October 5, 2016, http://www.chicagotribune.com/news/local/politics/ct-rahm-emanuel-police-reform-city-council-vote-met-1006-20161005-story.html (accessed October 2, 2016).

5. Police Accountability Task Force, "Recommendations for Reform: Restoring Trust between Chicago Police and the Communities They Serve," April 2016, p. 12, https://chicagopatf.org/wp-content/uploads/2016/04/PATF_Final_Report_4_13_16-1.pdf (accessed January 18, 2017).

6. Byrne and Dardick, "Emanuel Wins Round."

7. Ibid.

8. "Activist Ja'Mal Green Arrested Following Incident at Protest," July 9, 2016, *Chicago Tribune*, http://www.chicagotribune.com/news/local/breaking/87850031-132.html (accessed September 13, 2016).

9. Ja'Mal Green, community activist, in interview with the author following Green's arrest, September 20, 2016.

10. Byrne and Dardick, "Emanuel Wins Round."

CHAPTER TWENTY-TWO: COMING CLEAN

1. Justin McCarthy, "Americans' Respect for Police Surges," Gallup, October 24, 2016, http://www.gallup.com/poll/196610/americans-respect-police-surges.aspx (accessed October 28, 2016).

2. Citizens Police Data Project, Invisible Institute, https://cpdb.co/data/DR8agN/citizens-police-data-project (accessed January 21, 2017).

3. Frank Main, Mick Dumke and Tim Novak, "Watchdogs: 134,683 Complaints against CPD Cops, Only 553 Firings," *Chicago Sun-Times*, October 12, 2016, http://chicago.suntimes.com/news/watchdogs-134683-complaints-against-cpd-cops-only-553-firings/ (accessed October 20, 2016).

4. Ibid.

5. Rich Morin and Renee Stepler, "The Racial Confidence Gap in Police Performance: Blacks, Whites Also Have Dramatically Different Views on Causes of Fatal Encounters between Blacks and Police," Pew Research, September 29, 2016, http://www.pewsocialtrends.org/2016/09/29/the-racial-confidence-gap-in-police-performance/ (accessed October 22, 2016).

6. Washington Metropolitan Police Department interim police chief Peter Newsham, in interview with CBS News, October 26, 2016.

7. Westport Police Chief Foti Koskinas, in interview with the author, October 7, 2016.

8. Frank Newport, "American's Offer Solutions for Problem of Deadly Police Shootings," Gallup, July 28, 2016, http://www.gallup.com/poll/194012/americans-offer-solutions-problem-deadly-shootings.aspx?g_source=position2&g_medium=related&g_campaign=tiles (accessed January 21, 2017).

9. Terrance Cunningham, former president of the International Association of Chiefs of Police, in interview with the author, November 8, 2016.

10. Morin and Stepler, "Racial Confidence Gap."

11. Ibid.

12. Jessie P. Guzman and W. Hardin Hughes, "Lynching—Crime," *Negro Year Book: A Review of Events Affecting Negro Life, 1944–1946, 1947*, in National Humanities Center Resource Toolbox, *The Making of African American Identity*, vol. 3, *1917–1968*, http://nationalhumanitiescenter.org/pds/maai3/segregation/text2/lynchingcrime.pdf (accessed November 1, 2016).

13. Cunningham, interview.

14. Terrence Cunningham, speech at the 2016 IACP Annual Conference Exposition in San Diego, California; footage available at "Chief Cunningham Remarks," YouTube video, 4:08, posted by "TheIACP," October 17, 2016, https://www.youtube.com/watch?v=1GZDdq7L7ZY (accessed January 21, 2017).

15. Terrance Cunningham, former president of the International Association of Chiefs of Police, in interview with the author, November 8, 2016.

16. Cunningham, interview.

17. Ibid.

18. "Deputy Matt," "The IACP Apology: Being Lectured by an Academic," Law Officer, October 22, 2016, http://lawofficer.com/leadership/the-iacp-apology-being-lectured-by-an-academic/ (accessed November 9, 2016).

19. FBI Director James Comey, "The True Heart of American Law Enforcement," (speech, International Association of Chiefs of Police Annual Conference, October 16, 2016).

20. Ibid.

AFTERWORD

1. Sadie Gurman, "After Deadly Police Encounters, Voters OK Civilian Oversight," *Associated Press*, November 11, 2016, http://bigstory.ap.org/article/632ab74cb35a4b18a4b5203f271eba65/after-deadly-police-encounters-voters-ok-civilian-oversight (accessed November 13, 2016).

2. Terrance Cunningham, former president of the International Association of Chiefs of Police, in interview with the author, November 8, 2016.

3. President Lyndon Johnson, "Special Message to Congress on Law Enforcement and the Administration of Justice," The American Presidency Project, March 8, 1965, http://www.presidency.ucsb.edu/ws/?pid=26800 (accessed November 9, 2016).

4. Timothy Roufa, "President's Commission on Law Enforcement and Administration of Justice: Facts from President Johnson's Commission on Law Enforcement," The Balance, October 11, 2016, https://www.thebalance.com/1965-presidents-commission-law-enforcement-974564 (accessed November 2, 2016).

5. Commission on Law Enforcement and Administration of Justice, *The Challenge of Crime in a Free Society* (Washington, DC: US Government Printing Office, February 1967), https://www.ncjrs.gov/pdffiles1/nij/42.pdf (accessed November 2, 2016).

INDEX